Recreating Asia

Visions for a New Century

Frank-Jürgen Richter
&
Pamela C.M. Mar

John Wiley & Sons (Asia) Pte Ltd

Other Wiley Editorial Offices

John Wiley & Sons, Inc., 605 Third Avenue, New York, NY 10158-0012, USA
John Wiley & Sons Ltd, Baffins Lane, Chichester, West Sussex PO19 1UD, England
John Wiley & Sons (Canada) Ltd, 22 Worcester Road, Rexdale, Ontario M9W 1L1,
Canada
John Wiley & Sons Australia Ltd, 33 Park Road (PO Box 1226), Milton, Queensland
4046, Australia
Wiley-VCH, Pappelallee 3, 69469 Weinheim, Germany

Library of Congress Cataloging-in-Publication Data:

ISBN 0-470-82085-3

Typeset in 10.5/13 point, Times by Linographic Services Pte Ltd
Printed in Singapore by Saik Wah Press Pte Ltd
10 9 8 7 6 5 4 3 2 1

Contents

STRATEGIES FOR SUCCESS: ASIA'S BUSINESS LEADERS SPEAK OUT

MANAGING POLITICAL AND CORPORATE GOVERNANCE CHALLENGES

FOREWORD

Klaus Schwab
Founder and President, World Economic Forum

What began as a small but ambitious attempt a decade ago to promote deep dialogue and interaction between business and government in East Asia, and with their counterparts in the rest of the world, has now become the pre-eminent annual gathering for the region to both take stock and look ahead. In similar fashion, this book marks both a stock-taking and a chance to look to the future for the World Economic Forum in East Asia. It gathers the most salient results and contributions from our Tenth East Asia Economic Summit, held in Hong Kong in 2001, and also underlines key trends which will define the next 10 years in the region.

As a non-governmental and non-profit institution, the World Economic Forum is committed to furthering integration of East Asian countries, as well as for the region as a whole, into the world in many spheres. Our East Asia Economic Summit has evolved to facilitate the exchange of experiences and expertise between leaders in business, government and civil society, in the interests of economic and social development in East Asia.

The 2001 Summit was one of the first independent, international meetings of business, government and civil society after September 11. The tremendous political and economic impacts of the attacks turned the Summit into both a point of reflection and a gathering ground for action. Surprisingly, even with a gloomy economic backdrop and fears about security, the views of many participants indicated that the global economy is stronger than it looks, and that the outlook for Asia can remain promising. Structural reform in Asian economies and within its companies has finally moved ahead. Support for global trade coordination, good political and corporate governance, and Asia as a leader in the technology and communications industries is now broadly clear. Moreover, the accession of China to the World Trade Organization and the continuing strength of China's domestic economy present opportunities for Asia to keep its economic engines strong. China will continue to become increasingly important in shaping the region's development in the years to come.

The World Economic Forum's Summits have become famous for frank, informal discussion and spirited debate on key aspects of the global agenda. This so-called Spirit of Davos, which has for years brought nations, cultures and individuals closer together on a global level, is now also an Asian phenomenon. It thrives on the goodwill of our members, constituents and friends, and we re-invigorate that sense each year during the East Asia Economic Summit.

I would like express my deepest appreciation to Prime Minister Mahathir bin Mohamad, President Macapagal-Arroyo, and all participants and friends contributing to this book. My special thanks go to Hong Kong's Chief Executive, Tung Chee-Hwa, who invited us to hold our 2001 Summit in Hong Kong, and I am also grateful to Mr Lee Kuan Yew and Australia's Prime Minister, Mr John Howard, for their comments.

We look forward to continuing to work with these and other Asian leaders, and their counterparts in business and other walks of life, to achieve our common aspirations of economic growth, regional prosperity, social stability and peace.

PREFACE

Lee Kuan Yew
Senior Minister of Singapore

Before the Asian financial crisis in 1997, the conventional view was that the 21st century would be an Asian Century. After the crisis, East Asia was written off.

A more objective assessment can be deduced from the way East Asian countries have developed since 1945, the end of Second World War. They have transformed themselves from agricultural backwaters (except for Japan) to industrial and industrializing countries with high trading volumes. No other developing region has matched this pace of transformation. The factors that created this rapid growth are still in place: first, governments that maintained stability, sound macroeconomic policies, and good infrastructure; second, peoples who continually educate themselves to higher levels, work hard, save much of their earnings and invest in their children's education.

China is the big story. It will continue to receive large flows of foreign direct investments (FDI). When other countries of East Asia suffered negative growth in 1997 and again in 2001, China still made over 7% growth. If it continues to have pragmatic and competent management of the economy for the next decade, it is set to remain one of the fastest-growing economies in the world.

For Japan, South Korea and Taiwan, China will be more a partner than a competitor in the next 10 to 20 years. It provides a cheap base to relocate industries, reduce costs, improve competitiveness and increase profits, as well as a huge market. Hong Kong transferred all its light industries to Guangdong in the 1980s and 90s. Taiwan's lower-end electronics and IT sector are moving aggressively into Shanghai and other coastal cities. South Korean and Japanese industries are doing the same.

But after it has improved its workforce skills, mastered the technology, and raised its R&D standards, China will become both a competitor and a partner.

For countries of Southeast Asia, China is already a competitor. Of the total FDI to Southeast Asia and China, 70% used to go to Southeast Asia, 30% to China. Now this ratio is reversed. As it becomes wealthier in the next phase, China will be more a partner, providing a huge market for tropical products, semi-finished manufactures and outward tourism. Southeast Asia will be part of a value chain, with the high-value end in Japan, China, South Korea and Taiwan.

In this book, prominent East Asian leaders in the fields of government, business and academia give their unique perspectives of likely developments. From them a reader will gain insights into one of the most dramatic economic and social transformations in the history of the world.

PREFACE

John Howard*
Prime Minister of Australia

I am very pleased to provide my support for *Recreating Asia: Visions for a New Century.*

Signs of economic recovery in the global and regional economic outlook are very welcome. As noted in this volume, the global economy is stronger than it looks and the outlook for Asia is promising.

However, now is not the time for complacency. Political, economic and business leaders must act with clear purpose. It is essential that economies not retreat into protectionist policies. Sustained economic reform is the only means to secure long-term growth.

The Australian economy is a powerful example. The Australian government's economic reform program has made our economy stronger and more adaptable in uncertain times. Australia has had one of the best-performing economies in the world over the past decade and is forecast to be among the fastest-growing developed economies in both 2002 and 2003.

Australia's performance and standing in the region provide the right environment for strengthened economic ties with Asia, enhanced by our common interests — bilateral trade, regional economic growth, regional stability — and our strong cultural, family and education links.

I commend the contributors, editors and publishers for their efforts in bringing to wider attention the tremendous potential and opportunities in Asia. I look forward to our governments and businesses working together to realize these benefits.

INTRODUCTION

Frank-Jürgen Richter
&
Pamela C.M. Mar

Trend-spotting in Asia is dangerous. Not only do would-be Asia-watchers abound but, ever since the Asian financial crisis of 1997, the region has undergone numerous "new beginnings" that have seemed to indicate waves of change only to fade on familiar sets of lingering concerns. Market watchers look for signs of revival in stock markets or foreign investment inflows, but are wary of the famous "dead cat" bounce. Political commentators watch for changes in the way Asian countries and companies are governing themselves, but are watchful too for old signs of back-room deals and money under the table. Social critics look for signs that Asian governments are addressing what they see as the root causes of Asia's refusal to regain universal regard, and yet could be accused of not acting in the "national interest" when they highlight these problems. We are all looking, it seems, for a "new era" in Asia to begin.

Our proposition is that Asia's new era is in full swing, and has already left tracks in a wide range of areas — from daily life, to business, government, society and back again. While occasionally these tracks are visible, such as agreements between ASEAN and China or between Singapore and Japan on liberalizing trade frameworks, or monetary swap agreements between Asia's central banks, more often they are hidden and subtler. This collection aims to give voice to those who have been instrumental in propelling Asia's new era ahead. And while some of these voices have "been around" — or have track records — those looking for trends are advised to look not to the historical past but to the urgent present.

In this regard we offer three frameworks which, when taken together, elucidate the most concrete changes that mark Asia's re-creation:

• Japan remains a contested ground but is closer than ever to moving beyond stasis
• China is and will remain the region's rising star, at least for the next five years
• Southeast Asia has awoken and is taking action to regain competitiveness.

These three observations are both glaringly obvious and yet obscured by the extent of the evidence that seems to counter the claims.

Nowhere is this clearer than in Japan, which has for the last decade been struggling with both a crisis of confidence domestically and a confidence crisis abroad. Domestically, even the Japanese people, especially youth and the urbanized middle class, not to mention those being "restructured", doubt even the power of established institutions and organizations to rescue the country. The soaring popularity of Junichiro Koizumi, followed by his fall in the rankings after replacing Makiko Tanaka, is indication enough that people need different figures. Regardless of what one thinks of Madame Tanaka, in many ways she represented change, and her expulsion from the halls of power dented Mr. Koizumi's apparent ability to effect the same. Mr. Koizumi luckily was able to swear in Yoriko Kawaguchi, who is popular (if less flamboyant) in her own right, as the new Minister of Foreign Affairs, and he may yet escape unscathed. There is much hope that Prime Minister Koizumi can continue the reform progress.

Is Japan on the way up or down? Perhaps a more apporpriate question might be, is Japan overcoming stasis? The answer, if one reads the papers and polls, is probably an emphatic "No". However, in considering how those in power are reacting and driving proposals forward, the answer could equally be "Yes". Although Mr. Koizumi did bend to the bureaucrats over Madame Tanaka, his policies, whether in economy or foreign policy, have remained intact. They are, in the best way, ambitiously realistic in both fields. One can see, for instance, the beginnings of the end to the web of cross-industry financial holdings that have thus far stymied corporate restructuring. There is progress in the financial sector, though Minister Heizo Takenaka, architect of Japan's financial reform, remains almost a silent player to the outside world. Perhaps this is the real indicator that things are moving.

On the corporate side, stasis is definitely a thing of the past. Companies like Sony, NTT DoCoMo, Toshiba, and Matsushita are only a few of the country's blue chips that have seen the future and know that it lies abroad. They have grown their operations. From an era when they could sit back on good designs and enthusiastic domestic consumers, Japan's corporate giants have been, in many ways, far more proactive than the government in setting new objectives, dismantling and moving operations, and ensuring their livelihoods. The most successful companies are those whose visions are distinctly their own — whether it is in suggesting that Asia needs to go beyond manufacturing, to innovate and lead the IT revolution, or in suggesting that Asian companies need to be more responsible citizens.

Japan's CEOs have also been more active than their government in venturing with the rest of Asia, continuing a tradition that began in the 1980s during the bubble years of the Japanese economy. Back then, foreign aid was more generous and tightly woven to corporate livelihoods, and enabled Japanese industrial giants to gain ground over much of Southeast Asia. Today, corporate expansion can be characterized not by the desire to gain market share but, rather, to preserve market standing. That is, whereas in the 1980s one might have found Sumitomo as contractors or Komatsu as equipment providers in countless construction projects in Thailand or Indonesia — and thereby increasing their market share — today, expansion by Toshiba or Matsushita into China is done as a way to protect their standing worldwide, by shifting operations to cheaper locations. Eventually, of course, these operations will feed into China's consumer markets, but it would be too ambitious for even the most enthusiastic China-watcher to regard the investment as primarily so.

After an uneventful 2001, in which regional and global geopolitics were dominated by China and the U.S., Japan's foreign-policy agenda has come back to life in 2002. Seeming to take the lead from the corporate sector, Japan's foreign agenda now proactively extends friendship to the rest of Asia. This time, it promises less direct aid and potentially more open borders, which could be even more valuable. When Japan takes down barriers on the range of agricultural products, the stasis will have ended. There is no telling when will be — and certainly doubts abound that it will be in this generation of political leaders — but the signs in trade agreements and friendship abroad indicate that the day will come sooner rather than later. The Japanese government, shaken out of stasis, might surprise us all.

If it does, much of the credit may go, indirectly, to China, the region's rising power. China's ascent, particularly since overcoming the possibility of deflation in the first half of 2001, has been startling to many who doubted the country's ability to move beyond its past. Even after accession to the WTO, doubts abound about China's ability, and commitment, to implement the accession accords. The number of naysayers and skeptics on China's economic future is matched by those who remain positive despite the many problems that continue to dog the country's planners. From unemployment, to rural unrest, to environmental destruction, to fiscal challenges, China continues to have a formidable series of hurdles to surmount.

There are those who say that the Chinese government either has no idea or has a very clear view of the scale of the problems that it faces. Our bet is firmly on the latter, and emanates from observations on how government leaders are approaching change. They know that the country has had a swift climb up the growth and development ranks and, rather than admiring the dust left behind by their achievements, are moving with even more determination to the next stage. Whether it is piloting regional "friendship" (read "economic-benefits-sharing") or putting the state behind IT development, China's leaders know that if they let up now, their other constituents — business community, the people, the media, even their peers in Asia — will return to their doubt-laden self-protection. The government has achieved a huge degree of confidence-building in the business sector and with its Asian neighbors, and if it ceases to reinforce these ties with continuing shows of support, they will fade fast. Along with them will go much of the hope that propels the country forward.

This reveals an intense truth about China: that regardless of the pace of economic opening and the creation of a market economy, China remains a country in which the government has paramount sway of the course of development, perhaps even more so than 10 years ago immediately following the Tiananmen student protests. This may be blindingly obvious to many, but it serves as a sign of caution to the businesspeople, inside and outside of the country, who would see too great a horizon for growth. The framework for operating and investment has become significantly clearer on the back of the WTO accession and efforts of local government to project clean and transparent government, but the fact remains that the frameworks continue to expand and contract, sometimes in unpredictable ways that would seem counterproductive to growth. This has to be the case for a developing economy and especially for one that is starting from a point that was so markedly opposed to the market economy. It is necessary to inject a degree of sobriety into the exuberance.

China rising in many ways may seem to cast a shadow over Southeast Asia, not the least because of the latter's seeming inability to change at a pace even half of that of its northern neighbor. If Japan is in stasis, as some may claim, then is Southeast Asia moving backwards?

The past decade has seen Southeast Asia at the extremes of up and down, both in its economic achievements and its financial failures, and also in the degree to which it raised and then dashed hopes for turnarounds in politics, economy and social openness. To date there does not seem to have been a clear break with the past and, in the case of several governments in the region, a strong claim can be made that the ways of the past have been actively pursued and implemented. At times, we may need to ask: Did we not learn anything from the Asian crisis?

Although the signs would seem to point downwards, our proposition is that Southeast Asia is well on its way to regaining its competitiveness, almost in spite of the global and regional forces that seem to work against it. That is, in spite of the global turmoil surrounding al-Qaeda and other terrorist networks, there is a case to be made that Southeast Asia is both stronger and more cohesive than ever before. Having realized that their competitiveness relies in working with each other to build comparative advantage, and reinforce intra-regional commerce, the region's countries have come together on trade, monetary cooperation and IT linkups, to name just a few areas of progress. Much of this has come during the most intense periods of global insecurity about terror networks, though certainly the groundwork had been laid before September 11.

Regionally, the rapid rise of China has also pressured Southeast Asia to reassess its competitive position. Not only are ministers on both sides of the South China Sea reaching out to bridge regional divides, they are doing it with far more progress and in more concrete terms than the lofty "friendship" sentiments of the past. China's accession to the WTO may have prodded Southeast Asia to reassess its northern neighbor and, if so, the region is better off as a result. Stronger commercial ties within the region will certainly carry weight in solving the lingering strategic and geopolitical problems when they do reappear. No one is saying that problems over the Spratley Islands, the Taiwan straits or the Korean peninsula have gone away. They are simply in remission, but when they do regain the center of attention it is certain that new networks of business alliances, cross-border investments and commercial ties will assert the need to be clear on the order of priorities.

Economic realities may be one bulwark against hasty or ill-advised action in regional power games, but a stronger guarantee is to have leaders in place who have a clear grasp of the stakes as well as nuanced, preferably long-term, forward-looking agendas. That is, those with clarity of vision will have little trouble finding soundness in their actions.

The evidence shows that while Asia may continue to be beset by common developmental problems and potential stumbling blocks, those in power are, more than ever before, working assiduously to overcome these. The region-wide move towards better corporate governance, which began in international market centers like Hong Kong and Singapore, is now well in place in places like the Philippines and China. Adherents are almost as numerous in the corporate sector as well, especially in places which have until now had trouble finding clear-headed regulators (one thinks of Indonesia, but it is by no means alone). The point is that those who seek forward-looking, equal-opportunity agendas that build on the region's fundamental strengths are more than ever inside the halls of power rather than outside or in the opposition. They, at long last, have the power to write the agendas that will propel countries forward.

As we write, the Enron/Andersen scandal is not yet over, and the real fallout will certainly take many months to become clear. However, in Asia, instead of the victorious chest beating that one might have expected from a region that was lambasted for poor governance the affair has served only to reinforce the determination to seek change.

At the same time that reformist proponents of a level playing field are being more frequently seen inside the halls of power, we are also seeing significant strides in the power and recognition being given to the civil society. In official international organizations Asians are more active than ever, whether as leaders inside the UN General Assembly or in forming south-to-south networks within the global community. Grassroots civil groups are also finding their views much more welcomed and are even being mainstreamed as a part of the real debate about how the system should evolve. Eventually this broadening of the debate in Asia will be instrumental in maintaining flexibility and tolerance in times of national strain.

This trend is also true in the corporate sector. Indeed, businesspeople no longer shy away from "Western" topics like good governance, corporate social responsibility, equal-opportunity employment, and merit-based pay and advancement. CEOs willing to advocate these may not be numerous yet; more importantly, however, those who are committed are on top of their fields and leading by example.

These change-makers are part and representative of the new Asian landscape. While it is true that trends may reverse themselves or halt abruptly in their tracks, it is also quite clear that the current trends are broad and deep in nature and will not be easily resisted. If current directions hold firm, what can we expect to be the defining characteristics of a recreated Asia? We are betting on an Asia that:

- is an equal opportunity territory
- is enabled by clear-sighted leaders with vision and focus
- has transparent governance frameworks and solid governing institutions

- is tightly integrated economically and globally at ease
- remains respectful of national traditions and cultural distinctions

Is this too ambitious an agenda? Empowerment is one side of the story and that has taken root already. Enabling the region's nations to achieve their visions is the "mere" other half.

CONTRIBUTORS

MAHATHIR BIN MOHAMAD

Dato Seri Dr. Mahathir bin Mohamad became the fourth Prime Minister of Malaysia in 1981. Born on 20 December 1925, he graduated from the King Edward VII College of Medicine in Singapore. Dr Mahathir bin Mohamad was elected as one of the vice-presidents of the United Malay National Organisation (UMNO) in 1975. He was elected the party's deputy-president in 1978 and in 1981 was appointed president. In 1987 he was re-elected as president and since then he has been returned unopposed to lead UMNO.

GORDON CAMPBELL

Prior to becoming Premier of British Columbia in 2001, Gordon Campbell served in the provincial legislature and as the Leader of the Official Opposition. He also held the position of mayor of Vancouver for three consecutive terms. He worked as a teacher and as a basketball and track coach in Nigeria while serving with the Canadian University Service Overseas. He was educated at Dartmouth College in the U.S., and holds an MBA from Simon Fraser University.

JUSUF WANANDI

Jusuf Wanandi is a founder-member of the board of trustees of the Centre for Strategic and International Studies (CSIS), Jakarta. He is publisher of *The Jakarta Post Daily* and chairman of the board of governors of Prasetiya Mulya School of Management, Jakarta. He is affiliated with many regional and international institutions and is a contributor to local, regional and international newspapers, magazines and journals on Indonesian developments, and on regional and international issues.

KARIM RASLAN

Karim Raslan is a founding partner of Raslan Loong — one of Malaysia's leading corporate law firms. He is the author of *Ceritalah: Malaysia in Transition* and *Heroes and Other Stories*. His weekly syndicated column is published by several Asian newspapers. He was educated at Cambridge University and has recently been a Fulbright Scholar at Columbia University. His recent projects include one entitled "Freedom of Expression in Islamic Societies".

GLORIA MACAPAGAL-ARROYO

Gloria Macapagal-Arroyo was sworn in as the 14th President of the Philippines on 20 January 2001, and is the second woman to be swept into the presidency by a peaceful "people-power" revolution. With an educational background in economics, she began her professional career as a teacher and later as a professor before she entered government service.

KIM MIN-SEOK

Kim Min-Seok has been a member of the National Assembly in South Korea since 1996. He received a Master's degree in public administration from the John F. Kennedy School of Government, Harvard University. He served a three-year prison sentence for leading the democratic movement as chairman of the National Association of Universities and Colleges during the 1980s. He was elected as a Global Leader for Tomorrow by the World Economic Forum.

SHI GUANGSHENG

Shi Guangsheng has been China's Minister of Foreign Trade and Economic Cooperation since 1998, and was one of the driving forces behind China's accession to the WTO. Previously, he served as Vice-Minister and Director General in the Ministry of Foreign Economic Relations and Trade (Mofert) nationally and also in Shanghai. He has also worked in the China National Metals and Minerals Import and Export Corporation and the Chinese Embassy in Belgium.

VERNON ELLIS

Vernon Ellis is International Chairman of Accenture. Mr Ellis takes a lead role in representing the company in public forums, as well as building relationships with governments and key clients throughout the world. He is also chairman of the board of the Prince of Wales International Business Leaders Forum; deputy chairman of the Seoul International Business Advisory Council; and a member of the World Business Council of the World Economic Forum. Veron Ellis wrote this chapter with Elizabeth Padmore, who is Partner and Director of Policy and Corporate Affairs at Accenture, UK.

HEINRICH VON PIERER

Dr von Pierer has been the chairman of the managing board, president and CEO of Siemens AG since 1992. He graduated with a Master's degree in economics and a doctorate in law. He also serves as chairman of the Asia-Pacific Committee of German Business and is a member of the Foundation Board of the World Economic Forum. One of the three largest electrical and electronics companies in the world, Siemens is one of the largest European investors in Asia. In China alone the company has invested more than 500 million Euros and set up more than 50 companies.

JOHN CHEN

John Chen is the chairman of the board, chief executive officer and president of Sybase, Inc. He has served as CEO and chairman since November 1998 and as president and director since August 1997. Before joining Sybase, Mr Chen served as the president of the Open Enterprise Computing Division of Siemens Nixdorf. He also served in various executive capacities with Pyramid Technology Corporation.

FU YUNING

Dr Fu Yuning is a director and president of China Merchants Holdings Co. Ltd., chairman of China Merchants Holdings (International) Co., and chairman of the executive committee for the board of directors of China Merchants Bank. Dr Fu graduated from Dalian Institute of Technology with a degree in Port and Waterway Engineering in 1982. He obtained a doctorate in Offshore Engineering at Brunel University of the United Kingdom, where he also worked as a post-doctorate research fellow.

PHILIPPE PAILLART

Philippe Paillart was appointed CEO of DBS Bank in January 2001. Previously, he was the bank's senior managing director and head of the Consumer Banking Group. Prior to this, he worked for Ford as chairman, president and CEO of Ford Motor Credit Company and president of Ford Financial Services Group. He also worked for Standard Chartered Bank as group executive director, and for Citibank as vice-president and general manager of International Personal Banking for Europe, the Middle East and Africa.

KIM SUNG-JOO

Kim Sung-Joo is the president and CEO of Sung Joo International, one of South Korea's most prominent and popular retail chains. The daughter of a leading businessman, she was raised to be an obedient wife and mother through an arranged marriage. Instead, she rebelled and went abroad, earning advanced degrees from Amherst College and the London School of Economics. She is known for her support of women's initiatives, and has started Iwillb.com, which provides jobs, business opportunities and training for women in Korea.

TADASHI OKAMURA

Tadashi Okamura was born in Tokyo in July 1938 and joined Toshiba on graduating from the Faculty of Law at the University of Tokyo in 1962. He received his MBA in 1973 at the University of Wisconsin. Mr Okamura was appointed president and CEO of the Toshiba Corporation in June 2000. He promotes continuous evolution of the management reforms initiated by his predecessor, and steers the Toshiba Group toward the long-term growth and profitability offered by the IT revolution.

CHEN WEN-CHI

Chen Wen-Chi is president and CEO of VIA Technologies, Inc., which he founded in 1987. Prior to this, Mr Chen co-founded and was president and CEO of Symphony Laboratories. He also held positions as vice president of Sales & Marketing at high-tech start-up ULSI, and senior architect at Intel. A committed Christian, Mr Chen holds a MSEE degree from National Taiwan University and a MSCS from the California Institute of Technology.

KEIJI TACHIKAWA

Dr Keiji Tachikawa became president of NTT DoCoMo in June 1998. Before then, Dr Tachikawa's 36-year career with NTT included postings as senior executive vice president of NTT DoCoMo, and with NTT's Business Communications Headquarters and Service Engineering Headquarters. He spent a couple of years in New York, where he founded and became the first CEO of NTT America Inc.. He is the author of several books in Japanese on the future of the communications and information industries.

Y.T. LEE

Y.T. Lee is the founder and chairman of Trigem Computer, one of the world's major PC suppliers. Trigem is evolving into a flagship within the Internet community and a leading integrated information-communications company. Dr Lee is also a vice-chairman of the Federation of Korean Industries and an honorary chairman of Korean Information Industries.

MANUEL V. PANGILINAN

Mr Pangilinan founded First Pacific in 1981 and served as managing director until 1999, when he was appointed executive chairman. He serves as the president and CEO of Philippine Long Distance Telephone Company (PLDT), the country's dominant telecom company. He is also chairman of Philippine Business for Social Progress, vice chairman of the Foundation for Crime Prevention, and a former governor of the Philippine Stock Exchange.

TUNG CHEE-HWA

Hong Kong's Chief Executive, Mr Tung Chee-Hwa, was born in Shanghai in 1937. He worked in the United States before returning to Hong Kong in 1969 to join the family group business. In 1996, Mr Tung was elected to the post of the Chief Executive of the Hong Kong Special Administrative Region (HKSAR) of the People's Republic of China. He assumed office in July 1997, for a five-year term, and was re-elected in 2002.

HEIZO TAKENAKA

Heizo Takenaka has served as Minister of State for Economic and Fiscal Policy (Cabinet Office) and Minister of State for IT Policy in the Koizumi

Cabinet since April 2001. He is in charge of the Council on Economic and Fiscal Policy (CEFP), which was created in January 2001 as the most important and effective body of economic and fiscal policy within the Japanese government. Former appointments include posts at the Japan Development Bank, Harvard University and Keio University.

CHRISTINE LOH

Christine Loh is the CEO of the Hong Kong-based non-profit public-policy think-tank, Civic Exchange. She is a lawyer by training but spent 15 years of professional life in business, once heading the Asian regional office of the commodities trading arm of Salomon Inc in the 1980s and early 1990s. She then spent nine years in politics, serving in the Hong Kong Legislative Council. She now speaks and writes frequently on issues relating to politics, political economy, corporate social responsibility and sustainable development.

LILIA R. BAUTISTA

Prior to her appointment as chairperson of the Securities and Exchange Commission, Ms Bautista's long public-service career included a series of positions with the Department of Trade and Industry. She was also the Philippine Ambassador and Permanent Representative to the United Nations in Geneva. She holds an MBA from the University of the Philippines, and a Master of Laws from the University of Michigan as a Dewitt Fellow.

E.C.W. NELOE

Edward Cornelis William Neloe began his career in 1966 when he joined the government-owned Bank Dagang Negara (BDN). He gained experience working in the operations, international banking and credit departments, and also spent time in Hong Kong for the Bank, until he became the managing director in 1991. He then became the vice president director and subsequently president director of a large petrochemical company. Then, in 2000, he was appointed CEO of Bank Mandiri. With his commitment to change and better governance, Neloe is the key driver behind the ongoing transformation of Bank Mandiri.

FELIPE YAP

Felipe Yap is a successful, self-made, businessman and has been chairman of the Philippine Stock Exchange for two consecutive terms since March 2000. He is chairman of the board and CEO of Lepanto Consolidated Mining and Lepanto Investment and Development Corporation, among others. He attributes part of his success in business to the rigorous discipline instilled by his university studies in Philosophy at the University of San Carlos.

SAIFUDDIEN HASAN

Saifuddien Hasan has been the president director of PT Bank Negara Indonesia (Persero) Tbk (Bank BNI) since 2000. He earned a Bachelor's degree in economics from Gadjah Mada University (1978), and an MBA from the University of Nebraska (1987). Since joining Bank BNI, Mr Hasan has held various positions, including as the head of regional offices in Denpasar and Surabaya as well as various positions in the planning department.

TUNKU ABDUL AZIZ

Tunku Abdul Aziz Tunku Ibrahim has held senior management positions in large organizations in the private and public sectors in Malaysia, Hong Kong and the U.K. He initiated the setting up of the Malaysian chapter of Transparency International, the global coalition against corruption. In October 1997, he was elected to the international board of Transparency International and, in March the following year, he became vice-chairman of Transparency International's board of directors.

SUPACHAI PANITCHPAKDI

Dr Supachai has held a range of positions in former governments of Thailand, including the position of Deputy Finance Minister (1986–1988) and Deputy Prime Minister (1992–1995). From 1997 until January 2001, Dr Supachai served as Deputy Prime Minister and Minister of Commerce of Thailand and has been actively involved in international trade. Beginning on September 1, 2002, Dr Supachai will serve a three-year term as Director-General of the WTO, succeeding Michael Moore.

XI JINPING

Xi Jinping is the governor of Fujian Province, People's Republic of China. During the Cultural Revolution, he worked in the countryside with a production brigade in Yanchaun County, Sh'anxi Province. Upon graduation from Qinghua University (where he became a Doctor of Science of Law), he served in a range of positions, including chairman of the Standing Committee of Fuzhou Municipal People's Congress. He is an alternative member of the CPC Central Committee.

KEAT CHHON

Born in 1934 and educated in France, Keat Chhon is Senior Minister and Minister for Economy and Finance of the Kingdom of Cambodia. He is also a coordinator for the Cambodian Government Private Sector Forum. His former positions include governorship of the Bank of Cambodia, Senior Minister in Charge of Rehabilitation and Development, and positions at the UNDP and the UNIDO.

HISHAMUDDIN TUN HUSSEIN

Hishamuddin Tun Hussein is Malaysia's Minister of Youth and Sports. He began his career in Malaysian politics in the United Malay National Organisation (UMNO), which is an anchor political party in the Malaysian Government's ruling coalition, the Barisan Nasional (The National Front). A lawyer by training, he was called to the English Bar in 1984 and to the Malaysian Bar in 1985, before entering the Malaysian political arena.

OH JONG-NAM

Oh Jong-Nam is the commissioner of the National Statistical Office in Korea, the central government authority in charge of statistics. Before assuming his current position, Dr Oh worked as Secretary for Finance and Economy in the Office of the President of Korea, where his major roles included coordinating macroeconomic policies, structural reforms and competition policies. He also served as Alternate Executive Director of the International Monetary Fund (IMF) in Washington, D.C., representing 14 member-countries.

RAFAEL BUENAVENTURA

Mr Buenaventura assumed the position of Governor of the Central Bank of the Philippines on July 6, 1999, following a long and distinguished career in private commercial banking spanning more than 30 years. He has been the recipient of many business awards, including "One of Asia's Most Outstanding Bankers" by *Asiamoney* in 1991. A graduate of De La Salle University, where he received a Bachelor of Science in Commerce, he took his MBA at Stern Graduate School of Business, New York University.

GEORGES UGEUX

Georges Ugeux became Group Executive Vice President, International, of the New York Stock Exchange in September 1996. He is a member of the NYSE Management Committee. Mr Ugeux is responsible for developing new international listings for the NYSE, maintaining relationships with listed non-U.S. companies, exchanges and governments, as well as dealing with regulatory issues in the United States as they relate to international securities. In addition, he oversees the NYSE's London and Tokyo offices.

YU YOUJUN

Yu Youjun has been Mayor of the Shenzhen Municipal Government since 2000 and has been one of the foremost supporters of technology-centered development in this fast-moving city. Before this, he held the position of Director-General of Publicity of Guangdong Province. He is a member of the Standing Committee, the Guangdong CPC Committee and is vice-party secretary of the Communist Party of China Shenzhen Committee. He has a Ph.D in Philosophy.

NOBUYUKI IDEI

Mr Idei became chairman and chief executive officer of Sony Corp. in 2000 after serving as the company's president for five years. He graduated from Waseda University with a Bachelor of Arts in Political Science and Economics. He also studied the economics of European countries at university, and spent a total of nine years working for Sony in Europe. In addition to his role at Sony, Mr Idei serves as an outside director for Nestlé S.A. and General Motors Corp. Mr Idei is a member of the Foundation Board of the World Economic Forum.

PART
1

A New Look at
Globalization for Asia

Introduction

Four years after the start of the Asian financial crisis, Asia's love-hate relationship with globalization is still very much alive. Indeed, it has become more pronounced. However, attention has gradually shifted from focusing mainly on economic and financial aspects to geopolitical and strategic aspects. The latter have received particular attention in the wake of the continuing conflict in the Middle East but had actually been gelling long before two planes veered into the World Trade Center and altered the shape of the global security consciousness.

If there was a lesson to be learned from the Asian financial crisis, it was that while the globalization of markets and money could propel Asia steadily up in the development ranks, it could just as easily take it away. Proponents of an Asia that is integrated into the global economy are still very numerous and solidly in positions of power. However, they have also reached a tacit understanding with their peers on the other side of the argument that, if anything, Asia needs to dictate very clearly the terms of her engagement in global markets. Foreign-investment incentives and open borders are good in theory as frameworks for national growth but, in practice, need to be tempered with policies that take into account the developmental stage and needs of those most likely to be adversely affected. The debate over globalization has matured from its initial focus on "yes or no" into one that centers on "the ways and means".

The discussion in Asia on globalization — or global engagement — in the geopolitical sense is following a similar path. That is, most Asian leaders and thinkers seem to accept and agree that global engagement is a positive necessity. Rather, the debate centers on the nature of Asia's participation in globalization, global networks and global consensus-building on specific issues. They know and want to temper the ripple-back effects that such participation will have on domestic constituencies or interest groups. The need to stake national positions on the war against terrorism has only highlighted this need.

Integrationists in Asia will find comfort in the fact that those in positions of power largely do support Asia's engagement in the global anti-terrorism fight. Philippine President Gloria Macapagal-Arroyo is one of the strongest voices for involving Asia and has taken the big step of allowing the U.S. military back into the country. A more common reaction in Asia accepts engagement but takes the more serious challenge for Asia as one of introspection. The global focus on terrorism has created the need for Asians to distinguish the good, moderate sides of Asian religion and values, as shown by Jusuf Wanandi of the Center for International and Strategic Studies in Indonesia, and lawyer and columnist Karim Raslan. In another way, Korean MP Kim Min-seok advocates a reassessment of security concerns for Asia, but with a specific view to ending the uncertainty and stasis on the Korean peninsula, as a way to bolster global peace. Malaysian Prime Minister Mahathir bin Mohamad Mohamad takes this one step further and says that, while Asia should be introspective, it should accept globalism only as an added impetus to national development.

Attention to global geopolitics need not overshadow the still pressing demands for Asia to continue to strive for better economic conditions. Asia's framework for growth and development — economic, financial and social — remains sound and stable, as pointed out by Heinrich von Pierer of Siemens and Gordon Campbell, the Premier of British Columbia. However, the scope for further work towards regional development is still quite broad, and Chinese Minister of Foreign Trade and Economic Cooperation Shi Guangsheng indicates just a few of these, with a focus on regional co-operation. Given his experience in bringing China fully into the world economy through accession to the WTO, Shi's counsel for more regional interaction seems wise.

At the end of the day, Asia's voice on globalization is highly pluralistic, which should not be a surprise given that national sovereignty and interests have always been paramount in a region with a hundred different histories within her borders. Each country and each people will come to terms with, and adapt in its own way, to globalization. Asia's new look at globalization involves recognition that the region is engaged, but in very specific terms that are defined by nations and peoples. As such, Asia's new take on globalization is propelling it towards greater global integration, even before a regional consensus is reached. Ironically, globalization — the force which has been accused of stamping out national traditions, cultures and peoples — is in Asia prompting no less than a reinforcing of national sovereignty and difference.

Globalization: Challenges and Impact on Asia

Mahathir bin Mohamad
Prime Minister of Malaysia

 Globalization is a much-used word. And, like such words, it is surrounded by confusion and misunderstanding, because each one places a meaning to it in a different way from someone else.

My contribution is on the challenges of globalization and its impact on Asia. I shall confine myself to the issue of economic globalization. To begin with, "globalization" is not a God-given, iron-clad law of nature or humanity. It is a set of concepts and policies made by human beings and, therefore, can also be reconceptualized, reshaped and changed. The concept is deceptively simple. The free market must be allowed to function without interference. Governments must remove all barriers that prevent the full and free operation and movement of goods and services, capital, firms and financial institutions across borders.

In theory this is supposed to be for the good of all. In reality, this concept was designed by the developed countries on behalf of their companies and financial institutions to overcome the regulations set up by developing countries to promote their domestic economy and local firms, which had been marginalized during colonialism. In practice, following these policies can bring a country new opportunities for wealth creation, but also new risks that can destroy prosperity in the twinkle of an eye, as we have seen recently in East Asia and, later, in Argentina.

The lesson of recent experience is that a country must carefully choose a combination of policies that best enables it to take the opportunity while avoiding the pitfalls — a task easier said than done. A country that is still poor or developing may find that it is not wise to jump blindly into complete integration with the world economy, for this may open it up to many risks that can damage its local economy. It is wiser to engage in a selective and strategic integration with the world market. In this approach, the country chooses the way and degree to which it wants to open up, the timing and sequence of opening up, the form of cooperation and competition between its local firms and foreign firms, and the particular sectors it wants to liberalize and those sectors that still need some protection, for the good of the country.

The breaking down of economic barriers may not be new (for example, it also took place in the laissez faire era of the 19th century). What is new in the present age is the globalization of policy-making. Increasingly, policies that used to be made by national governments are now formulated for developing countries through global processes and institutions, including the IMF, the World Bank and the WTO. Their policies tend to favor the agenda of the richer countries that dominate them. Developing countries are pressured by IMF loan conditions or the legally binding rules of the WTO to apply the policies which, in turn, determine the countries' economic and social path.

Since the policies are usually set in a one-size-fits-all manner, they hinder the ability of the individual country to choose the particular set of policies that suits its own development needs. As a result, developing countries have found it extremely difficult to steer through the turbulent waters of globalization.

National policies should largely be made by national governments and not on their behalf by global institutions or other governments. Moreover, one size does not fit all when it comes to policy-making and, therefore, the policies of the IMF and the rules of the WTO have to be reviewed and re-calibrated. Finally, the mandate and procedures of global institutions to set national policies for governments have to be looked at again, in the light of recent experience.

What is important is that countries be given the right and space to review the impact of globalization, and decide which aspects to make use of in future, and which aspects to discard. As recent events show, it is too dangerous to allow the so-called free market, or global institutions, to usurp the role of governments, for this may well lead the countries to prolonged periods of economic slowdown, economic anarchy and social chaos.

There are at least three major aspects of economic globalization: trade, finance and investment. Each aspect is distinct, poses its own set of challenges and has to be dealt with carefully. In Asia, the countries have had their full share of benefits and costs from these different aspects of globalization.

The Western view of Asia's globalization experience has undergone a 180-degree shift. East Asia was seen as the shining example of wholesale liberalization leading to spectacular growth. After the crisis, it was portrayed as a cesspool of corruption and crony capitalism, which conveniently explains why the free market cannot function well. Today, Argentina is going through the same image change, from the free-market success model to a country that failed because of corruption.

Where Asia is concerned, the caricatures have been too extreme and simplistic. Most of the East Asian countries that succeeded did not practice the kind of total free-market liberalization that their former admirers attributed to them. Instead, there was a policy of strategic integration with the world economy. In trade, sectors where local companies were too weak were protected until the companies could better compete with imports. As local products became more-efficiently produced, duties on them were also gradually reduced. Lacking rich domestic markets, many Asian countries oriented their economies towards exports: firstly, through the traditional primary commodities; secondly, through diversifying the range of export commodities and processing them, and then moving on to industrial exports.

Thus Asia's relative success in trade was not due to a policy of wholesale liberalization, but to selective and strategic trade liberalization in which opening up to trade was carried out in stages, with the sequence and degree of liberalization being set by national conditions and goals. The damage that could be caused to local industries by import liberalization was minimized, whilst policies to maximize the benefits from exporting were emphasized.

Likewise in the area of investment, East Asian countries did not have a policy of total liberalization. Instead, there was encouragement of both local and foreign investments, an attempt to attain a balance between the two, and in pursuit of national economic and social goals. In Southeast Asia, foreign investments have for a long time been welcomed and generous incentives are given to attract them.

For example, Malaysia provided tax exemptions and relief for foreign investors in the manufacturing industry. We also encouraged joint-venture arrangements so as to facilitate the participation of local people in equity and profits. We also encouraged foreign firms to transfer technology and use local inputs to stimulate the local economy. In sectors where local companies and people have technical and marketing expertise, such as mining and agricultural-export crops, we did not welcome foreign investments. This kind of discriminating investment policy, involving a mix of local and foreign investment and local and foreign partnerships has contributed to social and political stability. This, in turn, benefited the foreign investors and the local people alike.

In trade and investment, therefore, East Asian countries by and large succeeded in managing the relationship between the national economy and the world economy quite well. The countries were able to make use of the opportunities presented by globalization.

When it came to finance, Asia has had a more bitter experience with globalization. Not so long ago, the Asian countries practiced prudent policies in relation to external finance. They had liberal policies relating to long-term, foreign direct investment, but they also carefully regulated and restricted the inflow and outflow of short-term funds.

However, following the global trend, most East Asian countries rapidly liberalized and deregulated the flow of funds, allowing the inflow and outflow of foreign loan, portfolio and speculative capital. The international financial institutions, the developed countries and the gurus of finance heaped advice on Asian countries to open up and enjoy the benefits of capital flows; they did not warn about the risks nor provide guidelines. Fortunately for Malaysia, we retained the regulation that local companies can only borrow from abroad if (and to the extent) the proposed loan can be shown to bring in revenue in foreign exchange to service the loan. However, in some other countries, there was a huge inflow and build-up of private-sector foreign debt, putting the countries in a vulnerable position. The blow came when rapacious speculators took advantage of the situation to manipulate the local currencies, sparking steep devaluations, and making it almost impossible to earn enough devalued local currency to service foreign-currency debts.

Even then, the crisis could have been contained had there been an international or regional mechanism to provide liquidity to the countries, or to arrange for a temporary debt-standstill whilst creditors and debtors were called together to work out a solution in a calm, fair and proper way. Since there did not seem to be an alternative source of financing, the IMF's assistance was sought. Unfortunately, the IMF policies of high interest, reduced government spending and prohibition of foreign-exchange controls made the situation worse, as the contractionary policies led to recession, closure of firms and a sharp rise in non-performing loans. Foreign and local funds left the countries. And the IMF policies on privatization and on removing restrictions on foreign ownership led to the sale of local assets to foreigners, often at a cheap price, causing much unhappiness among the people.

In Malaysia's case, we were also affected by the crisis as our currency steeply devalued and the stock market declined with the withdrawal of foreign funds. We did not have to seek funds from the IMF as our debt was manageable. However, at first, we voluntarily followed IMF-type policies of high interest, reduced budget and continued capital mobility. Like other affected countries, our economy spun into recession and the local companies and banks were seriously hurt. After a year of this, we decided to switch policies to a package that included a fixed exchange rate. The economy recovered well in 1999 and 2000 before the current global slowdown started to affect us again in 2001.

Some lessons can be drawn from this episode. Firstly, financial liberalization should be treated much more cautiously than either trade or investment liberalization. The risks of financial liberalization are greater, its impact far more devastating, if it is not done properly. The benefits for the recipient country are not so certain. Developing countries must draw from this experience and formulate guidelines on financial liberalization based on a thorough understanding of the financial markets, especially the speculative components.

Secondly, there are many systemic faults in the global financial architecture. The Argentina crisis is only the latest of a series of financial shocks that have rocked Asia and other regions. The global system needs to be overhauled urgently before more crises erupt. The various types of capital flows have to be reviewed and made subject to regulation, whilst manipulations — as distinct from speculation — in currency and capital markets should be curbed, if not prohibited.

Thirdly, financial instability and crisis can cause immense damage to a country; it can offset the wealth and economic achievements and overcome the institutions that have been built over a generation. Thus, there should be national, regional and international systems to prevent such crises or to manage them well, to avoid the massive damage.

Fourthly, the IMF itself has to revise its outdated policies. Its governance system has to be democratized so that developing countries have a greater say in its policies.

As the above account shows, the different aspects of economic globalization have affected Asian countries in different ways. Trade and investment liberalization have been kind to Asia, partly because of their nature and partly because of the selective and strategic manner in which the Asian countries have managed these aspects of globalization. On the other hand, integration into the global financial system has wreaked havoc with several Asian countries, again partly due to the nature of the system itself and partly to the wrong policies that Asian countries had taken on financial liberalization.

The present global slowdown also prompts Asian leaders to ponder over our previous strategy of export-led growth. When the world economy is doing well, such a strategy results in many benefits and high growth. However, a global slowdown also affects the more globalized economies more seriously.

If there is a swift global recovery, then our problems will be short-lived and our economies will soon grow rapidly again. However, if the global slowdown persists or worsens, then our economies will be vulnerable to stagnation for several years as demand for our exports is affected. It is thus timely to look towards alternative sources of growth, such as making conditions more conducive to local investments and the building up of the strength of the domestic market, to production for the domestic market (even as we strive to maintain our competitiveness in the world market), and to increasing regional trade and investments (in order to reduce excessive dependence on the developed countries that are affected by recession). With the global economy in trouble, Asian countries should intensify their regional cooperation in trade and finance, including such initiatives as an East Asian Economic Grouping and a regional monetary fund.

As I said earlier, globalization is not the kind of ironclad inevitability it is often made out to be. It is shaped by man-made policies. So far, most of these policies have been set by the developed countries and the institutions they control. Asian countries must take a more pro-active role in shaping the globalization process. To do so, they have to coordinate among themselves better to be more effective in promoting their rights and interests in the global decision-making institutions such as the IMF, the World Bank and the WTO.

The globalization of policy-making also has its drawbacks, as rules and policies made in international bodies (especially those over which the developing countries have little influence) can be inappropriate or, worse, can hinder or prevent us from implementing policies required for our development and nation-building.

The current globalization process is being driven mainly in institutions like the IMF and the WTO, with the developed countries mainly in the driver's seat. We have already seen how destabilizing the world financial system can be, and the deficiencies of the IMF's policies.

At the Doha Ministerial Conference in 2001, the WTO decided on a very heavy work program that will really tax the human and financial resources of developing countries in Asia. Negotiations will soon begin on important subjects, and the results will have great significance on the options, policies and possibilities of our future development. If the developing countries, including those in Asia, get their act together and negotiate on the basis of their common interests, then there is a chance that the WTO can be changed to become an instrument for truly mutual development. However, if the present trend continues — in which the powerful countries work in concert while the Asian countries, of which many are still developing, are not allowed to work together — then I am afraid the WTO will become an even-more powerful instrument to expand the process of globalization along the present lines, leading to even more inequitable and inappropriate results.

Globalization is indeed a complex phenomenon to define and understand. However, with our rich experience and outward-looking attitudes, Asian leaders, policy-makers and intellectuals should be able to have a better grasp of globalization than many others. What is important is that we make a proper diagnosis of globalization in all its facets and complexities, and draw the correct lessons of what policies have worked and which ones have not worked, and then transform our conclusions into the next generation of policies.

Why Asia Must Stay Engaged in the Globalized World

Gordon Campbell
Premier of British Columbia, Canada

 After the tragic events of September 11, policy-makers around the world have been reassessing what globalization means. The terrorist attacks on the United States were a major focus of discussion at the World Economic Forum's East Asia Economic Summit which took place in Hong Kong at the end of October 2001, less than two months later.

It may be tempting to raise protective walls around our nations, yet in this age of worldwide travel, telecommunications and the Internet, there is an understanding that we are all dependent upon one another for our safety and prosperity. Globalization is not reversible.

As one of the most dynamic, prosperous and innovative parts of the world, Asia is at the cutting edge of global development and the social culture and economic benefits of real openness to trade are enormous. Asia must maintain and expand its political and economic linkages. Undoubtedly it will exert global leadership on the challenges that face us all at the onset of the new millennium.

SECURITY

September 11 was an attack not just against the United States, but against the entire world. It is striking that the primary targets of the terrorists on September 11 were the twin towers of the World Trade Center in New York City, which had been the target of an earlier failed attempt in 1993. In order to destroy this prominent symbol of globalization and the open society, the terrorists murdered thousands of innocent men and women.

The victims of the terrorist attack were not just from the United States, but from more than 60 other countries; they were either working there or just visiting the great city of New York.

The events of September 11 bring home the fundamental reality that we live in a world that is inextricably tied together more closely than ever before. In this interdependent world, no country can be an island unto itself. One of the basic functions of government is to provide citizens with protection against threats to their physical safety. Governments around the world must all work together to fight back against the random and brutal threat of terrorism. The fight is currently taking place on the battlefield and in intelligence networks, but it must also include an assault on the financial underpinnings of terrorism.

As Canadian Finance Minister Paul Martin has stated: "There exists today an overwhelming consensus on the need to wrest from the grip of terrorists the funding they rely on to finance their violence. Without money they cannot buy weapons. Without cash they cannot fuel their cause. It stands, therefore, that part of the coordinated war against terrorism is an equally comprehensive assault on its finances...By definition, this implies a high degree of coordination between sovereign governments. But so too governments must tailor their measures to international practices. Otherwise, blood money will simply shop jurisdictions until it finds an accommodating home."

All governments must do their part to support the international campaign against terrorism. Following the courageous example of Pakistan's President Pervez Musharraf, we must all stand against those in our societies who encourage hatred and violence. Equally, we must take stern action against those who seek to profit financially from abetting terror. We must work together to combat money laundering, smuggling and other transnational crimes that are used by terrorists to finance their activities. As U.S. President George W. Bush has warned, the international campaign against terrorism has only just begun. Terrorism is a global phenomenon, with its own secretive networks and hidden interdependencies. Thus, only by working together can the international community succeed in rooting it out to ensure our collective safety.

Similarly, governments must work together to prevent unnecessary barriers that would restrict the flow of legitimate trade and travel. Immediately after September 11, Canada and the United States closed their borders and airspace for security reasons. Several months later, we are still struggling to ensure that an open 49th Parallel is not another casualty of the September 11 attacks. Nearly $2 billion is traded across the Canada–U.S. border each day, much of it in just-in-time delivery of goods and services. In our interdependent economy, it is vital that governments and businesses work together to develop innovative solutions that facilitate legitimate trade and mobility. This will free scarce law-enforcement resources to focus on movements of higher risk. Enhanced security, combined with improved flows of goods and people, will produce a more secure and responsive trading regime.

This is important since, as Minister Martin has pointed out, "It is the poor primarily who bear the long-term consequences of terrorism". We have all become aware of the grim reality of the daily lives of ordinary Afghan families, and all countries need to help repair the damage caused by the first phase of war. But Asian countries will need to take a leadership role in reconstructing Afghanistan, and also draw on their own histories to most effectively assist the most vulnerable victims of violence. Only by working together, learning from one another, and rooting out the causes of hopelessness will we ensure the long-term defeat of hate and terror.

LEGITIMACY AND GOVERNANCE

From the perspective of 2002, Asia is a remarkable success story. Asian countries have emerged successfully from a tumultuous century of colonialism, independence movements and war.

Since the fall of communism in 1989, most people recognize that there is only one viable model for a stable and successful society: a pluralistic democracy committed to the free market and which promotes respect and tolerance for diversity and civil society. Clearly, there is much room for variation within this model, and countries have their own national histories, traditions and cultures which will produce different political systems and values. However, the last 50 years illustrates that, irrespective of these national differences, democracy and free markets foster technological innovation and economic and social vitality. The unprecedented global boom of the second half of the 20th century testifies to the link between free-market societies and economic progress.

The terrorists who attacked the World Trade Center on September 11 were attacking the basic legitimacy of a society in which men and women are equal, in which colour and religion do not divide people, in which people do work which they enjoy in order to enjoy the fruits of their labour. They sought to destroy a global society in which countries live at peace with one another and trade goods and services in an efficient and orderly manner.

We cannot become complacent about our shared values. Globalization has brought untold prosperity to people around the world.

However, globalization is not just about increasing worldwide economic integration. Globalization is also about the development of a world community in which human rights and cultural and social improvements are pursued with equal determination.

While globalization has led to the rise of many highly successful societies, some have not made equal progress. While there is no universal approach in the area of governance, some basic guiding principles are clear. A society is more likely to become a free-market democracy if it can foster a middle class that owns private property. A state is likely to succeed if it can win the trust of its people through respected institutions and efficient bureaucracies that administer laws impartially and fairly. Governments that apply these principles are more likely to become stable and successful.

With the rise of worldwide travel and telecommunications, the expectations that citizens have of their national governments have also risen. Citizens are less likely to accept corruption or bureaucratic obstructionism. With high global demand for individuals with advanced skills and entrepreneurial verve, many countries face a challenge in retaining their best and brightest. All these factors make it imperative for governments to improve their own functioning. Immediately after my election as premier in May 2001, the Government of British Columbia reduced personal income taxes by 25%. We have made a commitment to reduce the hidden tax of unnecessary government regulation by one-third. Our goal is to make British Columbia a leading jurisdiction of choice for investment.

Like governments elsewhere, we need to compare our own ways with global best practices, and to ensure that they satisfy the needs and wishes of our citizens as well as or better than our competitors.

We all share the responsibility of helping to build and reconstruct governments or states that face significant challenges, whether in Asia or other parts of the world. Asian governments are important providers of financial assistance as well as governance expertise, and other members of the world community can provide assistance and economic support in helping new governments get beyond the initial transition to democracy and achieve stable and competent administrations.

GLOBALIZATION AND REGIONAL VALUES

Klaus Schwab, the President of the World Economic Forum, has pointed out that neither the "hyperglobalization" of a fully integrated monocultural world nor a world of anti-globalization isolationism built on intolerance is viable. In Schwab's words, "We need globalization based on networks with regional hubs…that combine global values with national and local values".

Asia's extraordinary cultural richness includes the great legacies of ancient Chinese and Indian civilizations, the elegance and beauty of Japanese ceremonies and rituals, and the cultural vitality of daily life across the whole vast continent. Asia hosts a diversity of languages, religions, colors and races that is the envy of the world. Many Asian countries have a history of multiculturalism that has made it possible for many diverse groups to live together in peace and harmony.

In addition to the wondrous riches of its cultural heritage, Asia is also at the cutting edge of global technological innovation. Engineers, designers and programmers in Japan, Taiwan, Korea, India and many other Asian countries have made Asia a global powerhouse in technology research, development and commercialization.

Asia's cultural riches and cutting-edge technology make it an ideal candidate for leadership in a global world that is not dominated by any one culture. I believe that globalization is an opportunity to learn from each other and to become wiser and more capable global citizens as a result.

For instance, the West has much to learn from the Confucian values of community, harmony and stability that underlie the economic success and social stability of the East Asian economies. The excellent educational performance of Asian students should serve as an inspiration to their counterparts in North America and Europe and should provoke a healthy global competition in educational excellence.

Conversely, Asian countries may benefit from absorbing the individualism which is the basis for so much of the technological and cultural innovation in North America. Individuals in North America are encouraged to speak out in ways which may appear disruptive but which are actually beneficial for their community. As Marjorie Yang, Chairman of the Esquel Group of Hong Kong, noted at the East Asia Economic Summit, her biggest challenge as a CEO is to encourage her knowledgeable and well-educated staff to speak up. In British Columbia, we welcome thousands of Asian students to our schools and post-secondary institutions, since we recognize that these students will be our best ambassadors in the long run. We hope that the friendship these young Asians form with young British Columbians will lead to greater understanding and personal growth for all.

FULL PARTICIPATION IN GLOBALIZATION

United Nations Secretary-General Kofi Annan has said that "If we cannot make globalization work for all, in the end it will work for none. The unequal distribution of benefits and the imbalance in global rule-making, which characterize globalization today, inevitably will produce backlash and protectionism. And that, in turn, threatens to undermine and ultimately unravel the open world economy that has been so painstakingly constructed over the course of the past half-century."

Obviously, globalization that does not include the developing countries of Africa, Latin America and Asia is not globalization. For globalization to be more than merely the increasing economic integration and political harmonization of the rich countries of North America, Western Europe and East Asia, it is important that the barriers which separate the North and South, richer and poorer countries, those who can access digital technologies and those who do not have access to electricity, telephones or clean water, must be overcome.

Globalization has made us more aware of the challenges *and* opportunities that lie ahead. It has led to increased awareness of global inequality, to the rise of a kind of "global conscience" on the part of non-governmental organizations and governments alike, and also to the growth of global mechanisms and institutions that seek practical solutions to alleviate poverty and inequality and foster economic development in poorer parts of the world.

As James Wolfensohn, the President of the World Bank, points out, "Future growth in the world's population, nearly all of it in developing countries, is an issue for us all. The world needs to address poverty, equality and equity issues." No corner of the world is immune from the consequences of what takes place in another part, whether through the increase in desperate refugee claimants or through the transmission of previously unknown bacteria and viruses.

It is, therefore, in everyone's interests to actively engage the challenges of globalization as well as enjoy its benefits. As the most populous part of the world, with the most extreme disparities in wealth, Asia has a unique perspective on the challenges of globalization. Although over 800 million people in Asia live on less than one dollar per day, Asia is also a beacon of hope to raise the prospects of the poor: between 1990 and 2000 the proportion of people living in absolute poverty in Asia declined from 28% to 15%. Other parts of the world may wish to learn from the Asian experience in poverty alleviation.

Governments have a responsibility to work together to make globalization a process that works for everyone's benefit. Trade ministers at the Doha summit of the World Trade Organization in November 2001 recognized this responsibility by promoting an unprecedented capacity-building initiative to enable poorer countries to participate more actively in trade negotiations. Wealthier countries also have an additional responsibility to provide meaningful international development assistance. Financier George Soros has called for Western governments to provide more support for the developing world, saying that, "If all countries would provide 1.5% of their GDP to the provision of global goods then this would make a tremendous difference". Clearly, governments in Asia and elsewhere must renew their efforts to make globalization work for everyone.

RENEWING GLOBAL INSTITUTIONS

In the aftermath of September 11, many aspects of the global political order are being re-examined. The United States has taken a leading role in assembling a wide-ranging coalition in the international campaign against terror. The fear among many that the United States was retreating into an inward-looking isolationist posture has been shown to be unfounded. It has also become clear that everyone must support the struggle against terrorism, as no country is exempt from this menace nor the duty to remove it from our midst.

Now is a time of opportunity in which old assumptions can be dropped and global institutions can be renewed or built to suit a new internationalism. Many global institutions which were established in the aftermath of the Second World War could benefit from a reassessment of their utility and purpose in this fast-changing global milieu. Similarly, there may be reason to consider new multilateral mechanisms to combat new global challenges such as terrorism or the spread of deadly diseases. There is scope for a renewed multilateralism in which all democracies have an important role.

Asian governments have special reason to undertake this exercise in renewal, given their experience of the Asian economic crisis of 1997–98. Existing international financial institutions such as the International Monetary Fund may not have been able to provide adequate assistance to help Asian governments cope with the enormous economic and social challenges that their countries faced during the economic crisis. Following this, Canada called for a new international body to be formed to renew the global financial architecture. As a result, the G-20 international forum of finance ministers was formed, and several Asian member countries of the G-20 have brought an Asian perspective to renewing the Bretton Woods structures.

To again use the words of Canada's Finance Minister Martin, there is need for "a better framework to address challenges such as the rescheduling of national debt. We need new rules of the game that would allow the international community to find solutions for debt problems in a timely way." Furthermore, Minister Martin points out, "making globalization work requires more than the management of financial crises...For billions of people, the greatest danger has not been that globalization will succeed, but rather that it will fail. Now more than ever we must redouble our commitment to strengthening the world economy, but also to strengthening the ties that bind us together as a community of nations."

In addition to taking a leadership role in renewing the international financial architecture, Asian governments must take leadership to ensure the success of the new round of global trade negotiations. These complex multilateral negotiations are a vital opportunity to undo the barriers of protectionism and promote greater economic efficiency to the benefit of all. As Supachai Panitchpakdi, the Director-General-Designate of the WTO, has pointed out, it is particularly important for Asia that the WTO should work for everybody.

Asian governments also have an important role to play in global negotiations on the environment. As the fastest-growing economies in the world, Asian countries must take a far-sighted and long-term approach towards global issues such as environmental protection. Protection and promoting the environment is important today and for future generations, and the international community welcomes the responsible engagement of Asian countries as we jointly face the biggest challenges to our future. There are also many opportunities, as we in British Columbia have discovered, in the fields of environmental technology and emerging energy sources such as the Ballard fuel cell. Vancouver hosts the biennial GLOBE trade fair, which offers the strategic intelligence required for balancing the global business, energy and environmental agendas. Increased Asian participation and leadership in this area would be welcomed.

In addition to participation in existing international institutions and multilateral negotiations, Asian governments are also setting a valuable example in regional integration, both within Southeast Asia and within the broader Asia Pacific region. Efforts by the ASEAN countries to come together with the Northeast Asian economies may become a critical driver in the region's economic recovery, and set a good example for other parts of the world where regional integration efforts may have stalled. The APEC forum has proven its value as a global forum for world leaders to engage in serious dialogue and consensus-building. That leaders engage in peaceful discussions in multilateral forums as well as bilaterally provides valuable support to global stability and security.

THE NEW COMPLEXITY

Globalization is a complex process that is much more than the integration of the world's financial markets and increased trade liberalization. Global economic integration has been made possible by an exponential boom in new information and telecommunications technologies that have made the world a smaller place. Markets operate around the clock, just as people move around the world in growing volumes at accelerated and unpredictable rates. Time and distance have become less relevant in the new global order.

Since the end of the Second World War, the world has become a vastly richer and safer place. Advances in medicine and public health have reduced infant mortality and increased life expectancy dramatically. Innovations are being showered upon us so rapidly that we take them for granted. The personal computer was only produced 20 years ago, yet today no office or home in the developed world seems complete without one.

However, we cannot assume that technological innovation and economic interdependence will be sufficient to drive this ongoing process of globalization. It is worth remembering that the European economy was highly interdependent in 1914, just before the First World War took place. The events of September 11 are a grim reminder of the challenges that still lie ahead. Business leaders and elected officials must continue to strive to break down unnecessary barriers. Political will and good sense will continue to be required to make the world a safe place, in which all our citizens can enjoy the benefits of modern science and technology.

In order to sustain globalization, leaders all over the world must commit themselves to staying the course of sound economic policies and fiscal discipline. This is a challenge at the best of times, let alone during difficult economic circumstances. Asian leaders are well aware of these difficulties, having undergone the economic crisis of 1997–98. However, the sacrifices made by governments and by ordinary citizens are worth it in the long run. We must put into place economic policies that reward efficiency rather than subsidizing inefficiency. Institutional reform is a critical part of the process. Reducing red tape and eliminating corruption are key components of the reform process.

Governments have a vital role to play in furthering the well-being of their citizens. In particular, governments must invest in education in order to foster the creativity and potential of our greatest renewable resource, our young people. Investment in education brings the highest return in the long term, in enhancing productivity and improving the standards of living. Furthermore, the whole world benefits from this investment, as I know from my personal experience as a volunteer teacher in Africa in the 1960s.

As Rapporteur to the East Asia Economic Summit in October 2001, I summarized the conclusions of so many prominent Asian business and political leaders on the work that lies before us: "September 11 has created a new urgency to move forward. It is critical that we hear the message of this summit: we are all for the eradication of terrorism, but if we are going to do it, it is important for us to eliminate the sense of hopelessness that is felt in some communities. We have to understand the importance of a development agenda for the WTO. We have to invest in education. And we have to start building the social infrastructure we need. The velocity of change must be relentless."

In the final analysis, globalization is the process which is unleashing the unbounded potential of human beings by making irrelevant the barriers which have hindered us through so much of our history. As we work together, we discover the values and aspirations we hold in common. Asian leaders have a vital role to play in this process, by maintaining and expanding their linkages with the rest of the world and by taking leadership roles in dealing with the challenges and opportunities that face us in the new millennium. We in British Columbia look forward to working with you.

East Asia, Terrorism and New Global Rules

Jusuf Wanandi
Member of the Board of Trustees, Centre for Strategic and
International Studies, Indonesia

The terrorist attacks on September 11 were very dramatic and traumatic because they hit at the heartland of the U.S. They were directed against her symbols of power and killed so many innocent people in such a short time in a way that nobody could ever have imagined.

Therefore, the pressures on the Bush Administration to do justice in self-defense should be appreciated. That Bush and his security assistants were able to mobilize overwhelming bipartisan support domestically, to formulate an all-encompassing strategy and to create a broad-based coalition in the space of a few days is to be applauded. These are factors that are critical to the success of the struggle against terrorism.

The first phase of the struggle is aimed at getting rid of the Taliban, and to transform the image of Osama bin Laden from a protected hero of the underprivileged, like Che Guevara in Bolivia before, into a fugitive, like Carlos, to be hunted down by the whole world. But beyond this, this phase is also characterized by the ushering in of a new era in strategic development.

The September attack on the World Trade Center and the Pentagon was a watershed in strategic development and international relations. It made an end to a post-Cold War era that was characterized by the presence of one superpower and a great deal of uncertainty about the direction of global developments because that superpower had no clear agenda.

The new era will be neither bipolar nor multipolar, as some analysts and governments had expected. It is still unclear what international order will develop, and the situation is extremely fluid. It will definitely not be a unipolar one. Recent developments have shown that isolation or unilateralism will not go far in fighting terrorism. Stronger multilateralism will be required, and the U.N. will play a bigger role in the future.

After some initial hesitation, the U.S. has come out quite well and has shown itself willing to take the leadership again in the new era of international relations and strategic development. This is critical to maintaining the system. During the post-Cold War period there were doubts about U.S. willingness to stay engaged and to lead the world in the right way. She is now willing to lead within a multilateral mode. This does not mean that every policy or action will be consulted over or decided together, but that the main policy directions will be formulated with the involvement of many coalition partners.

It also will not mean that every partner in the grand coalition has to agree on every tactic or strategy for fighting global terrorism. Therefore, regional and even national initiatives should be welcomed, so long as there is some degree of coordination.

In fact, what each country can do is to first develop public support for the fight against global, regional and, most importantly, domestic terrorism, through supplying adequate information and an active public education program. Then, each should freeze the bank accounts of terrorist networks, especially of al-Qaeda, and close their training centers. Furthermore, each country should engage in intelligence and police cooperation, both regionally and internationally, and give political and diplomatic support to the global coalition against terrorism under U.S. leadership.

In the U.S. itself, there is a concern about the bipartisan and majority support for President Bush's policies when the Taliban have been defeated and Osama bin Laden is killed or captured. But this fight against terrorism will be a long-term affair and will encompass all spheres: military, diplomatic, political, economic, financial and social. Another worry is whether during this long struggle U.S. policies will remain multilateral. Essentially, the question is whether the coalition can last in the longer term.

It should be recognized that the coalition cannot be a tight and regimented one and be determined solely by the U.S. In reality, there are many types of coalition with different functions and intensities. U.S. allies, such as NATO and Japan, have something specific to perform and are expected to be ready for military action. Both Germany and Japan are involved outside their immediate environment for the first time since the Second World War, while the U.K., France and Italy are ready to participate on the ground.

Pakistan and, to a certain extent, Uzbekistan, Tajikistan and Kazakhstan are providing intelligence support and will make themselves available as bases from which to stage attacks against the Taliban. U.S. relations with Russia have improved quite substantially. Putin's decision to line up with the U.S. in the "war" against terrorism has put Russia squarely on the side of the West. China is willing to cooperate because she worries about her own terrorists, who also have links with al-Qaeda. As a result of this cooperation, the relationship between the U.S. and China has improved. However, it remains to be seen how long this honeymoon can last, and whether it will help solve other problems.

Japan has been persuaded by her neighbors to send her SDF Navy beyond her own borders and this may pave the way for Japan to become a "normal" country in the future. India has begun to develop closer relations with the U.S. and now sees an opportunity to accelerate and deepen the process. However, Pakistan's critical role in the coalition has imposed some limits on India's efforts. But in the long term, India will be strategically important to the U.S.

Other Muslim countries, particularly in the Middle East, have been asked to give political support to the coalition and to sever al-Qaeda's networks in their own countries. In this context, the U.S. is willing to be more balanced on the perennial problem of Israel and Palestine and is pushing for a cease-fire and the resumption of talks in line with the Mitchell Commission's recommendations. This is maybe the most important, concrete and acute problem in U.S. policies for all Muslim countries, and has given rise to deep feelings of injustice and accusations of double standards from Muslims in general. This has been compounded emotionally by the fact that the third-most holy place in Islam, the al Aqsa Mosque in Jerusalem, is now under Israel's control, and limitations have been placed on Muslims who wish to visit the place. This sense of despair and hopelessness has resulted in a great deal of hate being directed against the U.S. This has to be corrected.

It has to be admitted that the end of the Cold War and the demise of the Soviet Union have tended to make the U.S. more inward-looking. The U.S. tends to ignore the plight of the world, especially of the poorest. It has not paid enough attention to regional conflicts, particularly the Israel-Palestine conflict. It has done almost nothing on the non-proliferation of weapons of mass destruction, refusing to ratify treaties to that effect. It has never really tried very hard to explain its policies to the world and instead closed down USIS, merged USAID into the State Department, cut the budget of the VOA and the State Department. In addition, it has ignored the U.N., and refused and to pay its dues. At the end of the Cold War, the U.S. entered into a decade of lost opportunities.

It is to be hoped that the U.S. will now become less unilateralist and will adopt a more multilateral approach to world affairs. Its friends and allies have to assist on this by reminding the U.S. again and again about the need to adopt this new approach. This is so because there is a very real need for a global coalition to face global terrorism. The efforts to get at Osama bin Laden and al-Qaeda and to get rid of their protectors, namely the Taliban, are only the first step. More steps are needed and more assistance and cooperation for the next phases of the struggle should be anticipated. These can lead to the creation of a new world order where all big powers participate in the fight against terrorism globally and in addressing the root causes of terrorism. These efforts will have to address such issues as poverty; various forms of transnational crime; the proliferation of weapons of mass destruction; and regional conflicts, especially intractable ones such as the Israel-Palestine problem.

In this effort, Russia is an important partner. It will be more difficult for China to be completely on board, but special efforts should be made to cooperate with her. India has shown her desire to become a partner and can be expected to join. For all these efforts to be feasible there needs to be a consolidated and streamlined U.N. because she, as the representation of the international community, has to give her support and sanction to the most important efforts against terrorism. The U.S. has to show its commitment to the U.N. before this will be possible.

While military activity will be necessary, the fight against global terrorism should go beyond this. It should involve a struggle for ideas and beliefs as well as a global effort to eradicate poverty. This cannot be achieved by the U.S. alone. It should be based on a new concert of great powers and backed by the U.N. Such a concerted move could be led by the G-8 plus China and India. Others can participate later.

There is still a great deal of apprehension among the friends and allies of the U.S. that the multilateral approaches of the Bush Administration, which thus far have been quite encouraging, are not deep and are not based on a changed ideology.

There are, indeed, mixed signals about whether a unilateralist or a multilateralist attitude is the more pronounced in the Bush Administration since September 11. On the one hand, the Doha Agreement brought fast-track authority in making trade agreements; on the other, the ABM Treaty was repudiated.

Ideology-wise, Bush's team is much more unilateralist. But the group consists of smart, experienced people. If they realize that the challenge of terrorism is a medium- to longer-term problem, encompassing a struggle in every field of life — in ideas, ideologies and values — then it should also be clear that a credible global coalition is necessary to overcome this challenge. If the U.S. ever thinks of going it alone, she would have to change her way of life of the last 100 years. Essentially, she would have to close her society and civilization, affecting not only her own people but a great many more around the world. That is why the prospect of a unilateralist United States, strengthened by the military prowess demonstrated in the war against the Taliban, should not be our conclusion. This is only the first phase of the struggle. There should not be only one coalition because there are too many aspects of the struggle. Regional initiatives should be encouraged and supported.

It is very important that the unilateralist tendencies of the U.S. are kept in balance by the multilateral interests and approaches of her allies and friends.

The economic aspect of these efforts should not be underestimated because, to be able to get at the roots of terrorism, a healthy global economy is a *conditio sine qua non*. Beyond that, efforts are needed to ensure that developing nations can participate in the globalization process.

The Doha Agreement to start a new round of trade negotiations got a strong real boost from the terrorist attacks and the loss of confidence that followed. The international community is very lucky to have two strong supporters from the two biggest trading groups; namely, the United States Trade Representative, Robert Zoellick, and Pascal Lamy, the Trade Commissioner of the E.U.

East Asian regional support for such a Round, as expressed since at the APEC Summit in Shanghai, the World Economic Forum's East Asia Economic Summit in Hong Kong, and the ASEAN+Three meeting, is an important factor, too. But the greatest push for the Round definitely was the aftermath of September 11.

The global struggle against terrorism is also seeking answers on how to overcome the global recession that was already on the way before September 11. The economies of the U.S. and other developed nations are important sources of finance for the struggle, but they are equally critical to the developing world, who will face a lot more pressures in the struggle against terrorism. These pressures are both political and economic in nature. The Asian economic crisis of 1997–1998 has already hurt some nations badly, and the internal pressures they face could be very destabilizing, especially in Muslim nations such as Pakistan, Indonesia or Malaysia. A prolonged economic recession globally will only add an extra burden on top of the struggle they have to face in the future. The economic downturn could also limit their capabilities to fight domestic and regional terrorism.

The world has become more complex. Efforts should be directed towards creating a world that balances the post-modern — characterized by high-tech information and communication and a globalized economy — with a modern world, as it exists in East Asia, where full sovereignty and a balance of power are still the norm. It should also enable a pre-modern world, where ethnic and religious divisions are the order of the day, to participate in the use of the advanced technology of the post-modern world.

That the attacks on the World Trade Center were undertaken by a group of people who did not belong to any particular state grouping raises the question of the function of the state in future developments of international relations. Globalization, regionalism, local aspirations and the emergence of non-state actors, such as NGOs, reduce the power of the state. However, the attacks have increased the power of the state as it attempts to cope with global terrorism.

The danger is that this fight against terrorism will revoke the limitation on the role of the state and will weaken attention to the rule of law, civil liberties and human rights. This could be very counterproductive. It may also undermine the legitimacy of the fight against terrorism.

A really fine balance has to be struck here. In certain circumstances there may be good reasons to limit civil liberties, but it must not be permanent and long-term. Wiretapping, the opening of mail, preventive detention and other measures could be acceptable, but should be limited in scope and undertaken only with legitimate reasons.

Abuses could be prevented if there is sufficient recognition of the differences between local conflicts and international terrorism. Local conflicts — such as those in Aceh or West Papua — usually have local roots and cannot be tackled in the same way as international terrorism. They should not, however, be ignored because of the fight against international terrorism. In fact, it is the evil genius of Osama bin Laden that succeeded in relating his campaigns against the U.S. with such local or regional grievances, especially in the case of the Israeli-Palestinian conflict.

One of the most important factors in the al-Qaeda strategy is the use, or abuse, of Islam for its own purposes. The West, and especially the U.S., has a special task to understand and appreciate the religion of one-sixth of the world's population. More than that, it should also appreciate the reasons why political movements in Muslim states have such real grudges and hatred against the West, and the U.S. in particular.

Such states feel as if they have been left behind and that their grievances and sense of injustice at the way Muslim societies have been treated are being ignored. This has been part of their history since the crusades and the period of colonialism after the First World War.

Islam and the Muslim leaders face a major challenge. They have to decide on how they would like to be perceived by the rest of the world: as a religion of peace and cooperation, or as a source of extremism, fanaticism and terrorism. They should not allow Islam to be "hijacked" by the terrorist groups such as al-Qaeda. Mainstream Muslim leaders have to take over the leadership of political Islam and develop modern, open Islamic societies that are on par with the West.

The development of Islam in Indonesia, in particular, is inspirational. There, a new generation of leaders has been coming up, well-versed in Islamic thinking because they were brought up in Islamic schools (*pesantren* and *madrasah*) and partly trained in the leading universities of the West. These new leaders see Islam not as a socio-political movement but as a social-cultural one, where it is the individual, and not the state, that has to decide on his/her religion. They have now taken over the reins in the anti-terrorism campaign, realizing that they have to take the lead in changing the international community's perception of Islam in Indonesia. Islam in Indonesia now has a fighting chance to show to the Muslim world that Islam can be open, flexible, democratic, moderate and capable of supporting economic development.

It was very unfortunate that for the first three or four weeks after the September 11 attacks the reactions in Indonesia were influenced by small, extremist Muslim groups. The Indonesian government was not sufficiently alert to oppose these and to encourage the mainstream Muslim groups, especially Nahdlatul Ulama and Muhammadiyah that represent over 70 million Muslims, to take the lead. This leadership only happened at the end of October. It should be noted, however, that while they condemned the terrorist attack these groups strongly opposed the bombing of Afghanistan because the target was not clear and the damage to the populace could be severe.

Now that the Taliban is practically defeated and since the attacks are undertaken on the ground in cooperation with the Northern Alliance, U.S.-led campaigns have become more acceptable. Indonesia is now ready to consider its involvement in peace-keeping efforts in Afghanistan if asked by the U.N.

As stated earlier, regional participation in the coalition can take many forms and involve different activities. They need not always be organized or participated in by the U.S. Their main contribution could be in the efforts to overcome domestic and regional terrorism.

The efforts by ASEAN and other East Asian countries in this regard should be appreciated. ASEAN has initiated real efforts to coordinate its police and intelligence operations. Army chiefs of the ASEAN countries came together in Manila in the middle of November 2001 to coordinate their efforts to combat global terrorism. They have also given humanitarian aid to the Afghan people. U.S. recognition of these activities will contribute to the success of the coalition.

While the coalition has been successful thus far, this is only the first phase in the long-term struggle against terrorism. If other states are found to be supportive of Osama bin Laden and al-Qaeda, clear evidence should be presented. If Iraq is found to be involved, the U.S. will have to consult with its main allies and friends to bring them on board. Iraq will be harder to face and the unity of the coalition could be compromised if it is not well prepared. Most probably, surgical action against the sites of the weapons of mass destruction, rather than a wholesale invasion of Iraq, will be the best answer.

As we try to assess the consequences of the war against terrorism, two basic questions remain. First, how permanent will be the impact, and what basic changes will this bring to the international system?

Second, what is the impact on East Asia as a region, and what can East Asia contribute to the development of a global system?

Speculation abounds about whether the changes in the international system caused by the U.S. response to terrorism will be short- or long-term, and whether the new system of international order that is inclined towards multilateralism will be sustainable.

If the U.S. takes a long-term view and the struggle against terrorism embraces values and ideas, then multilateralism will be sustainable. There is no other strategy that can deal effectively with such a complex long-term task.

However, that does not mean that multilateralism will be maintained in every field of activity and on every occasion. For instance, in the military field the U.S. is most powerful and is thus best equipped to do the job of leading the coalition's military activities, sometimes alone or with the support of the Northern Alliance and other anti-Taliban groupings. But in the diplomatic, political, economic and cultural fields, a broad-based coalition is a necessity. Also, regional and national efforts to overcome the challenges of terrorism should be considered as important building blocks in the fight against global terrorism.

The international system is changing in light of the war against terrorism but developments are still fluid and uncertain. Whether the U.S.

is really willing to establish a new global order, not only to face Osama bin Laden but also to overcome the root causes of terrorism, in concert with other nations and with the support of a consolidated U.N. system remains to be seen. It is only with such changes that a credible longer-term fight against terrorism can be sustained.

As far as East Asia's contribution to the future international and global system is concerned, a lot can and should be expected from the region. East Asia has not yet completed its economic restructuring following the crisis of 1997–1998. This may take a decade and the complexity and messiness of the changes continue to create a great deal of uncertainty, as the current situation in Indonesia best illustrates. However, these changes are very important for East Asia's future. While ups and downs should be expected, if East Asia is successful in building a new system of the economy, of governance, of politics, of social developments and cultural changes, then it will become a much more important part of the world. If this happens, it will strengthen the international system, because East Asia has always been at the forefront of globalization and free trade.

The region is continuously opening up its economies and societies. Despite the financial crisis, in general, the region's countries have been able to maintain and increase their openness in the last four years.

The restructuring of the economies will go on, although not always in a straight line. The new ways of governance have become more important. In ASEAN, the AFTA process showed that free trade is now completely rules-based such that if exceptions are requested by any member, the compensation clause becomes operative. This was applied to Malaysia in response to its back-tracking on reducing the tariff in the automotive industry.

There is no doubt that a market-based economy will be the general rule in East Asia, especially now that China has joined the WTO. Because of the region's system of values, where big families and social relations are vitally important, East Asian capitalism will be closer to the European model than to the Anglo Saxon one. This means that free-fight capitalism, as exemplified in the U.S., will have to be corrected in East Asia, where it would not be implemented resolutely because of the constraints of the social and family system. It should be coupled with more state intervention — for instance, in a better-organized social security and welfare system — to compensate for the competition. In addition to the free-trade objective, the region remains committed to cooperating in financial affairs, especially since the financial crisis of 1997 left East Asia on its own while the IMF made substantial mistakes in looking for solutions.

East Asia will not have a common currency such as the E.U. has been able to establish after half a century of preparation and cooperation. But some other ideas could materialize in the medium term. These include an early-warning mechanism and peer review, as well as a regional monetary fund to complement the IMF. It has to be remembered that East Asia has the highest savings rate globally and she could assist herself in a crisis if a regional system existed.

As a matter of fact, regionalism is budding in East Asia, driven by the integration of the economies, especially in trade and manufacturing, as well as by the desire of regional countries to deal jointly with the rise of China. With or without the war against terrorism, China has been looming large in East Asia's future. The anxiety over China is whether she will develop into a status-quo power or become a revolutionary power. In the meantime, the critical issue is whether the bilateral relations between the U.S. and China will be characterized by co-existence or enmity, cooperation or competition. Bilateral relations have progressed — as both see global terrorism as their common enemy. But it remains to be seen whether that factor alone can overcome the substantial differences that exist between the two. The most probable answer is that it may not, but other efforts have been made to keep the relationship at least on an even keel, despite the differences in outlook and policies. And a new basic agreement to cooperate in many fields and to differ in others could really improve relations in the future. A U.S. presence in the Western Pacific or Pacific Asia is always an important factor for the future stability and development of the region.

As far as abiding by international and regional rules is concerned, China is considered to be a status-quo power already, especially with her accession to the WTO and her support for the U.S.-led coalition against global terrorism. But China needs time to learn and adjust because she has only been opening up over the past 20 years. Often, she still sounds brittle in her reaction to regional or international issues.

The challenge posed by China has raised ideas on the need to develop an East Asian regional institution. This began with the establishment of the so-called ASEAN+3 (APT) process. This process includes annual meetings of Heads of States/Governments of ASEAN and China, Japan and South Korea, as well as meetings of ministers of foreign affairs, trade and industry, and finance. One of the important objectives of the APT process is to help China integrate peacefully into East Asia. Other regional forums, APEC and the ASEAN Regional Forum (ARF), of which the U.S. is a member, also contribute to this effort.

There are still some constraints in the relationship between the two big Asian countries, China and Japan. However, this relationship continues to improve. In the economic field, there is huge potential for the development of relations between the two.

China's challenge to the region is not only strategic, which is of a long-term nature, but also economic, which is much more immediate for the region. But economic competition is not a zero-sum game. In fact, both sides can benefit from the development of closer economic relations. For the more developed part of ASEAN (Indonesia, the Philippines, Malaysia and Thailand), the economic challenge is a real one. These countries need to respond to this challenge by upgrading their economies and industries and by raising the quality of their labor force. In the meantime, they need to find the niches that would increase their economic complementarities with China, in trade and manufacturing as well as in investment. Studies have begun to explore ways to strengthen economic relations between China and ASEAN, including the possibility of establishing a free-trade area over a 10-year period.

The World Economic Forum's annual East Asian Economic Summits have been very instrumental in bringing together global business, governments and academe to talk about East Asia's problems, challenges and contributions, as well as to exchange ideas and experiences with other parts of the world. In the last five years or so, it has brought in other partners in development, such as labor, civil society (NGOs), and artists, to participate in the meetings and to find some common ground for cooperation. These meetings have been very useful for East Asia, because they provide new ideas and comparisons with other models, experiences and success stories from other parts of the world or other parts of societies, which otherwise would not have been consulted and listened to.

These exchanges and exposures are priceless and very supportive, especially for East Asian business. Cooperation in the economic and business fields has been important for the region and has helped in turning East Asia into a dynamic economic region. Efforts need to be made to promote cooperation in the political field as well. The region is faced with many new challenges, including the emergence of democracies, which can lead to the creation of a more stable and peaceful region.

Though political instability remains a possibility in the region today, Taiwan, South Korea, the Philippines, Thailand and Indonesia are all on their way to establishing a more consistent and maturing democracy. Malaysia and Singapore are not very much behind. These are exciting prospects and offer a positive contribution to the peaceful development of the region and the world.

As has been said earlier, regional countries need to have a social-welfare system that takes account of more communal social values. The traditional, communal social systems are breaking down as a result of industrialization and urbanization and, therefore, have to be transformed into a modern system. Many East Asian countries, especially Japan, are facing rapid demographic changes that need to be accommodated. If these are adequately dealt with, the region can offer solutions to other parts of the world.

The region is very diverse culturally. Islam is a main factor in influencing cultural values in Southeast Asia. The region has a fighting chance to show to the other parts of the Muslim world that Islam is a religion of peace, openness, moderation and cooperation, and that it can become a modernizing factor in Muslim countries through the development of democracy and the economy.

In Northeast Asia, Confucianism plays a dominant role. These countries (Taiwan and South Korea) have shown how important education and traditional family relations are in modernizing the state and society. They have been able to show that economic modernization and great progress can be achieved in two generations and that such societies can transform themselves into democracies.

In the end, cultural values are of critical importance to raising self-confidence. But these values are also developing and changing rapidly under the influence of new, international values. Governance, transparency, rules and accountability are all new values to be practiced in East Asia. Talk of specifically "Asian values" has been so misleading in the past. We must now look to the future because the region clearly needs the introduction of the new values that reflect new global realities.

A Southeast Asian Plea for Moderation

Karim Raslan
Partner, Raslan Loong, Malaysia

 The terrorist attacks in the U.S. have focused global attention on three main sections of the Muslim world; the Saudi peninsular, Palestine and the Indian Subcontinent. As a consequence many people across the globe now associate Islam almost exclusively with the Arab people, and with the extremism and violence advocated by Osama bin Laden and his cohorts.

Unfortunately, the obsessive blanket coverage of these global hot-spots has also resulted in an image of Islam that is totally at odds with the Prophet Mohamad's essential message of compassion, knowledge and faith.

Furthermore there has been a tendency by those too ignorant to know better (a large section of the American media), as well as Islamic extremists, to present the unfolding events as an integral part of a conflict of civilizations between the Muslim world and the rest, thus exacerbating the wrong-headed identification of Muslim with Arab with terrorist. However, Samuel Huntington's nightmare scenario is not inevitable.

This misperception is injurious to all moderate, law-abiding Muslims and especially those from other parts of the globe, many of whom have no fondness for the Arab world. For example, Muslims from Southeast Asia (the home to the world's largest Muslim nation, Indonesia, with over 210 million Muslims) were deeply shocked by the brutal attacks on the World Trade Center, and denounced the atrocity categorically.

For many non-Arab Muslims there is a growing sense that the Middle East can no longer lay claim to the leadership of the Islamic world. In fact, many Southeast Asians see the attacks as yet another indication of the Arab world's moral, spiritual and socio-economic bankruptcy.

Nonetheless, Southeast Asian Islam faces its own challenges. There have been a number of bloody conflicts between Muslim and non-Muslim in the region, predominantly within Indonesia. However, it is rumored that many of these conflicts have been hijacked and exploited by forces closely associated with the former Soeharto regime. Nonetheless, these confrontations have tended to be confined to particular parts of the archipelago, such as the Maluku and Central Sulawesi.

The greater challenge for Southeast Asian Islam is the struggle within the *ummah* (or congregation), as moderates and extremists face off in a struggle to win over the hearts and minds of Muslims.

As with much of the rest of the Islamic world, the region is currently dealing with the rising tide of religious conservatism. This has, in turn, spawned a host of extremist groups, some of whom are certainly engaged in militant activity.

Of course, militants will always insinuate their way into society and, whilst Indonesia's Laskar Jihad and the Philippines' Abu Sayyaf monopolize the headlines, they are entirely unrepresentative of the majority of the *ummah*.

Certainly, the region's tolerant and accommodating Islamic practices and thriving multi-racial communities are increasingly threatened by the radical theological views emanating from the Middle East and the Indian Subcontinent.

Most people have associated globalization with Westernization. However, in a bizarre twist of fate, the very same channels of finance, telecommunication and transport that have eased global commerce have become a way for a particularly narrow-minded interpretation of the faith — Wahabism — to gain adherents across the Islamic world.

This interpretation of Islam first secured a foothold in the great citadels of the faith, Mecca and Medina, in the 18th century under the guidance of the preacher Abdul Wahab. Wahab argued that the only way to revive the past glories of Islam was to reform the faith, returning the *ummah* to the pristine and uncorrupted condition that existed at the time of the Prophet Mohamad in the seventh century.

Since then, the proponents of Wahabism (predominantly Saudi) have done their utmost to promote their interpretation at the expense of regional cultures. Moreover Wahabism rejects all local religious practices and innovations. Shi'ite Muslims, for example, and Sufi sects such as the Nashbandiyah have been vilified and are, in fact, treated as *kafirs* or unbelievers.

Many would argue that Wahabism has sought to destroy the cultural contours of the non-Arab Muslim world. In countries as diverse as

Pakistan, Malaysia and Indonesia, such pan-Islamic movements have undermined and, in certain cases, even eradicated centuries-old cultural practices.

The rigid and absolutist rhetoric of the Wahabis has also influenced the writings of the late Pakistani and Jamaat-I-Islam leader, Abu al' Maududi, as well as the Egyptian and former Muslim Brotherhood ideologue Sayyid al-Qutb, whose works have been a major source of inspiration for Afghanistan's Taliban.

However Southeast Asia — for so long on the margins of the Islamic world — has remained remarkably resilient in the face of Wahabism. Moreover, Indonesia also possesses a thriving indigenous center of Islamic scholarship that is both modern and entirely on par with the great seminaries of Cairo and Medina. The indigenization of Islamic practice in Indonesia as well as the large number of believers — fully 90% of the country's 220 million population are Muslim — has also strengthened the domestic scholastic traditions.

Southeast Asia's differences in this regard are due in part to geography but, more importantly, to history. Whilst the rest of the Muslim world was won by conquest, Islam's success in Southeast Asia was by force of example, as traders and preachers spread the Prophet Mohamad's eternal message.

Because of this, Islamic expression in the region was forced to adapt to the existing cultural environment. Hindu and Buddhist ideas and practices have become an integral part of Islamic expression in the region. Perhaps the most striking example of this syncretic process is the way in which Javanese Muslims look to the *Wali Songo* — the nine religious divines or saints who first introduced the faith to the island in the 15th and 16th centuries. Their graves in East Java, in marked contrast to Wahabi asceticism, remain the subject of considerable veneration to this day.

Any attempt to address the causes of terrorism will demand a two-pronged strategy and liberal Muslims, those who believe in the Holy Koran's essential message of tolerance and beauty, will need to be at the forefront of this engagement.

Firstly, there has to be a renewed emphasis on economic growth, with equity and development programs that tackle poverty through education, health-care and the creation of economic opportunities for all. Policies that neglect the role of women will almost certainly fail.

Liberal Muslims cannot afford to stand back and decry government corruption; their passivity merely strengthens the position of extremists. Liberal Muslims must press for greater transparency and accountability. Turning a blind eye to government failings will only strengthen the position of the extremists as so-called secular institutions of governance become riddled with corruption. The middle-classes have to become a bastion of moral probity, checking the inclination to conservatism within society at large.

At the same time there has to be considerable focus on Islamic scholarship and education. Elites (most of whom are Westernized and cosmopolitan in their outlook) in all Islamic nations have tended to avoid an engagement with the *ullamas*, the chief explicators of the Holy Koran.

There is no doubt that the Westernized elites will now have to spend more time reading and re-reading the Holy Koran. They must extract the essential truths of the Prophet Mohamad's message and endeavor to shape an interpretation of the Holy Koran that marries modernity with tradition.

This vital intellectual and spiritual exercise cannot be left to the tradition-bound *ullamas*, who, unfortunately, have always inclined towards exclusivity and exceptionalism. Moreover, their power-base rests on their authority to interpret the Koran. This trend has to be halted at all costs. However, attempts to exclude the *ullamas* entirely from public life will fail. The Kemalists revolution is not the solution. Islam cannot be banned and sidelined.

Instead, the *ullamas* must be made part and parcel of the development of their community. They have to be taught the value of modernity, of economic growth, of women's rights and religious tolerance. They have to be sensitized to the modern world, just as they have been in Indonesia.

In all parts of the Islamic world, there is now an urgent need to review and reassess the education of the religious elites. They must be encouraged to spend more time on the social sciences, on the humanities and on science and economics. Only then will their world-view become more nuanced and in keeping with the complexity of global issues.

Unorthodox solutions will emerge in the next few years. One of the most important areas that needs to be reconsidered is the conventional division of church and state that is present in secular, predominantly Christian, nations. This separation may not be the best means of addressing the age-old challenge of politics and religion within the Islamic world. Islam is too powerful a force to be thus excluded from public life and liberal Muslims will have to employ prodigious amounts of intellectual dexterity to advance their cause.

Indeed there is a growing sense amongst enlightened religious thinkers that the margins of Islam — Southeast Asia in particular — may constitute some of the most compelling models for governance in the Islamic world.

Firstly, a country such as Malaysia demonstrates that Islam and development are not mutually exclusive. The complexities of global commerce, scientific enquiry and religious faith have been balanced in a manner that marries modernity and tradition.

Growth with equity has been a hallmark of Malaysia's development model. At the same time, pragmatic socio-political policies have ensured that minority rights are preserved, notwithstanding efforts to the contrary by conservative forces.

Moreover the country's international outlook and cosmopolitanism is reflected in its extraordinarily large trade figures of well over US$100 billion. Interestingly Malaysia, with only 23 million people (of whom at least 55% are Muslim), is the largest trading nation in the Islamic world and the 14th-largest in the world.

Secondly, Indonesia for all its faults possesses one of the richest indigenous traditions of Islamic scholarship in the world. The two largest associations in the Muslim world, the Nahdatul Ullama and the Muhammadiyah, are both located within the island republic. Both have a long-standing commitment to moderation.

The Nahdatul Ullama (or NU) in particular, under the leadership of Abdurrahman Wahid, has embarked on an extraordinary voyage of intellectual discovery. Nurtured in the ancient traditions of Islamic discourse and the *fiqh* (jurisprudence), scholars from the NU have sought to marry Western philosophical traditions with Islam. In a feat worthy of emulation, scholars such as Nurcholish Majid have argued that the essential truths of the Holy Koran — of justice, peace and honor — are of far greater importance than mere ritual.

In conclusion, Malaysia and Indonesia represent two important aspects of the ongoing struggle between extremism and moderation within the Islamic world. Malaysia has shown that sound economic management and good governance are vital for the well-being of society as a whole, whilst Indonesia has revealed the importance of indigenizing and modernizing Islamic scholarship. The challenge now for Muslims everywhere is to ensure that both issues are tackled. Delay will be fatal.

Building a Coalition for Global Prosperity

Gloria Macapagal-Arroyo
President of the Philippines

 The events of September 11 have brought new levels of risk and uncertainty to a world that is just beginning to understand how intertwined their economies are following the Asian financial crisis of 1997 and 1998. The fact that the terrorists used the most promising features of globalization — the ease with which people, goods and capital move around the world — to turn the system upon itself, has shown that globalization can be a force for good as well as for evil. But the tragedy has brought countries closer together and injected the urgency of working together to combat a threat that goes far beyond Ground Zero.

Just as a coalition is being built to eradicate terrorism, so too can a coalition be formed to revive the global economy and put it on the road to sustainable growth. This renewed sense of global community could be the key to getting this economic recovery under way.

DEALING WITH TERRORISM IS OUR MOST URGENT PRIORITY

Given its impact on the global economy, our first challenge is to deal with terrorism and make this a safe and secure world.

Directly after the attacks on New York and Washington, I assured President Bush that the Philippines stands behind American efforts to eradicate terrorism. Our decision to join the fight against terrorism was not an emotional one — it was first and foremost a strategic decision and one that certainly carries with it risks. My country was facing its own challenge from terrorist groups in the South, where we have a substantial Muslim population. I did not want our participation in the global alliance to be construed as being directed against our Muslim brothers and not against terrorism. But I was convinced that the fight against terrorism is a global fight — it touches each and every one of our nations — and that we would be remiss in our global responsibilities if we were to take a passive stance out of concern for our own domestic situation.

Coupled with our participation in global efforts to stamp out terrorism, we are also working to promote cohesion and cooperation at the regional level. We have an operational arrangement with our neighbors, Indonesia and Malaysia, to fight terrorism within our common borders by sharing intelligence on terrorist activities, tightening border patrols and, if needed, by partaking in joint peacekeeping operations.

At the recently concluded APEC Leaders' Meeting in Shanghai, we agreed to take a strong stance against terrorism and discussed ways of prioritizing APEC's work to meet these challenges, including money laundering, aviation and port safety and security and cyber crime.

The cooperation and support shown by Russia, China and Pakistan, and the condemnation of terrorism by such countries as Iran, points to a geopolitical realignment that could be ripe with promise and opportunity. This unprecedented cooperation and coalition-building at the national, regional and global level to ensure security and safety could work equally well to ensure the economic security that globalization has both provided and, at the same time, threatened to dismantle.

A GLOBAL PROBLEM REQUIRES A GLOBAL RESPONSE

The challenge we face today is the same challenge that earlier generations have faced — to bring about stability, prosperity and progress in the world. However, we do so now under vastly different circumstances and that is due to the increasing pace of globalization. The rise of an interdependent, global economy has brought with it unprecedented prosperity as division of labor and specialization have led to rising productivity on a global scale. However, globalization carries with it a price. Globalized economies are today more exposed to greater risk of destabilization and contagion due to the greater volatility of short-term capital movements. Rightly or wrongly, globalization has also been blamed for impoverishing the poor, destroying the environment and undermining the sovereignty of nations.

The September 11 tragedies added an additional and dangerous side to globalization. Using the very tools of globalization — technology and open borders that facilitate travel, the transport of goods, the provision of services, the ability to communicate over long distances, and the flow of capital — the terrorists have brought a contagion of fear and uncertainty. And coming as it did in the face of a global economic slowdown, the global economy has been pushed to the brink of a full-blown recession. The United States is now in recession for the first time in many years. Japan, which was already in recession, has been in a decade-long struggle to right its economy. Europe is also experiencing a downturn. For the first time since the oil shock of the 1970s, all three engines of global economic growth are sputtering. In the absence of a carefully coordinated response, there is a very real danger that global economic progress may grind to a halt and, indeed, go into reverse.

All these reinforce the fact that events outside one's border – be they economic or political – cannot now be treated as someone else's problem. The daunting task of managing globalization so that its benefits are maximized and its risks minimized requires global leadership and greater shared responsibility. Many lessons have been learned by both governments and international organizations, which could prove to be valuable in dealing with the current crisis. One of them is the importance of cooperation and concerted action.

It begins with a greater acceptance that the domestic economy must be in tune with the global economy. The rapid export-led recovery from the 1997 financial crisis has lulled us into the false sense of security that we have done enough to master globalization. But, in only a short time, export markets have collapsed and have once again exposed fundamental weaknesses in many economies. Many of the antidotes to a repeat of the 1997 financial crisis have not yet been administered. It is time that they were, before it becomes too late. The current situation provides the right political conditions to take the bitter pills of reform. In my own country, this has included tough banking and fiscal reforms, strengthened corporate governance and opening up to global competition.

The efforts of the major economies — the U.S., Japan, Europe — to stimulate their domestic economies will have far-reaching consequences for the global economy. We in ASEAN also have a responsibility to contribute to global economic security. Keeping our markets open has been the key springboard for our success and we must be firm in our resolve to continue to do so. We have to make AFTA a reality, not in some distant future but in the next few years.

Advanced economies can also make vital contributions to developing-country efforts to integrate successfully into the global economy. They could do so: by promoting trade; by encouraging the flow of private capital, particularly foreign direct investment which brings with it steady financial flow and technology transfer; and, by supplementing more rapid debt relief with an increased level of new financial support.

We also have a rare opportunity to address the current global trading environment following the launch of the New Round at the WTO Ministerial Meeting in Doha. This may well be the defining moment on how we face the issue of globalization. We have seen more and more demonstrations against globalization and free trade. However, globalization is not driven by people meeting in Seattle, Davos, Genoa, or even Shanghai, but by developments in technology and markets. But it is in these meetings that we can address the concerns of those affected by globalization and find ways to make sure that the policies we put in place will lead to sustainable development and the alleviation of poverty. They have dubbed the new round as a Development Round and it remains to be seen whether its attempt to forge a balanced agenda does produce balanced results.

Trade liberalization is meaningless if there is no political security that will allow an economy to conduct its daily business normally. That is why together we should stamp out terrorism and deal firmly and with resolve with those that threaten the very foundation of civilized societies.

An economy's potential cannot be fulfilled if it has poor economic governance or if it is burdened by debt. That is why it is important that these issues are addressed at the same time. It does not matter to those who do not have the capacity to produce goods and services that the markets demand or do not have the infrastructure to support such production and the marketing of these products. That is why investments must be made available to develop this capacity and resources to build these infrastructures.

It also does not make much sense if an economy can produce goods competitively but then advantage is negated when the high cost of transacting the sale and export of those goods is escalated by differing standards, complicated customs procedures or multiple rules of origin. That is why economies must be assisted in developing capacity to facilitate the movement of goods and services across borders.

Likewise, information and communications technologies have introduced a new paradigm for the conduct of global trade — increasing productivity, lowering costs, providing affordable access to markets, and generating new products and methods for delivering them. To a large segment of the global population this will remain only a distant promise unless the digital divide within and between our societies is bridged.

The New Round provides an opportunity to bring to the fore the development dimensions of trade, which many developing economies — who make up four out of every five members of the WTO — say is missing. The WTO, of course, is not the panacea for all that ails the world nor should it have any ambition to be so. But the WTO can play a critical role in bringing trade into the core of development agenda. By looking at trade as such, assistance can be focused in meeting the requirements of making trade truly an engine of growth for developing economies.

A HOLISTIC APPROACH TO DEVELOPMENT

I strongly believe that meeting the challenge of development requires a holistic approach in which open trade plays a pivotal role. We have in the past called for greater coherence among international development institutions — the IMF, the World Bank, and the UNDP — and the WTO. The WTO to all intents and purposes should also be considered a development institution. It is about time that a workable and effective mechanism for bringing such coherence in the functioning of these multilateral institutions be made a reality.

The WTO is, of course, one of the Bretton Woods institutions that currently make up the institutional architecture of global governance and global economic management. For the most part, they have managed the many facets of global interaction as best they can. But they suffer from two distinct disadvantages.

The first is that while they are specialized institutions with specific mandates, globalization has a multidimensional character that requires an integrated approach. This requires an effective mechanism to ensure coherence among themselves in their policies and programs, which currently does not exist. The second is that given this complexity, achieving international consensus and enforcing the consequences of this consensus has been difficult and complicated. International institutions by themselves are not adequate to manage the global political and economic system but require a network of support groups. That support lies in the concentric circles of regional groups which, if harnessed properly, could be the building blocks for managing globalization.

REGIONAL COOPERATION IN A GLOBAL CONTEXT

Coordination of the complex agendas of economic, social and political action to ensure that globalization benefits all and harms few in international bodies is an enormously difficult task. However, if these are adopted and then addressed within smaller regional groups, it may then be easier to reach international consensus. Smaller groups are more manageable in dealing with difficult issues since there is no pressure of making global commitments right away. It then becomes easier to reach ever-expanding circles of consensus. Once agreement is reached globally, these regional groups can serve to monitor compliance within their respective regions. And as confidence is built, countries can then move on to integration on a higher scale, eventually leading to global integration. Under this scenario, globalization is managed not by super international institutions but rather by all players assenting to accepted rules, mores and norms of the market.

Compared with North America and the European Union, Asia is still at the stage of putting together a meaningful regional architecture. ASEAN has done much to advance the cause of Southeast Asian regionalism. And now with the ASEAN+3 concept closer to reality, we are on the verge of creating a larger, new East Asian sense of community that will give greater meaning to Asia as the third pole of the global economic growth triangle.

GLOBALIZATION CALLS FOR A GLOBALITY OF DISCIPLINES

One of the most important lessons we have learned in the aftermath of September 11 is that it is no longer possible to make the artificial division between economic security and political security when nations come together as part of international and regional institutions to address global issues.

As author Thomas Friedman has pointed out, globalization has so blurred the traditional boundaries between politics, culture, technology, finance, national security and ecology that it is no longer possible to explain one without referring to the others and you cannot explain the whole without reference to them all. The interaction of these disciplines is the defining feature of international relations today.

ASEAN has begun to realize this. For example, while it continues to adhere to the principle of "non-interference" — which effectively puts political and national security issues off the agenda — increasingly, ASEAN countries are beginning to rely on each other to deal with domestic political and security issues, as was most recently the case in East Timor and in Mindanao.

CONCLUSION

The events of September 11 were both shocking and horrifying for observers around the world. These events put us all on an uncharted course (both in terms of political and economic security and personal safety) and increased our sense of vulnerability and uncertainty.

This is one more manifestation of globalization and presents us with an added challenge. But these events also presented us with an opportunity to work together and come out stronger on a variety of fronts.

The coalition that has been built and the relationships that have been fortified in our collective response to terrorism can and must extend to global, regional and bilateral economic relations.

But as the financial crisis has demonstrated, we can maximize the benefits of globalization, and minimize its adverse effects, if we have greater coherence in how we respond to its many dimensions — trade, investments, capital and labor. It is therefore important that there be greater coordination among international economic institutions such as the WTO, WB and the IMF, and regional development banks. We face a rocky road ahead – that is certain. But I am confident that the global economy can, and will, pull through if we approach our economic uncertainties with the same cooperative and integrated approach that we have applied to confronting terrorism.

A New Collective-Security System in Asia

Kim Min-Seok
Member of the National Assembly, Republic of Korea
(Position is at the time of printing)

The war against terrorism rages on whilst new questions continue to arise. United States President Bush should be commended for his exemplary leadership during this crisis. He has restored the hope of the citizens of America in the aftermath of a devastating tragedy and an economy on the wane. He has also successfully rallied many nations to join in the battle against terrorism. However, it remains to be seen how the world is doing against terrorism on a long-term basis. Each nation must ask itself what is needed to prepare against future attacks of similar proportions. The world is more globalized than ever and globalization offers many positives to the global community. At the same time, unfortunately, there are many dark sides to globalization, such as the widening disparity in socio-economic conditions and terrorism. The way to impede the dark offspring of globalization is through collective efforts.

President Bush understands that these new transglobal issues cannot be handled alone. Indeed, one reason that his plan of action seemed sound and swift was that mechanisms for joint action, such as NATO, were in place and ready for mobilization. Asia seems to have fallen behind in this regard in comparison to North America and Europe. Measures and mechanisms, whether preventative or reactive, are clearly needed. There have been many obstacles to collective efforts between Asian nations, but it is clear that Asian nations can pool their efforts for a specific cause. The concept of the Sunshine Policy, let alone all the progress that has been made, could not have been possible without the collective efforts of the neighboring Asian nations and the international community. The reunification of Korea, much like the war against terrorism, is a global effort. Peace on the peninsula is peace in the world, in much the same way as eliminating terrorism in our society. This is why, despite all the great things that President Bush has done, his "Axis of Evil" statement does not fall in line with the progress that has been made.

THE NEW DANGERS

The terror attacks of September 11 have made all nations realize the emergence of deadly new threats to the peace and security of all humankind that even the strongest military force in the world could not prevent. It is a sobering reminder of a shift, since the end of the Cold War, from the dangers of the traditional nature of war between states to threats that are non-traditional and that are now engineered by a multitude of non-state actors. There are arguments that, every day, our world increasingly resembles that described in *The Clash of Civilizations* by Samuel Huntington, where battles are no longer waged in a bipolar world separated by ideologies, but between ethnicities and religions or for the restoration of former territories. We only have to look at our newspapers to see the ongoing conflicts in Palestine, Bosnia, Kosovo, the border between Pakistan and India, and several other regions of our world.

These conflicts give rise to unpredictable forces that threaten the peace and security of the free world, as seen in the attacks in the U.S. The U.S. has reacted with a call for allies to help it in the battle against those responsible for the attacks and to stamp out any future perpetrators. It is not only the U.S. that is prone to these and other devastating attacks; it is every nation. We must address the question of how Asia can be prepared to protect the peace and security of its peoples from any kind of attack, traditional or non-traditional.

The new dangers and threats in society now require a collective effort to combat and deter possible attacks. It is essential that preventative and deterrent efforts be made to ensure the peace and security of the region. It is unsafe and extremely costly to simply react to such circumstances. Although the Cold War is over, security alliances are needed more than ever. The nature of the Cold War was such that it aligned states together on one side or the other and security and intelligence were targeted at known entities and threats. Alliances must once again be formed, but in different contexts. These must address the threats represented by non-state actors that transcend borders and are difficult to pinpoint, where information is scarce and the element of surprise is a deadly weapon. The U.S. and its use of NATO is a prime example of what is needed to face these new unforeseen threats or attacks: the war against terrorism would not have been possible without a collective effort. The readiness to mobilize NATO has produced tremendous outcomes in this war and only reinforces the fact that Asia needs to be able to muster the same capabilities and resources to deal with such dangers.

A NEW SECURITY PARADIGM IN ASIA

We only have to look to NATO as a model for a security alliance. The heart of NATO is article 5, under which an attack on one of the member countries is considered and treated the same as an attack on all member countries. This collective defense pact exemplifies the unity that is the basis of any security alliance. NATO also plays a key role in the field of crisis management, by contributing to effective conflict prevention and, in the event of a crisis, by taking appropriate action to resolve the crisis when there is consensus among the member countries to do so. In addition, the Alliance promotes partnership and cooperation with other countries in the Euro-Atlantic area, aimed at increasing openness, mutual confidence and the capacity for joint action. We only have to look at NATO's role during the war against terrorism, in Kosovo and many other missions since its inception on April 4, 1949 for confirmation of this.

For the peace and security of North East Asia, a new collective security alliance between Korea, China and Japan is needed. The forces in this region need to be able to collectively prevent, or mobilize against, unforeseen attacks like the ones in the United States. Asia needs to be ready, as NATO was in the war against terrorism. It is not only essential in the event of a terrorist attack in the region, but for many other traditional and non-security measures. The Koreas, China and Japan share many security issues that can be handled more effectively and efficiently with a collective effort. In the current international security order, arms control and nuclear non-proliferation, biological and chemical weapons disarmament and ballistic-missile control regimes are under close scrutiny. It is in the interests of the nations in Asia to work together in addressing these issues. A security alliance, for instance, can work together towards arms reduction through treaties to keep each other accountable.

The threat of terrorism alone calls for a joint effort, as it has now become a conventional threat. Terrorist operations now have the same resources and capabilities as nation-states, but with unique advantages. Their clandestine operations go undetected, as it is nearly impossible to identify the hundreds of new recruits into these organizations. To determine which threats are serious among the thousands issued every day is another impossible challenge. We also see that these organizations now have the potential to obtain weapons of mass destruction.

Security cooperation can also lead to the sharing of resources, proficient arms transfers, joint military exercises and peacekeeping operations. Arm sales are a growing concern of late. There is great potential for the sale of arms or arms technology to terrorist organizations, especially when nations that carry them are in unstable economic conditions. If this situation arises, the aligned nations can transfer the arms between themselves or at least consult each other regarding potential outside transfers. The member nations can also keep each other accountable through specialized commissions to deal with specific issues.

In essence, when a specific issue threatens the security of the region, a commission can be formed, as in the case of the Korean Peninsula Energy Development Organization (KEDO) whose mission includes supporting international non-proliferation, peace and stability on the Korean Peninsula, and developing alternative energy sources for North Korea. For the KEDO project, leaders and professionals from Asia, the U.S. and Europe joined forces to oversee the activities of North Korea and its nuclear reactors. Joint military exercises and possible joint peacekeeping operations are also proven confidence-building methods. These are the same practices that have made the United Nations and NATO so successful in dissolving any ethnic or cultural conflicts within the organization.

Another dimension of security that can be addressed cooperatively is in the non-conventional arena. However, globalization and technology have not only enhanced the prospects of international economic and political cooperation, they have also created the means by which problems and crimes can transcend national borders. Transnational threats such as terrorism, illegal migration, trafficking in drugs and people, organized crime, piracy, environmental degradation, pollution and resource scarcity are just as much in the forefront today as conventional security. No one nation can deal with these problems alone. These are issues that must be discussed between the nations involved to devise strategies to address and prevent these problems. A collective security system in Asia is the only solution to maintain sustainable peace.

THE CONTINUING EFFORTS OF THE SUNSHINE POLICY

George W. Bush's recent reference to Iran, Iraq and North Korea as "An Axis of Evil" has sparked much debate for those concerned with the progress of engagement with North Korea. Though including North Korea in this statement does not coincide with the agenda of South Korean

President Kim Dae Jung and his Sunshine Policy, it comes as no surprise, since it falls in line with how the Bush Administration has approached North Korea. The Bush Administration has never rejected the Sunshine Policy, but it has taken a more hard-line attitude towards the North Korean regime. The Bush Administration is more prone to using coercive methods rather than the more incentive-laden approach of the previous undertakings of the Sunshine Policy. The biggest issue has always been trust. It is difficult for any nation to trust another nation that has labeled it "evil". In one sense, it seems that the Sunshine Policy has been undermined but, by the same token, the Bush administration has shown that it is more than willing to engage in talks with the North Korean regime and is in full support of the Sunshine Policy. It is essential that the Bush Administration continue its support for the Sunshine Policy because the United States has the major role in any effort towards reunification.

The Sunshine Policy is important for the cause of reunification; but it is also a poignant example of how the Asian community can unite for the cause of peace. The stability of the Korean peninsula is one of the key issues for the region. The two Koreas have been divided and technically at war since 1950. Korea is the only divided country and is the last remnant of the Cold War. The quest for reunification is a collective undertaking between the nations of the region and the international community. Great strides have been made since the implementation of the Sunshine Policy, which entails engagement with North Korea through aid and cooperation. The summit meeting between the two Korean leaders in 2000 was a historic and momentous event that has instilled a gleam of hope among the Korean people and throughout the world.

The progress of the Sunshine Policy is also evident in the reaction of the South Korean public after the September 11 attacks. If the attack had occurred five years ago, there would undoubtedly have been mass hysteria out of fear of an attack from North Korea. As a result of engagement, the ROK and other nations and NGOs have been able to provide aid to the famine-stricken people of North Korea. The cultural and sports exchanges between the Koreas have also put a face to the North Korean people and their culture. We no longer have to approach each other with fear or hostility, but with friendliness and with common goals and dreams.

The progress of the Sunshine Policy would not have occurred without the support of the international community. There is a great understanding that peace on the Korean peninsula is congruent with peace in the world and there has certainly been a collective effort across all continents to support this issue. Support has come in the form of both encouragement and action. The historic summit meeting could not have taken place without the support of all the nations. Since then, there have been numerous diplomatic exchanges and visits to North Korea from delegates from the United States, the European Union, Russia and China to aid the North Korean people and support the cause of reunification.

Unfortunately, the initiatives of the Sunshine Policy have, of late, come to a halt. Discussions and negotiations on specific issues such as family exchanges and reunifications, land and rail routes connecting South and North Korea and, eventually, Europe are at a standstill. This is straining relations between the two Koreas. Despite the current unfavorable situation, we must realize that the Sunshine Policy is still in its infancy. At the very least, progress has come to a halt and not fallen back. The goal of reunification is not one that will happen overnight, but one that requires patience over a long period of time. President Kim Dae Jung has assured the people that he will not give up on his promise to do his utmost towards reunification.

Geopolitically, the Korean peninsula is of great importance to the region's superpowers, so much so that the peninsula is regarded as the "hub" of Asian nations. Both China and Russia know first hand the importance of regional stability. Throughout history, the two nations have had great interest in the peninsula. At the turn of the 20th century, both nations had great influence in the political affairs of Korea's last monarchy, before the colonization of the peninsula by the Japanese. China and Russia have also exerted great influence over the course of relations between the two Koreas. This past year, Chinese leader Jiang Zemin visited Pyongyang to encourage North Korean leader Kim Jung II to engage in further dialogue with South Korea. This followed the visit of Russian President Vladimir Putin, who did much the same a few weeks before.

An Asian Organization of Collective Security could speed up the cause and process of reunification through facilitating the necessary dialogue between the two Koreas. Mandatory meetings can offer cooperative solutions to any concerns regarding the peninsula and the Asian region in general. Direct dialogue between North Korea and the other nations of Asia will diminish mutual suspicions and build trust.

NORTHEAST ASIA'S COMMITMENT

Currently, the security outlook in Northeast Asia is fragile and fragmented. There is distrust among the nations of this region rooted in the destructive relationships of their pasts. China, the Republic of Korea and Japan are the keys to regional stability. China has good relations with South Korea, but would be hesitant to form a security alliance with it because of the strong U.S. military presence there. Japan also shares a mutual defense treaty with the U.S., and there is also added historical animosity between China and Japan. South Korea and Japan also share an unusual security arrangement with the United States: while they are both under the American security umbrella, they have no bilateral security relations of their own. This is rooted, once again, in historical animosity. In addition, there is another obstacle to overcome for the security of Northeast Asia, which is how China, Japan and South Korea could bring North Korea to the table to discuss regional security issues.

There would be many reservations about the inclusion of North Korea in a cooperative effort, but the whole idea would not be feasible without North Korea. North Korea has to be considered a necessary part of the collective security system in order to balance out the powers, as it has good relations with China and this would be a more enticing reason for China to cooperate. In fact, China's inclusion in a collective security system could very well depend on North Korea's participation. Also, geographically, it would be difficult to set out policies working around a nation caught in the middle of the security alliance. This would cause great insecurity for North Korea and only serve to increase tensions.

NATO was conceived as a response to a common threat. It was created in the context of the Cold War as a necessary measure against the Warsaw Pact. Having already experienced the benefits of major cohesive action during two world wars, European countries were more willing to align themselves. The two Koreas, Japan and China, in contrast, have fought each other in the past and have stayed out of each other's conflicts as far as possible.

Another obstacle may be that, unlike members of the E.U. and NATO, the four countries do not share the same ideology or political system. Asian countries are also reluctant to infringe on each other's sovereignty, and although there are threats, they are not, however, immediate or devastating enough to force countries into alliance with each other. It is, however, important that the leaders of the nations are prepared for any possible attack to the region, as it is far safer to anticipate such an occurrence than to react to it. It would be better to prevent or eliminate situations before they become threats.

STABLE ASIA, INCREASED PROSPERITY

The impediments to a cooperative system can be overcome with the construction of common goals and confidence-building measures. Each nation can fulfill its own goals of prosperity by working together with the other nations towards gaining prosperity in the region. Prosperity in the region to compete with the superpowers in our world is the aspiration of all involved. Without peace and security, however, prosperity cannot be guaranteed. A cooperative security effort can facilitate any future prosperity in the region. If nations can work out their differences and build up enough trust to protect each other, then certainly there will be enough trust to be built up for trade relations. The first step is to lay a foundation of trust through commonalities and everything else can be built up from there. This would also allow North Korea to become visible to the international community.

The stability of the region is vital for security and political reasons, but also for economic prosperity. Globalization has required interdependency for economic growth in today's world economy and, as a result, trade alliances have formed between strategic partners. One just has to look to the North American Free Trade Agreement and the European Union to see how nations strategically align themselves. Most of the countries involved have not only benefited economically but in security relations as well. Asia can reap the same benefits with such an alliance and each member country can strengthen its own economic standing as part of a unified and strong Asia. The Korean peninsula can act as the hub of the Northeast Asian region and enhance economic prosperity.

All of Asia should be included under the security umbrella of the collective-security arrangement. The mandate should include the building of trust among all nations in the region. It is vital that the three bodies do not alienate the other neighboring Asian countries, especially North Korea. The three powers do have to be at the forefront to play the role of big brother, as the U.S. does in NATO. A collective-security system in Asia must come into being with U.S. consultation. The United States is the largest military and economic power in the world and it would be in Asia's best interests to be aligned with the U.S. as a separate body and also to seek its guidance in the formation and maintenance of a collective-security system in Northeast Asia.

In order to build up trust, the first step is to open up dialogue. This can begin through the existing channels of dialogue between the three nations. Forums such as ASEM, ASEAN+3, ARF and APEC, in which leaders of all three nations participate, can initiate informal talks on the idea. Eventually, there would be formal regional forums on the implementation of, and the common threats to, the collective-security body. This also goes for the continued support of the Sunshine Policy. More cooperative efforts and dialogue with North Korea will only increase the prospects of reunification and eliminate all tensions between North Korea and other nations.

Interdependency and cooperation are the keys to sustaining peace and security and to fostering prosperity in today's world. Northeast Asia must come together to balance the economic playing field. This region as a whole is lagging behind the two superpowers, the U.S. and Europe, in forming security alliances as well as in economics and politics. The security of this region is vital for its future prosperity and Korea, China and Japan should bring Asia together in building an Asian community and a prosperous globalized world. This, however, begins with the stability that a collective-security system can provide. Trust must be built. South Korea is ready to play the role of mediator in bringing the nations together. Continued efforts towards interdependency and the stability of the region are needed for Asia to grow, prosper and reach its full potential. The common goals of peace, security and prosperity can be fulfilled through building a new collective-security system in Asia.

Deepening Cooperation and Achieving Common Prosperity

Shi Guangsheng
Minister of Foreign Trade & Economic Cooperation,
People's Republic of China

 After 15 years of arduous efforts, China's negotiation on WTO accession was eventually wrapped up on September 8, 2001. At the Fourth WTO Ministerial Conference held in Doha, Qatar, on November 11, 2001, the decision on China's WTO accession was adopted and all the legal procedures were completed. On December 11 2001, China formally becomes a WTO member.

China's accession to the WTO is the requirement and embodiment of China's deepened reform process and symbolizes that China's opening up has entered a new stage. China's accession to the WTO will provide unprecedented opportunities for the sound development of China's economy, and will make a new contribution to the stability and development of the Asian and world economy.

NEW IMPETUS TO THE WTO

As the biggest developing country in the world, China boasts one-fifth of the world's population and a huge market. Its national economy ranks sixth in the world and is expected to grow at about 7% annually in the next five years. China is the world's seventh-largest trading nation and, for eight consecutive years, it has been topping the list of developing countries in FDI absorption. China's accession to the WTO will add to the integrity and representativeness of the organization, contributing to the promotion of trade development and economic and technological cooperation in the global context. It will enhance the balance between developing and developed members, enabling the multilateral trading system to better reflect the interests of various parties. And it will strengthen the rationality of the formulation of international trade rules, promoting the establishment of a just and reasonable international new economic order and realizing the coordinated development of the world economy.

ADVANCING THE NEW ROUND OF WTO NEGOTIATIONS

The Fourth WTO Ministerial Conference saw the release of the Doha Declaration and the successful launch of a new round of multilateral trade talks, following setbacks in Seattle. China supports the launch of the new round of WTO negotiations, believing that the talks should aim at establishing a fair, just and reasonable international new economic order; promoting world economic and trade development as well as trade and investment facilitation; and striking a balance between the interests of developed and developing members. The process by which new international trade rules are formulated should more fully reflect the interests and requirements of developing members, enabling them — especially the least-developed members — to share fully in the opportunities and benefits and to respond to the challenges brought by economic globalization so as to achieve common prosperity. To this end, the round should take the development requirements of developing members into full consideration, guarantee the effective participation of developing members and accelerate the implementation of the Uruguay Round Agreements in order to realize an overall balance between the interests of various parties. China will, according to its own economic-development level and on the basis of the balance between rights and obligations, play a positive and constructive role in the new round of multilateral trade negotiations, joining hands with other WTO members to help make headway in the new round of talks and making a positive contribution to the development of the multilateral trade system.

POSITIVE RECOVERY AND DEVELOPMENT OF THE ASIAN AND WORLD ECONOMY

In recent years, in a complex and changeable international economic environment, China's economy has withstood the shock of the Asian financial crisis, realized continuous and stable growth, and made its due contribution to the stability and development of the Asian and global economies. Since 2001, the U.S., Japanese and European economies, which account for 70% of the world's total, have been experiencing the first simultaneous slide since 1975, putting the world economy into recession. The terrorist attacks have seriously affected economic development and people's confidence. The global economy has experienced a fairly large-scale restructuring worldwide. China, however, has maintained steady economic growth through playing out its own advantages and implementing a proactive fiscal policy and a prudent monetary policy.

The year 2001 witnessed sustainable development in China's national economy and a GDP growth of about 7.3%, which is higher than the 7%-goal set for the year. Fixed-asset investment increased by 13.7% and the total retail sales of social consumption surged by 10.1%. Imports and exports amounted to US$509.77 billion, an increase of 7.5%. In the breakdown, exports stood at US$243.61 billion and imports at US$266.15 billion, 6.8% and 8.2% higher, respectively, than the previous year. Approvals for the setting up of foreign-invested enterprises totaled 26,139, an increase of 16.01% over the corresponding period of the previous year. The contractual value of foreign investment grew by 10.4%, to US$69.19 billion, and the utilized value climbed by 14.9%, to US$46.85 billion.

After joining the WTO, China will actively participate in the process of economic globalization in broader fields to make a greater contribution to the recovery and development of the Asian and global economies and bring more business opportunities to industrial and commercial circles globally. In accordance with the WTO rules and its commitments, China will continue to open its market in a balanced, orderly and all-directional fashion. It will establish an economic and trade regime in line with prevailing international rules and its own circumstances, thus considerably improving the consistency and transparency of its economic and trade policies. China will further refine and improve its foreign-related economic laws and regulations to create better conditions for the investment, production and operation of foreign enterprises in China. Various Asian nations, with their special geographical and cultural links with China, will be among the first to benefit from these changes.

INDUSTRIAL RESTRUCTURING IN A WORLD OF RAPID ECONOMIC GLOBALIZATION

Economic development and globalization are inevitably accompanied by worldwide industrial restructuring. Today, industrial restructuring can no longer be completed by one single country within its own domestic market; rather, it can only be achieved through interdependence, mutual promotion and coordinated development among various countries and regions in the world. Therefore, industrial restructuring is of both a regional and global nature. Currently, China is undergoing strategic economic restructuring, which needs the participation of Asia and the world; equally, the adjustment of Asian and world economic structures also requires the involvement of China. After joining the WTO, China will, through investment, trade, economic and technological cooperation, strengthen collaboration, enhance the optimized upgrading of regional economic structure and jointly share the opportunities and benefits brought about by economic globalization with all countries and regions in the world under the multilateral trade framework.

CAPACITY-BUILDING AND THE SUSTAINABLE DEVELOPMENT OF ASIA'S ECONOMY AND SOCIETY

The strengthening of capacity-building, with human resources at its core, is the logical demand to realize sustainable development and to narrow South-North disparities in an effort to promote common prosperity. It is also driven by the need to participate in economic globalization and to facilitate trade and investment. The Chinese government attaches great importance to capacity-building and holds that the roles of the government, the business community and academic circles should be brought into play and that human-resource development should be highlighted. Developed and developing members alike should intensify cooperation and learn from each other's strengths. After its WTO entry, China will continue to strengthen its cooperation with other Asian nations on capacity-building, sharing infrastructure, personnel training, information, experience, expertise and specialized techniques. By getting better adapted to economic globalization, China hopes to make new contributions to the economic and social development in the Asia region.

COOPERATION WITH OTHER ASIAN COUNTRIES AND REGIONS

Many Asian countries and regions are APEC members. The first grand gathering of APEC in the new century was held in Shanghai in 2001, with leaders from a number of Asian nations and regions at the 9th APEC Informal Leaders' Summit. Centering on the theme of "Meeting New Challenges in the New Century: Achieving Common Prosperity through

Participation and Cooperation", the summit reached an overall consensus on a series of issues. After December 2001, China, like the majority of Asian countries and regions, will be a member of both APEC and the WTO. This will open broader fields for cooperation and inject fresh vitality into its economic and trade relations with other Asian countries and regions. It will help to expand common ground and deepen cooperation under bilateral, regional and multilateral frameworks that are conducive to the development of mutually beneficial economic relations and the creation of a more prosperous and stable regional environment.

The next five to 10 years will be an important period for China's economic and social development. Having defined its development blueprint for the coming five years, China proposes to push forward its economic growth and social progress with development as the theme, structural adjustment as the guideline, reform and opening up and scientific and technological progress as the driving force, and the improvement of people's living standards as the basic starting point. At present, China is accelerating the process of adjusting its industrial make-up, its regional composition, its urban and rural layout and its ownership structure. The development of science, technology and educational causes is high on its agenda and it is promoting IT for national economic and social development. While continuously strengthening environmental protection, it is pressing ahead with urban construction and the improvement of its public-service system. Preliminary estimates show that China's GDP will have reached RMB12.5 trillion by 2005. From 2001 to 2005, China will import about US$1.4 trillion-worth of equipment, technology and products.

On the basis of balanced rights and obligations, China will abide by WTO rules and fulfill its commitments so as to play an active and constructive role in the multilateral trade regime. It will, as always, lay emphasis and intensify efforts on the forging of equal and mutually beneficial economic and trade relations with all other nations and regions throughout the world. It will deepen its cooperation with them, thus making positive contributions to the recovery and growth of the world economy.

Regaining Stability and Growth in Asia

Vernon Ellis
International Chairman, Accenture, United Kingdom;
with Elizabeth Padmore,
Partner and Director, Policy and Corporate Affairs,
Accenture, UK

 Asian business has been one of the greatest success stories of the modern world. Fifty years ago, when most Asian states were still emerging from colonialism or conquest, it seemed unimaginable that Asian businesses would become household names, powerhouses of manufacturing and services, and owners of huge assets in the United States and Europe — as they are now.

The Asian success story derived from exporting successfully to world markets goods and services of high quality at highly competitive prices. That performance was built on many pillars: sustained investment, particularly in technology and training; constant improvements in the quality and branding of their products; the creation, often from surplus rural labor, of a skilled, educated and motivated workforce; combining low costs and high productivity; a strong social commitment to education and self-improvement; and a helpful regulatory environment.

In spite of these strengths, Asian businesses are still prey to the general problems which affect global business as a whole. They operate in a fragile global environment, in which markets, suppliers and finance are subject to violent shocks. They operate in a rapidly changing business environment, in which new business models and relationships, sometimes entire new industries, are being created by new technology. Finally, like all successful businesses Asian businesses are prey to their own success: they become bureaucratic rather than entrepreneurial and their decision-makers cannot carry enough information or react quickly enough to the changing world.

As the global economy pulls out of recession, it might be tempting for Asian businesses simply to reassert their traditional strengths and hope to recapture their export markets. But we believe that this would be a fundamental mistake. The world has moved on and globalization has left businesses more vulnerable to shock and sudden change, and made it more difficult for nations, and even whole continents, to insulate themselves from adverse events in other parts of the world. In our view, Asian businesses — in company with all global businesses — should respond to a changing world by a double program of change.

First, they should recognize that business is no longer autonomous but intimately connected with the outside world. Asian businesses, like others, need to become a new kind of "connected corporation", building a web of relationships with other stakeholders in local and global society. To be sure, many Asian businesses have traditionally cultivated strong relationships with shareholders, customers, the financial sector, government and communal organizations — and with each other. But these relationships need to be developed not only for the sake of short-term gains, but in the pursuit of long-range common goals which may change the very nature of the business.

Second, they should develop a new kind of leadership which fosters the maximum entrepreneurial spirit among all their employees. That entails the abandonment of traditional hierarchy and personal control, a new willingness to create a clear strategy and purpose, and a trust in employees to fulfill it. They need to encourage diversity of thinking and to make the most of their knowledge. Above all, they need to build belief at every level of their organization that entrepreneurship is valued.

A GLOBAL ENVIRONMENT

Business is currently experiencing the rapidly changing context of globalization and integration — since 1950, world trade has increased 14-fold, compared with a six-fold increase in world output. In all aspects of business we are seeing global manufacturing and sourcing, global capital flows, increasingly international labor markets, a constant search for economies of scale, convergence of products and markets, and the spread of knowledge and commercial practices across geographical and industry boundaries.

Asian business has been both a significant driver of globalization and a major beneficiary. In 1950, Asia's share of world GDP was a mere 17%. Now, rapid economic growth has propelled Asia's share to around 40%.

All of this has been driven by several factors: technical progress, particularly advances in the power and reach of information and communication technologies (ICT); policy, such as the now widespread emphasis on removing barriers to trade and investment; and evolving corporate strategies, leading to new organizational models and intense competition.

As a result we have seen enormous benefits to international business, with far greater efficiencies of production and the opening up of new global markets for their goods and services.

Different countries followed different strategies, but a key feature has been generally outward-looking policies, a business-friendly environment, and a strong focus on export growth, with impressive results. Singapore and Hong Kong are now among the richest countries in the world in terms of per capita income; Taiwan and South Korea can hardly be considered as "emerging" markets any longer; and China is emerging as a major player in the global economy, a move reflected in its recent accession to the WTO.

In our view, then, globalization has on balance benefited the region, just as it has benefited the world as a whole. Policy geared around attracting business has not just helped companies but created wealth, increased choice and led to greater empowerment.

INTO RECESSION AND UNCERTAINTY

But of course Asia has also experienced first hand that there can be a downside, too. The financial crisis in 1997–98 hit the region hard, with large withdrawals of foreign capital flows, sharp declines in output, steep increases in the number of business bankruptcies, and painful restructuring.

There are different views on whether this crisis was caused by globalization, but there can be little doubt that it was exacerbated by it. Poor domestic business practices, particularly in the area of corporate governance, ill-judged domestic policies (such as the provision of subsidies to inefficient companies, and weak banking regulation) and bad luck all played a part. But global financial markets were also at fault. When financial troubles hit Thailand, for example, they abruptly withdrew investment finance.

Painful though the period was for business and the region as a whole, the worst of the crisis was short-lived. This was partly because the region was integrated into the world economy — Asian exports formed the backbone to recovery.

Yet in many ways the Asian crisis was one of the first warning signs of danger for the global business environment. Apart from the short-term problems over the stability of some Asian banks and governments, the crisis exposed longer-term anxieties: the widening gap between rich and poor, both within and between countries; concern that entrepreneurial behavior might undermine social cohesion; and fears that foreign companies would help to erode traditional cultures and ways of life.

Such concerns are now widely shared around the world, and have been given powerful expression through the anti-globalization movement. The rise of this movement has combined with two other shocks — the tragic events of September 11 and their aftermath, and the global recession — to reveal the fragility of the world in which we live. For example, East Asia has seen its output-growth estimates drop to 4.6% in 2001 from 7.3% in 2000. Such shocks pose a unique challenge for business, in Asia and elsewhere in the world. There have, of course, always been risks in business, but these are now magnified, and there is a new sense of uncertainty about how the world will develop.

"THE CONNECTED CORPORATION"

The danger in these difficult times is that businesses will become highly cautious, shore up the boundaries of the organization, cut costs ruthlessly to maximize shareholder value, and take a short-term view of their narrow interests. But this would be a mistake. Instead, to survive and prosper, CEOs need to recognize that the nature of the corporation has changed fundamentally, and that a new approach to leadership is needed.

We are seeing the disaggregation and reconfiguration of many businesses, along with the creation of much more permeable organizational boundaries. The result is a much more complex web of relationships and dependencies — what we term the "connected corporation".

Companies are beginning to appreciate the interdependent systemic nature of the connections between businesses (including suppliers and alliance partners), governments, trade unions/employees, shareholders, customers, non-governmental organizations, cultural institutions, local communities, and the physical environment that contains them all.

In this decentralized corporate "ecosystem", new relationships are constantly being created and old ones strengthened or destroyed. Of course, many of these connections have long existed, but their nature is changing greatly.

Asian businesses, perhaps more than most, have a greater understanding of what it means to be a "connected corporation". Many traditionally have strong interlinkages with other businesses and organizations. The challenge for Asian business is to make these traditional forms of connection count as an advantage in terms of encouraging greater innovation. Otherwise there is a danger that all the traditional links remain in place, but fixed and static — merely preserving the comfortable status quo.

Actively making the right connections at the right time in this complex environment is becoming a key determinant of survival. These relationships are not all between the leaders of organizations. Rather, it is employees who will create and hold the majority of such relationships. This places a new emphasis on the talent and energy of the workforce. We are heading towards an "age of capability", in which human performance — in particular, the entrepreneurial spirit of employees — becomes the critical differentiator for business.

THE IMPORTANCE OF ENTREPRENEURSHIP

Entrepreneurial behavior has always been important — after all, it is what most of today's businesses were built on. But in a time of great uncertainty, entrepreneurship is not just nice to have but the key to survival.

Over the past two years, Accenture has been analyzing what entrepreneurship really means, how it is exhibited within different types of organizations and in different countries, and what can be done to encourage more entrepreneurial behavior. Our research included interviews with 1,000 board-level executives in 26 countries/territories, including Hong Kong, Singapore, Malaysia, South Korea, China and Japan.

When we asked them which organizations they considered to be entrepreneurial, the 1,000 executives we interviewed suggested several hundred organizations. Only Microsoft received mentions in most countries/territories, and even then the total number of executives mentioning them was very low. (In fact, 13% of execs interviewed in Hong Kong mentioned them, higher than the average.) But nearly one in five of our total sample could not think of a single organization. What could this mean?

It became increasingly clear as we conducted our research that entrepreneurship has different manifestations, different applications and, as a result, there are different approaches to encouraging and growing it. For example, in India, an entrepreneur is perceived as a single, strong, charismatic leader, whereas in Singapore, it is expected that the entrepreneurial instinct will be shared by everyone.

But a number of key characteristics did emerge across all the countries:

- **Creativity and innovation** is at the heart of entrepreneurship, enabling entirely new ways of thinking and working. Entrepreneurs can identify opportunities, large or small, that no-one else has noticed.

- Good entrepreneurs also have **the ability to apply that creativity** — they can effectively marshal resources to a single end.

- They have **drive** — a fervent belief in their ability to change the way things are done, and the force of will and the passion to achieve success.

- They have **a focus on creating value** — they want to do things better, faster, cheaper.

- And they **take what many people might commonly think of as risks** — breaking rules, cutting across accepted boundaries, and going against the status quo.

In many countries a myth abounds around entrepreneurship — that it is all about start-up companies and new enterprises. Yet the reality is that entrepreneurship is relevant to all types and sizes of organizations and it is highly collaborative, not just an individualistic activity. In fact, nowhere is entrepreneurship more important than in large, established companies. In a market where large companies are constantly having to defend their territory from small, nimble organizations, the issue of how they motivate and energize their workforce has become more critical than ever.

In Asia, however, this myth is not so prevalent. It is extremely encouraging that there is such an emphasis on collaboration, which may provide Asian businesses with a real advantage if they can achieve the right balance between collective effort and individual initiative.

So, in the 21st-century model of the corporation, entrepreneurial behavior is key. Most of the senior executives we interviewed believe that entrepreneurship is very important to both their society and their company. Nearly all of them are certain of the importance of entrepreneurship to their organization — Taiwan just slips below the 90% mark, with 85% agreeing it is very/fairly important to their company. Only Hong Kong apparently remains unconvinced, with only 50%, the second-lowest figure globally, although as with the U.S. (the lowest figure) this may indicate that entrepreneurship is so built into the fabric of businesses that they do not emphasize it.

ENTREPRENEURIAL BARRIERS

But very few believe their organization is very entrepreneurial today — fewer than three in 10 executives think this. Taiwanese and Hong Kong executives are the least confident group in the region about the level of entrepreneurship in their organization. In Taiwan, only 68% think they are very/fairly entrepreneurial today, and in Hong Kong a mere 53% think so. This contrasts with 80% in Japan, 93% in Malaysia, and 88% in Singapore.

Not surprisingly, the vast majority of executives say that their country must be more entrepreneurial in five years' time: 100% in Malaysia, 90% in Japan and Singapore, and 93% in Taiwan think this; again Hong Kong is a little lower, on 78%.

So what is preventing more entrepreneurial behavior? One striking and encouraging feature of our findings was that executives from Asia are far less likely than Americans or Europeans to view government actions — for example, taxation, legislation and regulation — as important barriers to entrepreneurship. Instead, they tend to see businesses as major influences on the entrepreneurial culture.

In line with the global figures, just over half of the executives in this region think that structural and bureaucratic problems are a barrier to entrepreneurship; although in South Korea the figure is 78% — which is perhaps unsurprising, given that such complaints tend to be associated with large organizations, and that the Korean economy is still dominated by such large companies.

This is an issue of which we are very conscious in Accenture. Over time we have grown into a global company that employs more than 75,000 people across 46 countries and serves more than half of the companies on the Fortune Global 500. As we have grown, we have had to search hard to find ways to ensure that our sheer size and complexity does not work against us by stifling our ability to be innovative and flexible and to be entrepreneurial. We need to continue to be vigilant, ensuring that we never fall in the trap identified by the Japanese executive who commented that "Big organizations often kill individual ideas even if they are good", and the business leader in Canada who stated that "Many organizations and managers beat the entrepreneurial spirit out of employees".

In South Korea, 95% of executives think that aversion to risk and failure is a barrier to entrepreneurial behavior; 85% of those from Singapore think the same, while other Asian countries are in the region of 60–65%. Many employees do not have the confidence to act entrepreneurially — even if they have a good idea, and they are willing to battle through the bureaucracy to win support for it, they think that they may be criticized for showing individual initiative and blamed if ideas eventually prove unsuccessful.

Good leadership is key in fostering such confidence. Yet, 73% of executives interviewed in Singapore and 68% from Japan told us that one barrier to entrepreneurship was the failure by leadership to actively encourage entrepreneurial behavior. And about half of executives in Hong Kong and Taiwan — and even more in South Korea and Japan — told us that the lack of role models is a problem.

It is not that senior executives do not understand the importance of entrepreneurship: overwhelmingly, they support it, try to promote it and want more help from government and from their own employees in that task. But they seem rather confused and frustrated about what to do.

Across all the Asian countries, over 70% of executives think their employees lack entrepreneurial instincts; in fact, in Singapore 88% of executives hold this view. Yet there is a dichotomy here. Many want their employees to act more entrepreneurially, but appear nervous about possible loss of control. Half of executives say employees can be *too* entrepreneurial. Admittedly, there are some substantial variations between Asian countries — only 28% of executives in Taiwan hold this view, compared with 83% of executives in South Korea. But the point is clear. It seems that employers want their employees to be more entrepreneurial but all too often we do not trust them to act that way.

A NEW KIND OF LEADERSHIP

There is a pressing need for a new kind of leadership to release the entrepreneurial spirit. This is about much more than just getting the big decisions right, giving orders and trying to be entrepreneurial themselves. Instead, senior executives must be leaders of entrepreneurs rather than just entrepreneurial leaders, and they must be able to rely on their staff to exercise their own judgment, trusting them enough to let go, while at the same time providing them with opportunities to gain new skills and experience.

This means setting the overall direction of the organization, empowering people to work within a common framework, and inspiring them to make the most of their talents so that both they and the organization benefit.

But how can this be done in practice? Accenture research and analysis suggests five imperatives that a leader of entrepreneurs must undertake.

1. Use strategy and purpose to create entrepreneurial confidence

Having a clear strategy and purpose is essential if employees are to feel comfortable taking the entrepreneurial initiative, and if leaders are to feel comfortable giving this freedom to employees. It achieves this by defining the boundaries in which to take risks. It can also reinforce the message that entrepreneurship is a collaborative activity. For example, the mission for Matsushita Corporation includes the phrase "Teamwork for the Common Cause". In the entrepreneurial organization, strategy cannot be confined to the executive suite, and employees at all levels should provide input to the strategy process. They can also act as conduits to sources of information and thinking outside the corporation.

2. Be big, work small

Once the right strategic decisions are made, an entrepreneurial organization must be able to execute on those decisions swiftly. The challenge — especially for large companies operating on a global scale — is to get the organization out of the way and regain what Niall FitzGerald, chairman of Unilever, terms a "small-company soul". A good example is Acer (Taiwan), where it is known to have abandoned hierarchy, traditional deference and much other formality seen at other large Asian companies. At Acer, it is reputed that people two or three levels below the company chairman can argue openly with the chairman with no fear of comeback. Other ways to achieve this are to break the organization down into smaller units or encourage spin-offs.

Structural approaches are not the only solution: the best entrepreneurial organizations find ways to champion small-scale initiatives. For example, Nokia runs a scheme that provides seed money to employees who want to take an idea to the next level, or to try an activity that is new to them.

3. Encourage diversity of thinking

Bringing a diversity of experience, perspectives and viewpoints into an organization plays an important part in creating a more entrepreneurial culture. New ideas can be the grit in the oyster, challenging conventional thinking in ways that may not be comfortable but will often produce a pearl of innovation or insight. A diverse workforce also allows companies to read and respond better to the needs of complex markets. At Intel in Penang, Malaysia, the buzzphrase "paradigm shift" is used in everyday conversations and meetings. It is deeply set in the Intel culture that one should always seek new paradigm shifts in one's thinking or in one's way of operation.

Recruiting and hiring a variety of employees is an obvious avenue to increasing the diversity of thinking, but there are other approaches. Leaders can capitalize on the diversity present in a company's virtual network of alliance partners and other organizations and people with which it has connections. Finally, a truly entrepreneurial leader will have his or her antennae up at all times, constantly ready to hear new ideas or viewpoints from any source. The Indian company Bharti Enterprise continuously hires new people at the highest levels. "We believe that new faces are good around the decision-making table," says the group's chairman, Sunil Mittal.

4. Make the most of your company's knowledge

Given today's highly mobile workforce, a corporation will need to find quicker and more efficient ways to manage its knowledge and help employees to develop and maximize their entrepreneurial potential.

Companies need an effective knowledge-sharing system that includes benchmarking and allows an organization to learn from successes and failures and that communicates these lessons quickly. Coaching and mentoring schemes help the transfer of knowledge and experience within the organization as well as providing an opportunity for leaders to inculcate key entrepreneurial values such as creativity and risk taking in employees. e-Learning tools can also play a hugely important role in developing entrepreneurial skills. They can allow people to be immersed in simulated environments that prompt active decision making — like the flight simulators used to train pilots. They are effective because people learn best from doing, not watching or listening.

Equally important is the ability to learn from outside the organization — from customers, partners, competitors, portals, discussion sites and even casual business contacts. For example, Texas Instruments created a "Not Invented Here But I Did It Anyway" award and gave it to both the contributor and user of the best idea.

5. Build belief that entrepreneurship is valued

If they are to behave in an entrepreneurial way, employees at all levels need to be reassured that such behavior is appreciated and valued, and that it does not involve unacceptably high personal risks. To achieve that end, leaders of an entrepreneurial organization need to build an organizational mindset that encourages breakthrough thinking and change. They need to develop performance measures for entrepreneurial behavior.

Entrepreneurial contribution must be recognized and rewarded — this means that the organization must be willing to reward, or at least not penalize, intelligent failure. The aim should be to create an environment in which three successes out of five is recognized as better than one out of one; and where intelligent failure is recognized as providing valuable experience. The CEO of Nestlé, Peter Brabeck, says that "Every time I have to approve a promotion, I ask 'What was the biggest mistake that this person has made?' Because if somebody hasn't made a big enough mistake along the way, he hasn't had the courage to make big decisions or to learn along the way."

In some countries, there are concerns that entrepreneurship is not valued by society at large, because it is seen as being in some way anti-social: it causes social division, is associated with individual greed, and it leads to more job insecurity. Japanese executives felt particularly strongly about such worries. Perhaps in part linked to this, executives in a number of countries also told us that entrepreneurs are not well regarded — 70% of executives from South Korea said this, compared with only 13% from Hong Kong. We would argue that much of this is because people do not understand that true entrepreneurship is collaborative not individualistic and can have a very positive social impact — perhaps we all need to do more to make this case.

CONCLUSIONS

It has been said that "an average leader can lead when times are good...real leaders emerge in tough times". This is certainly being worked out in these times of recession. Good leadership is vital: but it is much more than just getting the big decisions right and giving orders.

The aim of leaders in an economic downturn should be working at how to revive the spirit of entrepreneurial action whilst maintaining a spirit of survival and growth. The key to this must be in encouraging entrepreneurial employees rather than relying on an entrepreneurial CEO. Traditionally, it does seem that the entrepreneurial spirit within Asian firms is often most closely associated with the founding owner and is perhaps less evident in the rest of the firm. But in this current economic climate, the emphasis on top-down cost cutting must also go hand in hand with the creation of bottom-up revolutionaries.

Asia – A Region Oriented Toward the 21st Century

Heinrich von Pierer
Chairman of the Managing Board, Siemens AG, Germany

 A few years ago there didn't seem to be any question where Asia was heading: up, straight up. Economic prospects in the region were bright and many Asian countries were rapidly developing into high-tech nations. Western models of social organization were being widely adopted. Virtually every article written on the region included the words "emerging markets" and "tiger nations". Among investors, enthusiasm for Asia was boundless and normal investment precautions seemed superfluous.

The euphoria has since given way to a more realistic appraisal. The events connected with the Asian crisis of 1997 significantly dampened the boom and the current global slowdown is also having an impact on economic developments in the Far East. Does this mean that the countries of Asia will now fall back and that the development potential ascribed to them was only an illusion? Are the major gains that have already been made in performance and prosperity now at an end?

The answer is a clear "No". Asia continues to have enormous power. It still has the extraordinary capacity to be the world's most dynamic innovation-friendly region within the next few decades. The basis has been laid and the performance parameters are intact. But what are the concrete factors in the Asian success story? In my opinion, there are five decisive areas:

1. The drive to perform and the desire to learn — the basis
2. Population development and demography — the driver
3. Enthusiasm for technology and the power of innovation — the engine for growth

4. Reform and economic policies — the climate for success
5. Networks and systems of relationships — the stabilizers.

THE DRIVE TO PERFORM AND THE DESIRE TO LEARN — THE BASIS

A Chinese proverb says: "Nothing is impossible for a willing spirit." The drive to perform and the yearning for a better standard of living, for prosperity and happiness, are key features of Confucianist societies across Asia. But this is not the abstract concept of happiness encountered in many Western societies, but well-being in the here and now. Even the symbolic character of Asian scripts — for example, those of China and Japan — reflects the very concrete thinking of people in the region, where the focus is on pragmatism rather than abstract theories or ideologies.

Asians, accordingly, take a solution-oriented approach to tasks. This applies to private, everyday life as well as to many other areas of society and business. In the academic, research and political spheres, solutions are sought to meet current needs and the demands of particular, concrete situations. This gives people a high degree of flexibility and adaptability, enabling them to adjust easily to changing circumstances. In an age in which speed and dynamism are the critical factors in the business environment, these characteristics often provide the decisive competitive advantage.

This future-oriented and positive attitude also explains the high emphasis placed on education in Asian societies, where knowledge and experience are considered the keys to success. In many Asian societies, a good education has historically been the prerequisite to high public office. Learning has been the primary method of advancement since time immemorial. Transferred to the business world, this explains the outstanding achievements of Asian students and their rapidly rising numbers in universities throughout the world. In international companies like Siemens, Asian employees are often leading performers and top executives, for the people of Asia know that education and hard work bring success. As Confucius himself told the ruler who asked what good governance meant: "Educate the people and make them prosperous."

This attitude also accounts for the basically positive attitude of Asians toward elites, toward social status that has been achieved by one's own efforts and toward wealth. An envy complex of the kind sometimes encountered in Europe, which begrudges the success of others, is unknown in Asia. On the contrary: extraordinary and conspicuous consumption — frequently a distinguishing feature of today's new performance elite — promotes social advancement. Status, prestige and influence in society are highly respected and considered to be highly desirable in many Asian countries. Performance orientation is regarded positively — an attitude which has made the Asian work and business ethic so successful worldwide.

POPULATION DEVELOPMENT AND DEMOGRAPHY — THE DRIVER

Some 3.7 billion people, or more than 60% of the world's population, currently live in Asia. This figure is expected to increase to 5.3 billion by 2050. In 2010, Asia will account for two-thirds of the people in the world below the age of 35, and it is already a region of young, high-performance individuals. Women also have a major role in economic development. Women already account for half of Asia's working population and head some 35% of the small- to medium-sized companies in the region.

All these figures point to a high potential for development — and not only from the perspective of a Europe-based company like Siemens that sees a major market opportunity. Objectively considered, Asia is the world's greatest reservoir of people with knowledge, drive and the willingness to work and improve themselves and their own countries.

China and its recent development clearly illustrate what this vast human potential can accomplish. The country and its some 1.3 billion inhabitants already possess considerable economic clout. The age structure of the Chinese population also indicates the enormous development possibilities for the future. Statistically, China has the youngest population in all of Asia. Today, the People's Republic is the seventh-largest economy and the eighth-largest trading nation in the world. According to the World Bank, the Chinese economy will account for 25% of the total world economy by the year 2025 — ahead of America (20%) and India (13%). In the next few years, the distribution of power within the world economy will clearly shift toward China. WTO membership — which will not only benefit trade with China's trading partners but will also accelerate economic and social change within the country's borders — will provide an added push in this regard. Thus, China and its population are currently getting themselves in shape to become, perhaps, the world's most important economic engine in the not-too-distant future.

India is another good example. The subcontinent's roughly one billion inhabitants harbor an enormous economic power. At its current rate of growth, India will be the world's most populous country in a little over 10 years. Even though wide-ranging reforms in the country must still pick up speed, positive trends are unmistakable. A growing middle class with considerable purchasing power forms a stabilizing core for India's domestic economy. Economic structures have been shifting away from agriculture and toward the production and services sectors, which now account for almost 50% of the country's gross domestic product.

If one disregards for a moment the problem of illiteracy, which remains one of the country's most urgent problems, India enjoys a relatively high level of education in some areas. This explains the high number of excellent engineers in the country. This knowledge base can, if it is systematically developed, considerably strengthen India's competitiveness on the global markets. Know-how can be a supporting pillar of India's economic power.

The strengths of India's educational system are already bearing fruit. The country's software industry has an outstanding reputation worldwide. The possibilities for development — which mark this rapidly growing sector as a result of, among other things, global Internet-based networking — are enormous. India's software companies are among the world's most efficient and innovative. The intensive cooperation which already exists with all world-leading high-tech companies, especially in the high-growth information and communications sector, will noticeably accelerate India's development in this area. For this reason, the software industry could be the germ for a wide-ranging technological and industrial boom in India. The prerequisites are already in place. All that remains is for business and political leaders to jointly recognize and exploit them.

Under certain circumstances, however, demographic change can retard a country's development. Longer life expectancies and an ageing population will increasingly burden social-welfare systems as these are currently structured, while fewer and fewer younger, working people will have to provide for a larger and larger number of retirees. There is, thus, a danger that economic development as a whole will suffer, especially if the result of an over-aged society is a lack of highly qualified young employees. This applies especially to the dynamic information and communications sectors which are marked by headlong technological innovation and equally rapid changes in know-how. This demographic phenomenon, which has long been only marginally noted, has now begun to act as an obvious brake on the economic growth and competitiveness of countries such as Germany.

But Asia has not been spared either. The Japanese economy is currently in danger of finding itself in this situation. Japan, where the average life expectancy is 84, has the oldest population in Asia and, in fact, in the whole world. The urgently needed stream of young people from universities — especially in the electronic and automotive sectors, which are vital to the Japanese economy — is slackening. This situation is being aggravated, moreover, by the reluctance of Japanese companies to invest domestically and the continued restrictions on foreign investment in many fields. As a result, too few new jobs are being created in promising, future-oriented fields and Japan's global competitiveness is, therefore, in danger.

Nonetheless, the country has greater resources than any other in Asia. Japan accounts for more than half of the region's entire economic performance. Enormous currency reserves, functioning industrial structures, management abilities, know-how in a host of promising fields of technology, and decades of experience in the export field are success factors that must and will pay off in the future. The prerequisite, however, is a mental opening of the country to the rules of the global economy, as well as rigorous structural reforms in the economy and society. When these steps have been taken, I am convinced that the land of the rising sun will flourish once again.

ENTHUSIASM FOR TECHNOLOGY AND THE POWER OF INNOVATION — THE ENGINE FOR GROWTH

Textiles, shoes and fireworks — not long ago it was products from low-tech industries that led the list of Asian exports. But those days are over. High-value electronics, consumer goods at world-market level and, increasingly, innovative products in the most varied high-tech areas have placed the offerings from the Far East in a completely new light. Information and communications technologies, electronics, new materials, biotechnology and gene technology are now on the agenda, together with future-oriented technologies in the fields of energy and transportation. Asian countries are developing their product portfolios more and more in the direction of high technology.

This trend has been driven, of course, in the first instance by developments on the world market since the aim has been, naturally, to make money. But there is another important explanation for Asian engagement in the high-tech sector. The peoples of Asia are readier than most to embrace the most advanced technologies — especially, in the area of information and communications technology.

In China, for example, over 120 million Chinese now use mobile phones and this figure is expected to double by 2005. In Shanghai, 90%

of all apartments are linked to fiber-optic networks, far more than in most industrial countries, and Internet use is rapidly expanding. In 2000, four million Internet hook-ups were registered and, by 2005, this figure is expected to jump to 85 million. The use of innovative transportation systems such as the Transrapid is yet another indication of the extent to which China's people have embraced modern technology. Second- and third-class products and technologies below the world standard have not been acceptable in China for a long time. High-tech is demanded by consumers and pushed by industry. This applies both to China and to Asia as a whole.

It is also clear that Asia's road to becoming a global high-tech center has long since passed the point of merely importing innovative technologies. The transformation of economic structures is to a large extent focused on positioning local companies as producers of high-tech products in the world market. A number of countries — in particular, Singapore, Malaysia, Taiwan and the Philippines — are pushing the development of future-oriented industries for electronics products such as components and memory chips.

It is now no longer only the young tiger nations that are encouraging foreign companies to locate within their borders as a way to attract foreign capital and give the economy added impetus. Many Asian countries are calling for an investment-friendly economic climate. Highly promising markets also play their part in attracting foreign capital. In 2001, foreign direct investment in Asia totaled more than US$150 billion.

For Siemens, too, Asia has long been an important pillar of our worldwide business operations. Nearly 70,000 of our 450,000 people around the world are employed in Asia. China is one area of focus for our Asia strategy. Already today, China ranks third in sales, after the U.S. and Germany. Siemens' activities in China include our new mobile-phone production facility in Shanghai, which manufactures cell phones not only for the Chinese market but for all of Asia, and Siemens Medical Solutions facility, also in Shanghai. The systems manufactured here are marketed not only in Asia but also in other emerging markets, such as those of Latin America. Clearly, China is a dynamic local market as well as an export location for the Asia-Pacific and other regions of the world.

Innovation is success factor No.1 in the global economy. Many countries and regions of Asia already boast a world-class climate when it comes to nurturing innovation. The prevailing positive attitude toward new developments and an eagerness to try them out also play a major role here.

REFORM AND ECONOMIC POLICIES — THE CLIMATE FOR SUCCESS

A stable, reliable political system is an indispensable prerequisite for a flourishing economy. Factors that make a location appealing for business include legal and financial systems that function smoothly and predictably, together with technical and logistics infrastructures that meet the needs of the global economy. Most of Southeast Asia has already recognized this, and has responded with political and economic reform programs in recent years.

Thus an economic framework has been created throughout Asia which is enabling the region's countries to withstand the current phase of economic weakness comparatively well. This applies to Singapore and Taiwan — export countries particularly hard hit by the slump in the IT and communications markets — as well as to those countries that experienced the greatest pressure during the Asian crises, such as South Korea, Malaysia and Thailand.

In the last three years, the stable financial markets in Asia have played a considerable role in re-establishing a solid economic basis. Capital outflows were limited and exchange rates generally stable, with few exceptions. Unlike other emerging markets, such as those of Latin America, Asia's willingness to cooperate with international financial institutions bore fruit, stabilizing the financial systems. This substantially strengthened Asia's appeal as an investment location, especially for foreign investors. The Asian countries have taken important steps to nurture investment and attract capital. In doing so, they have also built a great deal of confidence in Asia as an investment location.

Nevertheless, the countries of Asia have not yet reached the end of the road, and further efforts must ensue. This applies above all to structures in the corporate and financial sectors and to the continued liberalization of trade. Moreover, the pace of reform currently appears to be slowing in some of the region's countries. This would be a perilous route. If Asia intends to continue the integration of the entire region into the global economy, individual countries cannot abandon their efforts now, neither as regards to the continued opening of their markets — for instance, in the services sector — nor when it comes to eliminating structural weaknesses that still exist in a legal or institutional context. It is precisely the elimination of these shortcomings that could prove to be a major driver of growth.

Integration is also the key word when it comes to liberalizing trade in Southeast Asia. The entry of China and Taiwan into the WTO are highly visible milestones along the way. The establishment of the AFTA

(ASEAN Free Trade Area) on January 1, 2002 — six years ahead of schedule — is a signal that Asia is serious about free trade within the framework of global competition. ASEAN+3, which includes South Korea, China and Japan, has become an established concept in the political arena, even beyond the region's borders. For foreign investors, these developments are important confidence-inspiring indications of the growing uniformity of general economic conditions in Asia and thus also of the increasing stability of the region as a whole.

NETWORKS AND SYSTEMS OF RELATIONSHIPS — THE STABILIZERS

However, in addition to the prevailing economic and political framework, the tendency of Asians to act as part of a network plays a key role in the stability and success of the region and its companies. This does not refer to the interrelationship of the Asian economies with their foreign trade partners. Nor are the successes of a host of transnational Asian companies, including 19 of the 25 largest multinationals from developing countries that are located in Asia, the primary characteristic of the "Asia Network".

Rather, it refers to a success factor that is firmly anchored in the values systems of Asia: the conviction that continuous, predictable, reliable relationships are the best guarantee for successful cooperation in the long term. This kind of cooperation works best in stable networks that have been cultivated over time, and typifies private, political and professional life in Asia.

The idea of the family as a strong protective social entity is a core element of the Asian concept of the network. What matters is achieving an equilibrium between individual interests and the needs of the group. Should a conflict of interests arise, the family takes precedence. When applied to the economy, this strong group-oriented mentality is undoubtedly one of the most important success factors of Asian companies, particularly in the information and service society with its knowledge networks.

One example of this Asian version of the network economy is the worldwide network of Chinese nationals residing in foreign countries. While the claim of American trend researcher John Naisbitt that "Overseas Chinese are the third-largest economic power of the world" is no doubt an exaggeration, the truth is that some 60 million Chinese live in roughly 60 countries around the world. More than 90% of these individuals are citizens of their country of residence. Their contacts extend beyond the borders of nations and continents to create information and cooperation networks on a global scale. What may even be perceived as a threat is in reality a paragon of organization that could serve as a model for the economy of the 21ˢᵗ century and for the Internet age. At any rate, the efficiency of Asia's knowledge and economic networks is undisputed.

In Asia, cooperation between the economic and political arenas is also typified by a mindset that might be described as "Together we're a strong team". Rather than considering themselves primarily adversaries, representatives of business, employees, unions and politicians often engage in teamwork. This interaction is based on an awareness of the expediency of making joint efforts to realize the legitimate interests of all partners. Western economic models could learn a lot about how to increase their clout from this successful approach.

While it might be overstating the case to say, "Asia is where the Asians are. And that is all over the world", there is a grain of truth therein. The interconnections among Asian businesspeople do not end at the borders of countries and continents, even if these individuals reside permanently in a foreign country where they may have been doing business for generations. The best proof of this phenomenon are the Asian neighborhoods — some of which have been in existence for decades or even centuries — found in all of the major cities around the world.

Stable networks cultivated over many years are thus also the best strategy for establishing and maintaining trusting business relations in Asia and with Asian partners. On the other hand, a short-term approach and ad hoc moves are not well received in the Far East. Long-term cooperation of the kind described also emerges amazingly unscathed from phases of economic or political upheaval. The German business community knew what it was talking about when it long ago declared the motto of its commitment in Asia to be: "We are here to stay". Continuity, reliability and trust have always characterized relations between Germany and the Asia-Pacific countries.

ASIA'S FUTURE HAS ALREADY BEGUN

When we consider the future of the world today, our thoughts inevitably turn to Asia. The region already has all the prerequisites for leading its populations further along the road to prosperity. Rapidity and size, two terms which in the last few years have been repeatedly referred to in the economic world as the "attributes of the successful", are important from the Asian point of view but are not beneficial on their own. Perseverance, reliability and the courage to pursue untrodden paths are Asian virtues which are at least equally important for sustainable success. Those who currently drive the world economy, in so far as they are not already located in Asia, could learn a lot from this. Like no other regional business approach, the "Asian way" will influence the fate of the global economy in the coming years and decades. Those who want to be at the forefront of economic development in the future must adapt to this before it is too late, if they have not already done so long ago.

And if we were to sum up the future of Asia in a single sentence, we can echo the words of Jahn Hay, an American Foreign Secretary at the beginning of the 20th century:

"The Mediterranean is the ocean of the past, the Atlantic is the ocean of the present and the Pacific is the ocean of the future."

Strategies for Success: Asia's Business Leaders Speak Out

Introduction

A by-product of the Asian economic crisis of 1997 has been the belief that "Asian management" was outdated and even counterproductive to increasing the competitiveness of the firm. From Japan to Indonesia, Anglo-Saxon-style management techniques dominated discussion and practice, and formerly praised management approaches such as the Japanese *kaizen* (continuous improvement), Chinese *guanxi* (management through trust and stable relationships) and Southeast Asian business networks (conglomerate-style expansion) even became synonymous with rigidity, corruption and backwardness.

The debate between adherents of the so-called Anglo-Saxon model and the Asian model of management has been raging for a long time, and especially in the festive days prior to the outbreak of the Asian crisis. The debate centered on the cultural element of management — that a certain region, religion or shared history ought to determine the style and peculiarities of management. With this book, we do intend to build a counter-position to this hot-tempered debate. We believe, along with our contributors, that each successful company — whether based in Asia or not — has to develop its own distinctive management profile. There is no universal nor culturally asserted wisdom of how a company should be run — the real winners create innovative solutions which distinguish them from the big herd of those who manage their companies according to the mainstream. It is interesting to note that many successful and widely admired Asian CEOs have created their own culture of how to advance their companies.

Asian CEOs, above all, are very pragmatic by nature. Just imagine the Taiwanese cult of entrepreneurship: the dream of young graduates is not to join big multinational corporations, but to build their own companies. A good example is Chen Wen-Chi of VIA Technologies who ventured into semiconductors and who is one of the main competitors of Intel today. Via is a virtual company based on R&D, the manufacturing of chips being done by so-called fabs in Taiwan and increasingly also in mainland China. John Chen left his original Chinese environment to start a career on the U.S. West Coast, creating Sybase, a leading software manufacturer. His move is a very typical model for entrepreneurs of Asian origin and their peers from India; overseas Chinese entrepreneurs are dominating Silicon Valley. Back home, Chinese conglomerates are developing new models of management, either through looking at the "golden path" between the inherited and the adopted, or through envisioning totally new models. Fu Yuning, the President of China Merchants Holdings, tells us his success story. In a similar vein, Japanese and Korean multinationals are emancipating themselves from the usual stereotypes circulating around the secrets of the Japanese *kaisha* and the Korean *chaebol*. Toshiba's Tadashi Okamura, NTT DoCoMo's Keiji Tachikawa and Trigem's Y.T. Lee are doing away with the bequest of lifetime employment and seniority. Instead, they bet on IT as the engine for growth.

Other atypical careers and characters include Kim Sung-Joo, who is one of the first successful Korean businesswomen in an otherwise paternalistic environment; Philippe Paillart, a "foreigner" who runs a large Asian bank; and Manuel V. Pangilinan, who transformed a government-linked telecom firm into a flexible, outward-oriented regional player. Almost unnoticed, Asia's business leaders have risen to become the new heroes in the management firmament. Now they speak out.

Maintaining Competitiveness in a Global Economy

John Chen
Chairman, President and Chief Executive Officer, Sybase,
Inc., United States

 Does Asia have what it takes to be competitive in a global economy? The answer is "Yes" — but significant hurdles abound. The even distribution of wealth, broader access to education, a culture committed to innovation and risk taking, and a cooperative and nurturing business environment are the keys to success.

We clearly live in an era of global business, when goods and services can be marketed and sold all over the world in ways that were simply unimaginable in the past. But for all of its opportunities, the global economy has created its share of challenges as well. With competition now ubiquitous across the globe, companies must look beyond their traditional market boundaries and be prepared to fight for market share against the very best the world has to offer.

That means being capable of competing by the same rules — and fighting with the same weapons — available to the rest of the world. This is the central challenge facing Asia as it strives to compete in the global business arena. There's no question, of course, that Asia has immense resources to draw upon in its quest for market share, but those resources must be developed until they can measure up to the quality of the resources available to business enterprises in North America and Europe. And until they are, it will be difficult for many of the economies in Asia to achieve competitive balance on a global scale.

While there are a number of positive signs that point to Asian competitiveness, a closer examination reveals significant problems that must be addressed. To extend its reach around the world, Asia must first provide a more even distribution of wealth and cultivate greater consumer demand at home. It must invest in and provide better access to education. It must cultivate a business culture that stimulates innovation and risk taking. And the combination of private enterprise, government, venture capital and educational institutions must work together to foster a friendly operating environment conducive to promoting business. The balance of this chapter explores each of these issues in greater detail.

CREATING A MARKET OF DEMAND: SPREADING THE WEALTH

If we think of imports and exports as part of the measure of market size and strength, as a region Asia is comparable with — although not yet equivalent to — North America and Europe. Equally significant, the gross domestic product (GDP) of Asia as a region is larger than that of the European market or the United States. This clearly demonstrates that Asia, from the perspective of creating a market of demand, has the wherewithal to be competitive with other developed economies.

But a closer examination of the GDP in Asia reveals a highly unequal distribution of wealth, which is a major cause for concern. Today, only three economies — China, Japan and India — produce the lion's share of Asian imports/exports and gross domestic product. Together, in fact, they account for nearly three-quarters of Asia's GDP.

An important metric to look at is gross domestic product per capita. This measures the ability of the average citizen to purchase the goods and services that his or her country produces. And here, when we compare Asia to other parts of the world, we see a wide disparity. Some Asian countries, such as Hong Kong, Japan and Singapore, have a GDP per capita that compares favorably with the developed economies of the West. According to a 2001 report by the U.S. CIA, European economies such as the United Kingdom and France exhibit a GDP per capita of $22,800 and $24,400, respectively. The United States lays claim to the highest GDP per capita in the world, at $36,200. Compare these figures to Hong Kong and Japan, at $25,400 and $24,900, and a competitive profile emerges.

But other Asian nations — such as China, Indonesia and Vietnam, for example — fall far below Western standards. The GDP per capita of China is just $3,600; the figures for Indonesia and Vietnam are even lower, at $2,900 and $1,950 respectively. Simply translated, this means that in economies with a lower GDP per capita, fewer consumers are able to purchase what they produce. As a result, overall growth in Asia will be constrained in the long run by the inability of these economies to create a growing group of consumers — both within their own borders, and within the Asian region as a whole.

The disparity between the smaller Asian economies and their larger counterparts in essence undermines the growth of *all* Asian business enterprises, raising a barrier to the competitiveness of the entire region when it comes to doing business on a global scale. In addition, these disparities leave the door open to potential social and political unrest, which is never a positive sign for economic growth and competitiveness. Cooperation among all Asian nations to help each other more — to and by doing so, elevating the prospects for *all* concerned — is crucial to moving forward. A better distribution of wealth and the creation of a market characterized by greater demand is key to changing the current situation.

EDUCATION: WHERE KNOWLEDGE IS POWER

The percentage of gross domestic product that a country invests in education is a measure of its commitment to its competitiveness. The good news here is that many Asian economies invest heavily. Singapore, for example, spends more of its GDP on education than nations such as Israel and France, which are known for their extraordinary levels of investment in education. Japan and South Korea invest at a level on par with the United States and other Western industrial nations. Equally important, schools in these nations focus on basic math and science in the lower grades, providing a strong seeding ground for raw intellectual capital. According to a report published by the U.S. Department of Education, fourth-grade students in Singapore, Korea, Japan and Hong Kong score significantly higher in math testing than their American counterparts.

These are positive signs. But in the same way that wealth is unevenly distributed in Asia, there is a wide disparity in the quality of educational systems across the continent. In too many Asian economies, access to education — in particular, higher education — is limited to relatively few people. In Indonesia and China, for example, less than 10% of the population has access to post-secondary education. By way of contrast, 39% have this access in Singapore, 30% in Japan, and almost 25% in South Korea. The figures become even more disturbing: in Thailand, 69% of the population has an elementary-level education or less. That number is over 50% in Indonesia, Australia, Vietnam and China.

These are troubling statistics that paint a less-than-rosy portrait of competitiveness over the long term for Asia. Most Asian economies today are manufacturing-based, taking advantage of low labor costs to engage in mass production more efficiently than many other parts of the world. But the world is becoming more of a knowledge-based economy in today's Information Age. In order for Asia to move beyond the profile of a manufacturing-based economy and make the transition to that of a value-added, knowledge-based economy, a much higher mass of the Asian people must have access to advanced education. Leaving half the economy's population behind will not accomplish that goal.

KNOWLEDGE BREEDS COMMUNITIES OF INNOVATION

The importance of education extends well beyond just the benefits that individuals can receive by developing the personal skills necessary to compete in today's economy. Educational institutions can serve as powerful magnets to attract talented people to an area, and foster communities that reward and spur innovation — the ultimate key to competitiveness.

Such has been the case in Silicon Valley, where institutions such as Stanford University and the University of California at Berkeley provide intellectual diversity, debate and ideas that stream into the community at large. These universities helped develop the sophisticated technical infrastructure that is part of Silicon Valley. They have actively participated in the R&D efforts and the intellectual development of local companies, and they've seeded the local economy with bright people driven by ideas and able to turn them into new products and services.

Stanford University in particular has been a force in transforming the regional economy, ever since a young electrical engineering professor named Frederick Terman returned from MIT more than 50 years ago and set his mind to turning Stanford into a center of innovation. Beginning in the 1950s, the university spawned a number of developments that mark this pioneering spirit. The Stanford Research Institute was established to conduct defense-related research and assist businesses in California. Soon thereafter, Stanford opened its classrooms to local companies, encouraging engineers to enroll in graduate courses directly or through specialized TV instruction in what at the time was a revolutionary move for education. By 1961, there were 32 companies participating in the program, with about 400 employees pursuing advanced degrees in science and engineering on a part-time basis.

Stanford also became host to one of the first industrial parks in the United States, helping to reinforce the emerging pattern of cooperation between the university and electronics firms in the area. Stanford Industrial Park's first tenant was a local company, Varian Associates, which was soon joined by such firms as General Electric, Eastman Kodak, Hewlett Packard and, later, Lockheed and Raytheon. All of these companies were small start-ups at the time. The trend continued in 1970, when Xerox established the world-famous Palo Alto Research Center (PARC) and helped spawn the personal computer revolution.

CULTIVATING INNOVATION: THE AGE OF IDEAS

Combined with better distribution of wealth and a market driven by demand, education sets the stage for the ultimate criterion for global competitiveness: the ability to innovate and create products and services that add value and are viable in all sectors of the worldwide economy. And the ability to innovate is driven by a culture that nurtures creativity and free thinking, while encouraging people to take risks. This kind of mind set is crucial for Asia to improve its competitive profile on a global scale.

It's important to understand that, in the United States, innovation starts in school. The best institutions encourage students to think for themselves, speak their minds, and come up with new and novel approaches to solving problems. As Asian schools develop their curricula, the kind of atmosphere where ideas are explored and individualism is rewarded needs to be encouraged. Hong Kong, for example, has distinguished itself through the competitive drive of its people to pursue higher education. But how much emphasis is placed on simply answering questions on exams, as opposed to solving problems, thinking creatively or developing an independent point of view?

In Asia, the approach to education tends to be what can be characterized as "transaction-oriented." Skill in solving mathematical equations is widespread among Asian students — one reason that people of Asian birth or lineage have typically had success on standardized tests such as the Math SAT test taken in the United States for entry into college. In the U.S., by comparison, education is driven more by conceptual thinking, exploring the context of matters and thinking creatively to solve problems. Asians generally have not been trained in this way of thinking. It should be pointed out that *both* kinds of education are valuable — but a better balance is needed if Asians are to adopt a more entrepreneurial spirit.

The formal education process leads directly to the shaping of cultural attitudes. One of the underlying qualities that has been directly responsible for Silicon Valley's success is its way of thinking. The Valley lives by a culture that honors innovation, ideas and creativity over all other attributes — a core value that draws people from all over the world. Clearly, talent flows to the most attractive environment. The high-tech sector of Silicon Valley is powering one of the biggest emigrations of skilled people in history, serving as a major intake of talent and innovation. Of the 2.5 million people who now live in the area, one-third were born outside the United States. And still the demand for talent continues to grow.

Silicon Valley's core values drive constant turbulence in the market and rapid evolution of companies. That's because businesses in what has become an extremely competitive region of the world must constantly reinvent themselves, infusing fresh ideas to stay relevant. High-tech employees are continuously open to new job opportunities. Why? Because getting to the top does not necessarily mean staying there. The numbers tell the story: of the top 25 independent software companies in 1988, only six remained leaders in 1998. And of the current top 25, only 11 were public 10 years ago.

NO RISK, NO REWARD

An underlying principle essential to Silicon Valley and the spirit of innovation is a willingness to take risks — and, with it, the suppression of a culture that punishes or stigmatizes failure. For ideas to enter the marketplace, someone has to be willing to take a chance and go where others have not gone before. People will do so only if failure does not carry a social or economic stigma.

In Asian cultures, failure has historically been penalized — by the business community, by the courts and by society in general. But in Silicon Valley, business failure is not seen as a disgrace, as long as it wasn't willful or hopelessly inept. Business failure can even heighten the respect an individual commands, based on what he or she has learned by living through the experience of that failure.

Silicon Valley is characterized by risk in pursuit of growth. According to a Santa Clara University study, 95% of start-ups in the area survive the first four years. But 25% fail to survive their adolescent transition, and collapse in the second four years of their existence. Of the 250 firms analyzed that were founded in the 1960s, for example, 31% survived, 32% were acquired or merged and 37% went out of business. This study, obviously, preceded the dot-com mania and subsequent market retreat of the late 1990s, so one would expect the failure rate of today in Silicon Valley to be markedly higher.

Firms such as Fairchild, Intel and Apple were founded because their "parent" company was not willing to pursue new ideas. In each of these cases, risk-takers chose to run with an idea and develop it on their own. And they were not afraid to fail. When the famous "Fairchild Seven" left Shockley Laboratories in Palo Alto in the 1950s to found Fairchild, co-founder Robert Noyce — who later went on to co-found Intel — had to borrow US$500 from his grandmother. He summed up the attitude of his associates when he said: "We asked ourselves what was the worst thing that could possibly happen. And the answer was that we would fail utterly — and then simply have to go out and get jobs again." In Silicon Valley, failure can simply be a speed bump on the road to success.

The same commitment to continuous innovation and a willingness to take risks can yield the same results in Asia. What's needed is a "new economy" attitude, one founded in a knowledge-based economy. Here again, much of the responsibility for attitude must be shouldered by educational institutions. The manufacturing-based economies that have largely succeeded in Asia have been a direct result of the emphasis placed on process and transaction in Asian schools. But you cannot succeed in a knowledge-based economy simply by throwing people and processes at a problem; creative thinking, rather than process control, is key for success. And creative thinking must be encouraged from the ground up in Asia — in society, in the classroom and in the workplace.

This kind of attitude can help create wealth, raise standards of living, and increase both production and consumption. It can generate opportunities and incentives that encourage creative people to stay and build the next generation of technology, instead of leaving for greener pastures in the West. At a time when high-tech centers all over the world are bidding for talent, a commitment to continuous innovation can ensure that Asia's prime export is high-value goods — and not highly talented people.

VENTURE CAPITAL: PAYING OFF ON RISK

If risks are to have a chance to succeed, there must be sufficient risk capital on hand to fund entrepreneurial effort. Again, the Silicon Valley way of thinking provides a road map for competitiveness: money chases ideas.

Thanks to venture capital (VC), new Silicon Valley companies with new ideas are born every day. The number of Initial Public Offerings (IPOs) in the Valley jumped 140% from 1998 to 1999, largely due to Internet companies. And while many — if not most — of these companies have already failed — venture capitalists are still willing to bet big on creativity and imagination. As recently as 1999, for example, Silicon Valley was home to 77 IPOs, surpassing the previous record of 72 set in 1992.

The venture-capital industry continues to feed future success. In the first six months of 2000 — before the downturn that, at the time of writing, continues to dampen the U.S. economy — investors poured US$25.2 billion into 94 U.S. venture-capital funds. That's almost three times as much as was raised in the first half of the year before, and more than was raised in that entire year. California continues to lead the way, with US$10.4 billion in venture capital raised. That's as much as the next two states — Massachusetts and New York — combined.

According to David Williams of Draper Fisher Jurveston, Asian venture capital is increasing 15–20% a year. But the total amount of venture investments in new businesses is not yet remotely comparable to the Valley. From 1999 to the third quarter of 2001, total venture-capital disbursements for the U.S. was US$208 billion, compared to US$19 billion for Asia. This gap must close if Asia is to truly realize its potential in the global business arena. Thus far, venture capitalists such as Walden International and Hambricht & Quist have been quite active in Asia — witness the creation and sustenance of the entire semiconductor industry in Taiwan, for example. But much more venture capital — and many more venture capitalists — are needed to stimulate entrepreneurial growth in the region as a whole.

It has become clear that the success of venture capital is linked to all the other elements of innovation. The most successful VC firms are not afraid of risk; they see failure as a learning experience, they depend greatly on an educational system that produces ideas and they harbor an abiding respect for intellectual property. Without all these combined factors, there would be no incentive for creating the new companies that ultimately drive the new economy. The whole is indeed the sum of its parts — and Asia must focus on developing each of these parts to invigorate the economic whole.

CREATING A PRO-BUSINESS ENVIRONMENT

Another factor that Asian economies must consider to improve their global competitiveness is finding ways to create an operating environment conducive to doing business. The importance of such concepts as industrial parks in stimulating economic activity and growth cannot be overstated. The good news is that there is indeed precedent for such communities of industry in Asia; witness Taiwan's Hsin-Chu Science-based Industrial Park, driven by semiconductor manufacturing/packaging and PC production, which has dramatically boosted that country's economy.

Similarly, global businesses operating in Asia must do their part to stimulate and grow the economy. Sybase, for example, operates development centers in Singapore and Beijing, along with a Hong Kong Solutions Center where it and regional Asian enterprises work closely together to develop better solutions for the specific IT challenges facing these enterprises. This kind of cooperation stimulates business, creates new opportunities and helps drive competitiveness for all participants.

Beyond the cooperation of like-minded businesses in helping to create a positive operating environment, the role of national and local governments is crucial to business success. Three factors of particular interest that relate to this subject are political stability, the openness of corporate governance, and the maturity and openness of legal systems.

Competitiveness is closely correlated with political stability; it's virtually impossible to cultivate a growing economy in a country or region beset by political strife. While there are a number of relatively stable democracies in Asia, there are clearly some trouble spots as well. And any time there is a disparity in wealth, education and opportunity — as we've clearly illustrated there is in Asia — the risk of political instability and social unrest becomes higher. Today in Asia there are countries that are in transition to popular elections, there are cases of ongoing conflicts between neighboring nations and there are a number of armed conflicts under way. The greater the political instability, the greater the barriers to competitiveness across the region as a whole.

Equally important, significant and long-standing corporate-governance issues continue to exist in Asia. The largest economies in the region — Japan and China — are not now truly open, although there has been some recent movement toward reform in Japan. External investment will inevitably be constrained by any uncertainty over governance, reporting relationships or the way in which subsidiary transactions are overseen. Simply put, government must provide a legal and public-policy environment that encourages and rewards innovation. And one of the ways to do that is to protect intellectual property.

PROTECTING INTELLECTUAL PROPERTY

If one considers intellectual-property-rights protection as an indicator of the openness and maturity of any legal system, another clear correlation arises. The economies in Asia that are growing at the fastest rate, and moving the most quickly to become knowledge-based economies, are those with the most highly developed civil legal systems and greatest intellectual-property-rights protections — namely, South Korea, Japan and Taiwan.

Unless there's a move across the rest of Asia to strengthen the protection of intellectual-property rights, the already-developed Western economies will always have a business climate more conducive to external investment — and therefore will always be more competitive. Intellectual-property theft is a phenomenon with a wide-ranging effect that is not restricted to any continent or any country. According to the Software and Information Industry Association and the Business Software Alliance, last year worldwide losses due to software piracy exceeded US$12 billion. Such piracy has caused combined losses of more than US$60 billion over the past five years.

And yet, there has been significant resistance to intellectual-property rights in Asia, a phenomenon that ultimately is self-defeating. Ironically, when software or other products are pirated, the biggest loser is the country where the pirating takes place. And Asia has been guilty of its share of intellectual-property-rights violations.

A reputation for bootlegging creates hostility and discourages investment. There's a saying in the US software industry: "In Asia, you can only sell one copy." Even more importantly, a failure to protect intellectual property discourages innovation. In essence, this tells people that if they're going to create something innovative that has a tangible market value, they had better go somewhere else. Think of the celebrated Silicon Valley entrepreneurs who create new high-tech products and concepts in their garage. Would they do it if others could simply snap up the rewards of their labors? Or would they go to a garage in another part of the world?

Intellectual-property rights may have been a foreign concept in most parts of Asia. But as a pan-Asian high-tech industry continues to emerge, governments must ensure they can protect the intellectual capital of their people and business enterprises. Government must take the lead, as it is now doing in places such as Hong Kong. Because when it comes to the creation of wealth, government protection of intellectual-property rights provides the legal infrastructure for innovation.

LOOKING FORWARD: PATIENCE IS A VIRTUE

In summary, an overall assessment of Asian competitiveness reveals a number of positive signs, such as a strong regional economy and a general commitment to investment in education. But inconsistencies abound;

significant discrepancies across national boundaries when comparing factors such as the distribution of wealth, access to education, attitude toward risk taking, the ability to cultivate centers of innovation, and corporate governance and civil law are all conspiring to constrain Asian competitiveness.

A comparison with the economic development of Europe may be able to shed significant light on the subject, since Asia in many respects is now walking in the same steps Europe has already taken. Before the E.U. formed, for example, Europe's industrial production was due in large measure to very few economies, and gross domestic product per capita varied widely across the continent. Since formation, the E.U. region has benefited from economic cooperation, the opening of access to education, the narrowing of income gaps, and the stabilization of politics, corporate governance and civil law.

While the creation of a formal Asian union is not necessarily appropriate, the region as a whole would certainly benefit competitively by thinking in terms of long-term cooperation. In this way, Asia can best use its considerable resources to help distribute wealth more evenly, create markets of demand, and create communities that attract and retain talent to gain competitive advantage in the global marketplace.

All the principles that have been discussed in this chapter are critical to innovation and wealth creation. But in practical terms, how can they be deployed in Asia? What should Asia's focus be? The answer to these questions perhaps can be found in the fact that today, more than ever, long-term profitability depends upon the ability to add value. Reproducing old ideas, by contrast, is a formula for falling behind.

A case in point: semiconductor manufacturing has been a big focus for years in the Asian economy. But rather than setting up another center to copy something that is already being done — namely, building semiconductor chips — perhaps Asian enterprises need to think more along the lines of what innovations they can bring to bear on the market. Instead of reproducing the products of the past, Asia must think more in terms of building the idea-factories of the future.

Today, for example, wireless technology has emerged as the next great driver of innovation, presenting an opportunity for Asia to take the lead by developing the next "killer app". The United States led the way in the first phase of wireless evolution by developing the chips for wireless communications. Europe took over the lead in Phase Two — not by copying what the U.S. was already doing, but by agreeing on a common protocol and thus adding new value. Asia can be the leader in Phase Three, combining wireless technology and the Internet.

But in order for this to happen, all the issues discussed in this chapter must be resolved. Government must provide the legal and public-policy environment to encourage and reward innovation. Intellectual property must be protected and tax credits provided to encourage R&D. Universities must educate the people who can develop ideas and provide the links to business that turn those ideas into reality. Risk must be encouraged, rather than penalized, so that entrepreneurs dare to succeed rather than fear to fail. And money must be available to see ideas through in the form of venture-capital investment.

It's important to note that all these things will take time and patience to accomplish. For all of its global clout and power, California's Silicon Valley has hardly been an overnight success; it has taken more than 50 years of applying the various principles outlined in this discussion for the Valley to reach its acknowledged position of pre-eminence in the global economic arena. No amount of commitment to competitiveness in Asia will yield results without a long-term commitment of patience and seeing the entire process through over many years of application. Here, Asians can lean on a bit of time-tested Eastern philosophy with which they're abundantly familiar: be Zen.

Be Zen — and yet move forward incrementally to make the changes that need to be made. Such are the challenges facing Asia as it attempts to improve its competitiveness in the global business arena. Many of these challenges are cultural in nature, requiring a transition that is far more complicated than simply solving problems through the infusion of money. What is more crucial is the infusion of an ideal, and the ideas that accompany it, in a new kind of economy where innovation and fresh thinking are prized above all else.

Consolidation and Restructuring: Rebuilding a Chinese Conglomerate

Fu Yuning
President, China Merchants Holdings Company Limited,
Hong Kong SAR

 People may still remember the 1980s, when the world marveled at the "miracle" of the flourishing Asian conglomerates — the Japanese *keiretsu* and Korean *chaebol* — and looked forward to a promising "Asian Pacific Century". However, dramatic changes to this view of Asian business have taken place since the crisis of the late 1990s, and the ups and downs of the Asian conglomerates continue to amaze and puzzle us. So, then, what's wrong with the Asian conglomerates?

There has been a lot of discussion in Asia and elsewhere as to the troubles of the Asian conglomerates. I would like, here, to repeat three key causes of these troubles — over-borrowing, over-diversification and the lack of sound corporate governance — and go a little bit further to explore their effects. Chinese state-owned conglomerates, in a broader and deeper sense, have been suffering from the same intrinsic problems that are plaguing their Asian neighbors.

FROM INFLATION TO DEFLATION: OVER-BORROWING OF ASIAN CONGLOMERATES

After the Second World War, the global economy experienced half a century of worrying about inflation: the increase of prices and the decline of purchasing power. Inflation punishes savings and promotes borrowings; hence, we were living in a society which had disdained savings for so long that businesses and individuals were used to building their wealth by borrowing, hoping one day their assets would be inflated.

Today, the macroeconomic environment has changed and people have become more and more concerned about deflation: the decline of prices and the increase of purchasing power. Actually, Asian countries such as Japan, Singapore and Hong Kong have been aware of deflation for years. Deflation hurts borrowers and encourages cash-holders — in short, the opposite of what happens during periods of inflation. Deflation is good for people who hold cash, but is undoubtedly a nightmare for people in debt. For example, thanks to deflation, a growing number of Hong Kong families who purchased their houses in the real-estate bubble of the mid-1990s have found that the money they owe on their mortgage is more than their properties are worth. The Hong Kong government estimated that about 60,000 families would end up in this situation; accordingly, the number of individual bankruptcies reached a record high in 2001. This is where the concerns get more realistic.

During the period of inflation, people simply borrowed too much. The same applies to businesses, especially the trapped Asian conglomerates. Larger companies are in trouble because they have a hard time getting enough revenue to recoup their costs, or liquidating enough assets to repay their debts. In Japan, the deflation that accompanied the bursting of the stock-market and real-estate bubbles has severely damaged the entire banking system and destroyed the net worth of many corporations.

Where does the deflation come from? One of the major causes is the excess capacity of production established by the over-borrowing during the period of inflation. A lesson of the Asian crisis is that growth driven solely by capital inputs and funded largely by debts eventually collapses, even if it would have lasted for decades.

In short, we are on the verge of a period in which falling prices will become as commonplace as rising prices were from the 1960s to the 1990s. In a deflationary environment, the heavy debt burden of Asian conglomerates is calling for a dramatic restructuring, especially of debt reduction.

FROM DIVERSIFICATION TO REFOCUSING: GETTING BACK TO BASICS

We all know that diversification used to be an important strategy for corporate growth. Some early researches prompted massive diversification, especially in the conglomerates. Economic theorists pointed out that diversified firms performed better in terms of risks and returns than firms that did not diversify their activities. However, starting from the 1980s, a record number of mergers, acquisitions and divestitures occurred as U.S. companies sought to reduce the excessive diversification that had resulted from over-expansion in the 1960s and 1970s. But that trend did not affect the Asian conglomerates, which continued to remain highly diversified until the crisis of the late 1990s.

Empirical evidence shows corporate management tends to be actively engaged in diversifying activities, while the capital markets makes a strong case against corporate diversification. An increasing number of studies have documented that the average diversified firm trades at a discount vis-à-vis a comparable focused firm. One of the key findings is that every firm has its own limit for diversification, beyond which profits will decline.

A closer look at the business strategy of typical Asian conglomerates reveals that they were trying to offer everyone everything. Both Japanese *keiretsu* and Korean *chaebol* have made efforts to maximize their market share and grow as rapidly as they can. Their ambition to grow makes them fight their way to every industry and production segment, offering whatever product and service is required. In both cases, the goal is simply "to get big fast". Unfortunately, however, the Japanese and Korean management systems that had performed magically in many industries in the 1970s and 1980s were found wanting in the 1990s. Asian conglomerates are far less profitable than their Western counterparts.

Over-diversification is wrong — simply because one cannot provide whatever is demanded in the market. The real issue for Asian conglomerates is whether they can redeploy their capital from non-strategic business, divest themselves of unrelated and unprofitable business units, allocate more resources to further their position in their core business, and earn a much higher return in refocused markets where they can enjoy a competitive advantage.

Today, there is ample evidence that corporate restructuring — refocusing or simply getting back to basics — has changed the landscape of Asian business and that narrower corporate scope will definitely lead to higher efficiency and profitability, especially for those "over-diversified" Asian conglomerates.

WEAK CORPORATE-GOVERNANCE PRACTICES

Corporate governance refers to the framework of rules and regulations that enable the stakeholders to exercise appropriate oversight of a company to maximize its value and to obtain a return on their holdings. Among the factors contributing to the vulnerability of Asian conglomerates is a lack of sound corporate governance, which led to the excessive borrowing that took place in Asian businesses. Management paid little or no attention to corporate-governance practices that could have prevented the extension of debt burden and corporate failures.

The Asian corporate-governance system — an insider-oriented system — provides excessive managerial stability and autonomy but shareholders have little power. At the same time, the management always favors too much diversification and excessive borrowing, and over-emphasizes market share and growth rather than profitability. For some Asian economies, especially Japan, Korea and Indonesia, emerging evidence clearly indicates a rapid and unsustainable build-up of investment in fixed assets financed by excessive borrowing. This investment-spending spree has resulted in poor profitability, a low return on equity. The management feels no urgency to earn higher returns. As long as they are making acceptable profits and see no danger of bankruptcy, that's OK. They are happy to make a living during the period of inflation and don't worry about things like shareholders' interests or potential takeovers.

Asian corporate governance generally lags behind that in the developed Western economies. Conglomerates controlled by in-house directors and management dominate many sectors of Asian economies. There is a lack of a suitable shareholding structure, a disclosed and transparent accounting system, and sound protections for minority shareholders. Recent turbulence and crisis has served to highlight the fact that better corporate governance is an important step in rebuilding the competitiveness of Asian corporations and enhancing overall economic performance.

THE EMERGENCE OF CHINESE CONGLOMERATES

The Chinese economy has grown dramatically over the last 20 years and there is an optimistic expectation for the future. One of the largest efforts has been in the reform of China's state-owned enterprises (SOEs), and the creation and development of large enterprises has been proposed as a major measure to improve performance. The formation of large corporate groups, mainly through mergers and acquisitions among SOEs, was intensified by government measures. Some of them were justified by economies of scale and scope. However, much of the motivation and drive was fuelled almost exclusively by considerations of size. In an industrial system in which "size" was often translated into "power", SOEs, understandably, were taking every opportunity to grow.

During the 1980s and 1990s, the application of the *keiretzu-chaebol* model to some 500 big enterprises was set as a strategy to reform the Chinese SOEs. This strategy rested on the assumption that large corporate groups, with huge capacity, diversified production lines and large internal resources (i.e. "national champions"), were indispensable in matching foreign competition. However, Chinese conglomerates, much like their Japanese and Korean counterparts, have proved that such a course may bear negative results. Again, over-borrowing, over-diversification and the lack of sound corporate governance that has plagued most Asian conglomerates also apply to the state-owned conglomerates of China.

This "shortage economy" led to a rapid and excessive investment in building supply capacity and by the late 1990's, after 20 years of sustained economic growth, China moved out of this era of shortage.

As a result of 20 years' aggressive expansion, however, Chinese conglomerates found themselves with a heavy debt burden, with average debt-to-asset ratio as high as 70%. It is obvious that many Chinese conglomerates have moved far beyond the "optimal" level of diversification, largely as a result of the excessive growth in the last two decades. The attempt to improve the SOEs' performance through sound corporate governance has generally failed because they had never faced a real threat of bankruptcy. The "soft budget constraints" led to excessive investment, inefficient capacity and high debt loads during the investment boom in the first half of 1990s.

The bankruptcy of GITIC (Guangdong International Trust & Investment Corporation) and the debt restructuring of GDE (Guangdong Enterprises) offer many important lessons for us. No enterprise is too big to fail, even one that is owned and governed directly by the government. SOEs are stand-alone, limited-liability entities whose debts will not enjoy the full faith and credit of the Chinese government. Indeed, the urgency of SOE restructuring stems directly from the lessons drawn from the collapse of GITIC in the crisis of the late 1990s.

HONG KONG-BASED CHINESE CONGLOMERATES

To review the development of Hong Kong-based Chinese conglomerates, we have to examine the "window company" model, which was officially designated by the Chinese government. In addition to companies such as China Merchants, China Resources, Bank of China (HK) and China Travel Service (HK)) that had operated in Hong Kong for decades before China's open-door policy, many "window companies" mushroomed in Hong Kong during the 1980s as intermediaries and representatives of the governments that borrow internationally and make investment mainly in mainland China. Nearly every ministry of central government and every provincial government built up their "windows" in Hong Kong. One of their major missions was to attract foreign investment.

However, the collapse of GITIC and GDE, the "windows" of China's richest province, marked the end of the outdated model, which, though performing well in many industries in the 1980s and first half of the 1990s, was awkward and incomplete, as shown during the hardship of the late-1990s' crisis.

Generally, "window companies" lacked a core competency and held an excessively diversified portfolio of assets. Their financing came mostly through borrowing, especially foreign debts and they were characterized by a poor governance structure.

In recent years, Hong Kong-based conglomerates have been undertaking corporate restructuring to rebuild their competitiveness.

CHINA MERCHANTS GROUP

China Merchants Group, headquartered in Hong Kong, is a state-owned conglomerate. The group's origins can be dated back to the Westernization Movement of the Qing Dynasty in 1872 as the state's first shipping company. China Merchants has been reaping the benefits of China's reform and openness, and has developed into a diversified group over the last two decades.

In 1978, China Merchants began to develop the Shekou Industrial Zone, China's first industrial zone open to the outside world and the "seed" of China's special economic zones. Later, China Merchants successively set up China Merchants Bank, the first incorporated bank in China, and Pingan Insurance Company, the country's first incorporated insurance company. With total assets amounting to HK$58 billion and total assets under her management amounting to nearly HK$120 billion, China Merchants has proved her strategic importance to the economy of China and is one of the 42 state-owned corporations under the direct supervision of the State Council. In fact, the chairman of China Merchants has to be appointed by the Chinese premier.

As President of China Merchants, I consider myself lucky for the effective business-oriented operations and conservative investment decisions made during the red-chip euphoria and real-estate bubble in the 1990s. Still, we were not lucky enough to be immune from the "Asian Conglomerate Flu" that originated in the Japanese *keiretzu* or Korean *chaebol*.

Two years ago, China Merchants launched a strategic restructuring package to reshape the Group's business landscape and rebuild its competitive edge.

China Merchants Group used to invest in more than 16 different business sectors, including shipping, finance, real estate, trading, ship repairs, manufacturing, hotels, tourism, and so on. Excessive minority shareholdings had exhausted the resources and capital; most of the corporate debts were foreign-currency denominated and the cash flow was mainly from mainland China. Obviously, urgent action was necessary and we have since disposed of approximately HK$5 billion non-core and non-performing assets. Also, the Group withdrew from a small-sized bank in Hong Kong with a cash inflow of HK$2 billion, and accordingly enjoyed a significant improvement of net debt ratio by 15%. In the meantime, we are working on the correction of the mismatch between foreign debts and domestic cash flow through financial re-engineering.

China Merchants has positioned four core businesses: infrastructure, real estate, finance and logistics. In accordance with the refocusing strategy, we have consolidated messy and fragmented business operations, restructured the management team and shifted capital and resources to concentrated core businesses. The refocusing process involved more than 100 subsidiaries and about HK$20 billion in assets.

The Group has been consolidating its infrastructure investments (ports and toll roads) and injected these assets into our Hong Kong-listed flagship — China Merchants International. The Group's four real estate subsidiaries have been consolidated into one core strategic business unit — our Shenzhen-listed company, China Merchants Shekou. We have also restructured our logistic business unit, consolidating 20 logistics investments.

Corporate-governance practice has been among our major concerns. The Group's strategy is to list our four core business units on both the Hong Kong and China stock markets. I believe the listing of a state-owned corporation will certainly improve its corporate governance. The infrastructure flagship and real-estate flagship are listed in Hong Kong and Shenzhen. The initial public offering of China Merchants Bank took place in early 2002. China Merchants Logistics, our core business unit, will look for opportunities to list in the near future. By then, China Merchants Group will have four listed flagships, each focusing on one of our core businesses. The public ownership will definitely lead to an improved system of corporate governance which, in turn, will enhance management and boost efficiency of a state-owned corporation.

The process of corporate restructuring is tough, and China Merchants remains a conglomerate with four core businesses. We have acted very quickly and tried very hard to pursue the refocusing from more than 16 diversified businesses to just four. The Group has now defined its scope of business and we are no longer a conglomerate with excessive diversification. Even more important, we have successfully introduced public ownership into our Strategic Business Units and we encourage our companies to stay focused on their core competencies. Those listed companies will run in line with the demands of the market and under the supervision of investors. We are working with overseas and domestic strategic partners, independent board members and professional management, at the same time making sure there is growing pressure for prompt disclosure of operations and transparency of accounting in all our business units.

Following the September 11 terrorist attacks on the United States, the risk of global recession has increased. And unlike most previous post-war recessions, this recession has deflationary characteristics rather than inflationary ones. Given the investment surge and stock-market bubble of the 1980s and 1990s, traditional diversified conglomerates will face greater difficulties than ever before. The corporate restructuring of China Merchants is still under way and the reform may never end. So far, my experience has shown that our restructuring package has led to higher efficiency and profitability. China Merchants is now standing firmly in the market and, with its 130-year history, will certainly be there for a brighter future.

Business No Longer Usual: The Transformation Imperative for Asia Banks

Philippe Paillart
Chief Executive Officer,
Development Bank of Singapore (DBS), Singapore
(Position is at the time of printing)

 It was opportune timing for the East Asia Economic Summit to be held in the midst of a sharp loss of confidence after terrorist attacks in the U.S., which highlighted the interconnectivity between financial markets in most of the world. The forum gave participants the chance to ponder and share their views, in a timely way, on the consequences of the renewed downturn and the future of Asia's economies and financial institutions.

As two of the most mature economies and financial systems in Asia, Hong Kong and Singapore have undergone significant reforms over the past decade, the pace of which has accelerated after the Asian crisis of 1997–98. The crisis has shown the impact that interconnected financial markets can have on whole economies. In Singapore, the government took the bold step of initiating the opening of the financial sector in the middle of the crisis. Likewise in Hong Kong, the Hong Kong Monetary Authority, as part of a long-standing process, is implementing numerous additional initiatives to further liberalize the banking sector. The speed of capital movements caught the region by surprise and showed the importance of having well-developed financial markets with high standards of regulation and jurisdiction. In Asia, both Hong Kong and Singapore have led the way towards increased disclosure and greater transparency in order to upgrade their financial systems to world-class status. While this transformation is an incremental and very lengthy process, the evolution of the financial markets in both jurisdictions serves as a good example of how the financial-services industry and its regulators can proactively cooperate to raise overall standards. This cooperation ultimately results in a more efficient and sound financial system that underpins economic recovery and growth.

In the increasingly global market environment, it is vital that financial centers are continually upgraded to international standards so as not to be sidelined. This is especially the case for very open economies like Singapore, where total trade volume is three times GDP. In the manufacturing sector, businesses have been forced by the low cost yet increasing skill levels in other parts of Asia, such as China, India, Thailand and Malaysia, to go further upmarket in order to compete globally. The financial sector, likewise, has had to raise its level of competitiveness, both in its business capabilities and structural framework; that is, regulatory oversight, corporate governance and disclosure standards, market discipline, accounting standards, and banking- and capital-market jurisdiction. In addition, financial institutions have to look at building up their networks in the region if they want to seize the opportunities that these markets will present when growth returns. To sharpen the competitiveness of Singapore's banks, the government is introducing greater competition into the financial playing field, announcing in June 2001 the opening up of the wholesale market, with a target of distributing about 20 new wholesale licenses over the next two years. In addition, the government is extending the privileges of Qualifying Full Banks (QFBs), following earlier measures to allow a small number of QFBs to establish a limited number of locations and branches. They are now allowed to have more locations, branches and ATMs, issue debit cards operated through an EFTPOS network, provide central provident fund (CPF) investment accounts and accept CPF fixed deposits. All these measures will significantly raise the level of competition for the local banks.

In Hong Kong, the last phase of interest rate deregulation took place in July 2001, and now there are no restrictions on the ability of market participants to compete freely in product design of both deposit and asset-based products. In fact, the market has seen a proliferation of customer propositions that provide a wide range of choices for both liquidity and investment-based products, including several innovative accounts such as the Money Management Account and Save & Cheque Account that the DBS Group offers. Further liberalization of the financial-services sector is being considered by the Hong Kong Government, with a consultation currently under way to apply the same criteria to both foreign and locally incorporated banks regarding their ability to open additional branches or other types of financial-service outlets.

Among the key ingredients contributing to the success of the evolution of Singapore and Hong Kong's financial-services industry are, therefore, open and free markets, intense competition from foreign financial institutions and a solid and progressive regulatory framework. To foster strong and forward-looking financial institutions, regulators have several important roles. One of these, as mentioned above, is to promote good corporate governance, such as full disclosure and implementation of global best practices. In Singapore, the effort to formulate frameworks for these issues has been initiated by the government but spearheaded by the private sector. Several private-sector-led committees have done substantial work to recommend new or revised standards for corporate governance, disclosure and accounting standards, and company legislation and regulatory framework. Hong Kong has also been very active in developing its corporate-governance framework, with numerous initiatives being undertaken by both the private and public sectors. Perhaps the most notable of these is the ongoing comprehensive review being undertaken by the Standing Committee for Company Law Reform. Numerous proposed enhancements of corporate governance have already been endorsed by the Standing Committee, and legislative amendments are being implemented to improve the corporate-governance framework in Hong Kong. Another important role of regulators is to strengthen safety and soundness measures by, for example, providing a formal framework for a risk-based prudential supervisory system. Also, regulators have to refine credit and market-risk measures to reflect more accurately the exposures within bank portfolios and within the system as a whole. Finally, there is an initiative to work with the industry to provide a better system infrastructure that promotes efficiency and minimizes risk, with examples being the Real Time Gross Settlement System (RTGS) in Hong Kong and the Continuous Linked Settlement System (CLS) in Singapore.

The trend towards the convergence of financial services is already very much in evidence in Singapore and Hong Kong. Both the MAS and the HKMA have been actively encouraging banks to consider consolidation as part of their strategic planning. Regulators in both markets have undertaken numerous packages of market-driven initiatives to reform and further develop their respective systems to a relatively mature state. I see this process continuing and, in particular, the dividing line between different sectors of financial-services markets, such as insurance, securities and banking, will become increasingly blurred in the future. One can already observe numerous examples of cooperation among banks, brokers, fund managers and insurance companies as tangible evidence of this trend. At DBS, we have divested ourselves of non-core assets such as our insurance company but, at the same time, we have formed a strategic partnership with a world-class provider of insurance products, CGNU, to promote Bancassurance products to our existing and new insurance customers. Another example can be seen in the distribution of wealth-management products, including third-party unit trusts, through our established banking channels.

In order to restore profitability to pre-crisis levels, the immediate challenges facing financial institutions continue to be better credit-risk and asset-portfolio management. At our Thai subsidiary, we tackled the problems of NPLs head-on by selling 77% of the distressed assets. These were, in the main, the more toxic ones, and we also restructured a substantial number of loans. This effort, together with similar work around the rest of the Group, has paid off by substantially reducing total NPLs. We continue to emphasize credit-risk management and a proactive approach to tackling asset-quality concerns. To restore profitability, however, improving credit quality and lowering non-performing assets are only the first step.

In the longer term, Asian financial institutions need to embrace a more value-based management philosophy, where risk-adjusted returns become the order of the day. In addition to more sophisticated internal risk-management systems, the ability to understand customer behavior and manage relationship and product profitability, as well as channel preference and productivity, is paramount. To be competitive in the evolving mix of financial-services offerings, the providers have to be very focused on their core discipline and their competitive advantages. For example, our focus is on the customer and this affects our determination of what processes are centrally managed and what capabilities are managed close to the customer and the market. It affects our decisions about the capabilities which we will manage ourselves and the capabilities which we will achieve through partnership with another service provider. The Bancassurance example mentioned above is an example of building service offerings for customers that they want, rather than just selling traditional products that we make. In turn, this customer focus drives our technology and process innovation and re-engineering.

Scale will become increasingly important as an enabler that allows innovative technological investments to be spread over a wider customer base with lower unit costs. Indeed, our ambition to become a pan-Asian bank is not simply a wish to be big, diverse or even regional. Rather, scale and size is unavoidable if we are to gain the competitive advantages to meet the demands of today's customers, who are faced with a wide and varied offering of products and services that are relevant and responsive. Technology improvements have given customers an expectation of faster and better services at cheaper prices. To provide the quality of products and service standards that customers require, and at a competitive price, we need to attain a critical mass. The scale of operations predetermines the cost-benefit outcome of investing in centralized or shared services, systems and capabilities. In Hong Kong, we met our objective by our acquisitions of Kwong On Bank, in 1999, and Dao Heng Bank, in 2001. These have given us combined assets in Hong Kong that rank us fourth there, as well as reduced the Singapore share of total assets to only 57% by September 2001. Cross-border potential for greater operational efficiency includes the development of customer-relationship management systems which have been going on in both DBS Singapore and Hong Kong separately, thereby giving rise to a certain degree of duplication. The roll-out of treasury trading systems and risk-management systems in Hong Kong and Thailand is another example of operational efficiency, where capabilities developed in Singapore are extended in an efficient manner to subsidiaries in the region.

Asian financial institutions will also need to better utilize their capital and focus on their optimum size, rather than their absolute size, with more precise targeting of products and services to specific customer segments. This is an extension of the value-based management philosophy mentioned above, as companies become more sophisticated in their allocation of resources to those lines of business and customer segments that can produce superior returns. A key element of this analysis will be each institution's determination of those areas in which it believes it has a competitive advantage, enabling it to target its investments in a more cost-effective manner. By so doing, the institution will be able to provide its chosen customers with superior value propositions which, in turn, will enable it to further reinforce its competitive advantage. The days of trying to be all things to all people are gone, and it is crucial for Asian-based financial institutions to realize and implement this philosophy in their strategic planning.

There will likely be a proliferation of strategic alliances and partnerships among different sectors of the financial-services industry, in order to maximize market knowledge, competencies and capabilities, while taking full advantage of existing and new distribution channels. At DBS, we have the example of Bancassurance, where we decided that creating insurance products was not our core business, given that we did not particularly have competitive advantages in actuarial expertise and insurance underwriting. Nevertheless, we see insurance products as a critical part of the portfolio of wealth-management products, which we have the advantage in selling through our distribution channels; hence, the sale of our insurance business and our entry into partnership with CGNU.

Another example is our alliance with Frank Russell, one of the world's leading investment-services firms, to deliver a premium investment-management program to investors, combining our advantage in distribution, customer service and knowledge of the local market with Frank Russell's expertise in its multi-asset, multi-manager, multi-style investment approach. We have also tied up with TD Waterhouse to bring world-class, self-directed online brokerage services to our customers.

Finally, we believe that Asian financial institutions will need to migrate to a customer-oriented approach in place of their current, primarily product-driven, strategies, in order to add value and compete effectively with their foreign counterparts. All of the partnerships mentioned above were formed as a result of our focus on the customer. We designed a services architecture around the value chain from customers to suppliers of products, to help in understanding the services that are important to our customer-intimate focus. We want to become a key part of the customer's value network, differentiating ourselves by our customer services and business-intelligence services. Some products are made by us but could increasingly be made by others. We are working on designing, building and implementing a standard operating model or franchise model for all activities in the Group. The global banks in the region already operate their chosen franchise models and are the leaders of new customer propositions in both the retail and wholesale markets. Our model is being built around the customer, meaning that it aims to create a customer-intimate organization, which has competitive advantages in the key areas of customer information, distribution capabilities, and product and service offerings. Among the many challenges is determining how each service should be sourced; for example, in which areas we can re-use existing investment, where we can outsource the full operational service, where we can buy software components and where we have to innovate our own solutions. The model will guide the re-engineering of operating processes and technology. The aim is to have a common platform across the region, which will enable us to respond faster and more effectively to our customers' demands, extract better business intelligence, be more agile in implementing new ideas and requirements, attain new capabilities, achieve greater efficiencies through re-engineering and, ultimately, generate shareholder value. This will be a lengthy process, but it is one which we believe will reward us with a more efficient and nimble organization, enabling DBS to compete with global competitors in the region on an equal footing.

Corporate Responsibility and Attitudes Towards Women

Kim Sung-Joo
Sung Joo International, Republic of Korea

 Good business practices should not be limited to the traditional confines of maximizing shareholder value but should also include active contribution of corporate resources to the community. Of course, there are many ways in which corporations can be good corporate citizens and, in setting priorities, a focus on developing women's talents should receive attention. Today, more commitment is needed to better utilize the vast untapped wealth of resources in women's skills. Although women represent over half the world's population, the global economy still does not know how to maximize the use of this valuable resource.

Japan has been in an economic slump for quite some time, and a few years ago Korea also faced continued economic setbacks. One major factor that has been repeatedly identified as a key cause of Japan's and Korea's economic woes has been the inability of those countries to expedite restructuring away from their Confucian-embedded hierarchies, principles and loyalties. They are therefore unable to take advantage of the opportunity to capitalize on the potential productivity of some of the most talented brains.

THE HISTORICAL AND CULTURAL BACKGROUND

East Asian countries are known for their Confucian societies inherited from a strong cultural background that originated in China. The tradition of Confucianism has segregated men and women by social status, age, wealth and education, with a particular emphasis on family background.

Thus, a young woman coming from a modest background would have been in one of the worst positions in society. This type of class system created a strong patriarchal and top-down relationship in society. This structure led to a complete neglect of women's roles in the decision-making process, and paralyzed the creative and critical development of the minds of many young men and women. The only way of succeeding in this type of society was through family networks, school ties and hometown bonds. This phenomenon has been most distinctive and enduring in Korea and Japan. In contrast, China, the birthplace of Confucianism, and other socialist countries liberated women from this tradition by adopting a sort of Marxist doctrine, taking women as the first proletariat in human history.

Women in Asia still represent a minority of the workforce, particularly in executive positions. In Korea, for example, less than 60% of women between the ages of 20 and 50 are employed. Even more troubling is that among college-educated women, less than 20% are employed and those that are working tend to occupy marginal jobs. Korean society tends to be very close-minded, repressive, inflexible, highly political and extremely inefficient. Under such a structure, it is very hard to be global-minded or to fully maximize the productivity of creative brains, for both men and women. It has been apparent that the productivity arising from PC usage and networking in Korea has been comparatively low because of the current top-down structure.

Korea's problem is certainly not that it lacks sufficient brainpower. Korea's literacy level is almost 99% and the nation holds one of the highest levels of PhDs per capita in the world. The nation's challenge is to put this brainpower to use in overcoming its economic and social challenges. Japan is similar to Korea in that opportunities for female entrepreneurs are very limited.

Taiwan has brought women into its workforce to a far greater degree than Korea and Japan. The educational system and opportunities for women in Taiwan are excellent, and women are effectively integrated into the economy. Elsewhere in Asia, though, a heavy influence of traditional cultural norms and conformity have excluded women from leadership roles. A drastic change in attitudes toward women participating in both political affairs and economic life has to come about in order for the imbalance between the genders to be adequately redressed.

WOMEN AS THE FIRST VICTIMS OF FINANCIAL CRISES

It is interesting to follow Korea's transformation into a typical example of a crisis-ridden country. In the past, Korea was able to boast of having the world's 11th-largest economy and the eighth-largest trading volume, a solid industrial infrastructure, a very high savings rate and one of the highest literacy rates in the world. Problems arose when Korea's economic and financial infrastructure was not ready to face the challenges of a competitive global-market economy facilitated, in particular, by the Internet revolution.

It would be interesting to examine how this financial crisis has helped to reshape the structure of Asia's patriarchal societies. Many countries in Asia where so-called crony capitalism flourished did not realize how much ineffectiveness was produced by a business culture founded on family, school and hometown networks. Often these business practices produced non-transparent and discriminatory practices, which contributed to the countries' inward-looking attitudes and made them highly uncompetitive by global standards.

During the crisis, working women, often scarce before, became the first victims of the crisis, losing jobs and even being blamed for taking jobs away from men. In Korea alone, women made up nearly half of the employees laid off by a group of Korean banks in late 1998, even though they comprised only one-third of the banks' total workforce. Even today, Asian women are still grossly under-represented among corporate executives.

MOBILIZING WOMEN'S WORKFORCE IN KOREA

Through the Asian financial crisis, the consultants McKinsey & Co. conducted research into the main cause of the crisis, focusing on the neglect of the female workforce in the economy and suggesting how to enhance the competitive edge in a fast-moving globalized environment. They concluded that too few college-educated women participate in South Korea's workforce and this was likely to affect the country's prospects for long-term economic growth. They proposed to companies and the government that educated women should play a bigger role if South Korea was to become one of the world's most economically advanced nations.

That goal may be a stretch. South Korea belongs to the Organization for Economic Co-operation and Development (OECD), but for the country to become one of the OECD's top ten members (ranked by GDP per capita) by 2010, its GDP would have to grow by 6.1% annually. This high growth would generate three million new jobs, at least 1.2 million of them for professionals. But with recent trends, South Korea would not be able to fill those jobs only with men, since more than 90% of its college-educated men already participate in the labor force.

Although nearly half of today's college graduates in South Korea are women, only 54% of its female college graduates participate in the labor force — the lowest rate of any member of the OECD. By contrast, the corresponding rate for South Korean men almost matches the rates for men in Sweden and the United States.

The McKinsey study identified 10 obstacles for women in the South Korean workforce, including discriminatory hiring policies, ineffective legislation on working women's rights, and social prejudice. It recommended several remedies, from launching equal-opportunity programs to reinforcing employment-discrimination laws and using the mass media for a campaign against sexual bias. One way to integrate women into the workforce is to relieve them of the burden of childcare, which the respondents to a 1998 survey of nearly 40,000 South Korean women perceived as the biggest obstacle to employment. This is far more serious than prejudice and grounded in reality: the labor-force participation rate is particularly low for women in their mid 20s and early 30s.

This so-called M-curve contrasts with the reverse U-curve of countries such as Canada and Sweden. In practice, it means that women leave the workforce during their peak learning years because there is no one to take care of their children. This phenomenon gives rise to discriminatory human-resources policies because companies do not feel it is worthwhile to invest in the careers of women who are destined to leave the workforce. Those policies are responsible for the concentration of women in lower-status jobs and for career ceilings.

South Korea isn't the only Asian country that fails to make full use of its highly educated women. In Japan, 98% of college-educated men participate in the labor force, compared with only 68% of college-educated women; in the Philippines, those figures are 83% and 47%, respectively. In some parts of Asia (including Hong Kong, Japan and Singapore), women also leave the workforce temporarily in their mid 20s and early 30s or even permanently when they marry or give birth.

In South Korea, childcare problems manifest themselves in two ways: inadequate maternity benefits and poor day-care options. Although maternity leave is seen as adequate, the costs are borne by insurance and employers, thus adding yet another disincentive to hiring women. The lack of adequate day care is just as problematic. Although working women in South Korea have about 2,000,000 children under the age of six, only 640,000 of them can be accommodated in existing day-care operations.

Lightening the childcare burden significantly will be hard in the short term but a few improvements are possible. The reform in maternity leave, for example, should include cost breaks for employers, rather than simply focusing on increasing the number of days. The government should also enforce the existing laws, increasing penalties for employers that ignore them. Companies can help further by developing on-site childcare programs or joining consortia to share the costs of such programs.

In Korea, there are a few good examples in which corporations have taken the initiative in this issue.

Case I: Kookmin Bank

Kookmin Bank is one of the largest commercial banks in Korea. During the economic crisis, McKinsey & Co. examined and assessed how to re-structure the organization and work procedures to maximize the shareholders' value and to optimize customer service. One of the most significant recommendations was to bring more women into the workforce, not only at the managerial level but also integrating capable women at branch-officer and director levels in various departments. Moreover, call centers, database management and other Internet-related marketing departments became areas for women to flourish and to show leadership at more senior levels.

The result of this aggressive integration of women into senior positions produced significant improvements in the bank's share values. It also generated a 30% increase in revenue and customer-satisfaction levels almost doubled. Many other Korean banks and institutions (insurance companies and security firms, for example) that were regarded as mostly male-oriented environments began to follow Kookmin's lead. Foreign bank branches in Korea (for example, Citibank and HSBC) and other Korean financial institutions with direct foreign investments have started a revolutionary trend of tapping into the highly educated Korean female workforce, who previously were ignored by those traditional and global companies.

Case II

A couple of years ago, one of the largest and most successful international conglomerates in the beverage industry (the name is withheld for reasons of confidentiality) conducted an important internal brainstorming session.

At this meeting, topics about a change of direction in product development (from caffeinated beverages to healthier alternatives) and marketing initiatives to support women through internship and training programs were discussed. The reason for this unexpected focus was the increasingly powerful position of women consumers, not only as a majority consumer force but also as future corporate leaders in the 21st century. Instead of directing the marketing campaign towards an imperialistic and male chauvinistic view, this firm recognized that women had become more conscious of health matters relating to themselves and their children. These women had also become stronger, smarter, more ambitious and more independent than ever before. The need to gain favor in this market was seen as a key to success in the future economy. This beverage company had the insight to implement support programs to take advantage of this valuable, but often overlooked, resource.

CONCLUSION AND RECOMMENDATION

The rapid change brought about by the Internet revolution has certainly had a great impact on the old economy. It has reshaped the manufacturing-based, old economic structure and presented new opportunities for women. A key element in the entrance by women into important sectors and influential positions in Asian economies will initially be through development of small- to medium-sized enterprises, especially in Internet-related business services. In the process, the competitiveness of Asian economies will be improved, particularly in retailing, marketing, telecommunications, database management and other technology-related businesses, and many newly emerging jobs in the service sector.

The World Bank has recently focused on activities of human cooperation in IT and has put an emphasis on training the untapped resources of women in banking and finance. Many capable Korean women will eventually rise to middle and top positions within multinational banks doing business in Korea.

For instance, in 1991 the Workplace Equality task force at the Bank of Montreal implemented various initiatives including gender-awareness workshops, flexible work arrangements, childcare, elder care and career networks to support women. The results were impressive: between October 1991 and October 1994, the proportion of women promoted into executive ranks increased from 29% to 50%; promotions in senior management increased from 20% to 38%; and middle management increased from 43% to 67%.

The stellar performance of Korean women at foreign banks clearly shows that there has been a lack of training programs for women and a lack of equal opportunities for those capable women within conventional Korean banks, which have never promoted women into managerial positions.

In 1991 Hewlett-Packard held the first Technical Women's Conference to showcase the top female engineers and scientists in the company. It included addresses by the CEO and female senior managers. The women introduced their work in a series of technical sessions and the conference provided numerous career-development workshops. The company presented awards to recognize and raise the visibility of female engineers and first-level managers. Management strongly supported the conference. The company considered the conference consistent with HP's tradition of fostering and supporting innovative activity and expected it to result in improved recruitment and retention of experienced technical women.

Recently, some international business magazines have elaborated on the theme that Asian women are coming on strong. They are shaking up old companies, old social customs and old prejudices as they increase their spending power and independence, which advertisers cannot ignore. Marketers are now also wooing a new pool of affluent single women in Asia, who have hefty disposable incomes. There is a clear trend of more women entrepreneurs and women forming a critical consumer base. Recent statistics show that in Korea women Netizens make up more than 40% of the total. Korean female entrepreneurs have grown at 42%, faster than their male counterparts (35%).

The future growth of economies will depend upon their ability to utilize women's skills and any notion of good corporate citizenship should include looking to the future and investing in women. In addition, corporations need to be attentive to women in their marketing strategies. The key to success is to secure a long-lasting loyalty from women consumers, who are already dominating the global consumer market.

Companies can and should be good corporate citizens with regard to women in various ways. For instance, they should devote 10% of their marketing budget to provide internship programs and special training (especially relating to IT) and educational programs for women who are willing to work. They should also provide more support services, such as childcare and flexible working times, to enable women to enter the workforce.

The traditional view is that it is expensive and not worthwhile to hire women. In reality, women are a source of corporate competitiveness. Research into the top 100 corporate revenue earners shows that those that employed more than 10% women executives in their management had greater shareholder value than those with less than 10% women executives in their middle-to-top management. Overall, good corporate citizenship that enhances women's participation as productive members of the economy and addresses women's needs not only helps women but also allows corporations to grow and be much more competitive in the marketplace.

For centuries, women have raised their families through consensus building, compromise, effective communication, compassion and nurturing. Imagine the power of such talents unleashed onto the business world and unhindered by notions of how such talents should be tempered or conditioned to fit into preconceived notions of doing business. Women could be more effective in communicating messages and managing people. Ultimately, the global environment can only benefit from contributions by women.

IT as East Asia's Engine for Growth

Tadashi Okamura
President and Chief Executive Officer,
Toshiba Corporation, Japan

 The East Asian economies continue to be buffeted by strong adverse winds, winds first fanned by recession in the IT sector in the United States and then given further force by the terrorist attacks in the U.S. and continuing geopolitical instability. In these circumstances, it might well seem overconfident to respond positively to the question: "Will IT drive future growth in East Asia?" However, my considered response is to do just that, to affirm, "Yes, it will". Needless to say, that "yes" is not unconditional, but subject to a number of factors and the completion of some demanding tasks.

I am sure we all agree that it is more than just difficult — that it is, in fact, logically impossible — to sustain business prosperity in any given region of the world when the overall global economy is going through a downturn. Even so, if IT-related industries are to remain, or in some cases become, the driving force for growth in East Asia, we must find an answer to the major question facing us: how to increase the size of the IT segment that enjoys more resistance to external influences.

As I attempt to answer that, I first of all want to try to understand why the IT recession happened as it did, and to consider whether differences between the IT industries in the U.S. and East Asia resulted in different causes for the downturn. Let me summarize my conclusions at the outset, and say that I believe that the origins of the slowdowns in the U.S. and in East Asia do differ in their essentials, a fact that reflects important differences in the nature of the IT industry in each region.

In the U.S., until recently, new businesses based on advances in IT-related technology appeared literally one after the other. These start-ups were blessed with an investment infrastructure keen to nurture the potential of venture businesses, and which helped to assure that the physical infrastructure of the information society made fast progress to reach maturity. The required hardware was created — PCs, servers and routers — and broadband services subsequently emerged in the form of ADSL, cable-network communications, ISDN services over fiber-optic cables, wireless communications, and more. Internet services and application service providers also appeared, all ready to make full use of every advance in hardware and broadband capabilities to offer new or improved services.

With the enthusiastic support of investors who believed that prosperity would flow with the development of these new services, it was no surprise that more and more venture enterprises appeared. They all had a business model that combined mature IT infrastructure with new business ideas, and they were all seen as winners. As a result, communications providers foresaw increased demand and responded with their own investments.

However, as time has clearly taught us, while a business model may be judged as feasible in its own terms, the cold reality is that it is not feasible for many companies with the same business model to coexist in the market. As a result, the once-booming IT market reached the point where its bubble burst, with a shock wave that sent dot-com companies falling like dominoes.

The IT recession in Japan and East Asia had different origins. It did not result from a new business model grafted on to mature IT infrastructure, as in the U.S., but simply from a downturn in the well-established manufacturing sector that produced parts, semiconductors and hardware products that were broadly dependent on demand in the U.S. market. In this case, the damage came as something of a chain reaction from the situation in the U.S.

When we consider the IT downturn in the U.S., we are looking at a case where the economy became a victim because it had reached maturity. This leaves difficult tasks and an important lesson for the future, since even though there were people who issued warnings at the time when everything looked rosy, they were dismissed as pessimists.

Of course, whatever the difference in causation, the IT recessions in East Asia and the U.S. have produced similar levels of pain.

Thinking about the differences between these economic downturns, and the differences in the U.S. and East Asian IT industries, lends support to a three-fold classification of the IT industry as a whole.

1. At the base of this division are products developed through research and development — the hardware breakthroughs that result from scientific inventiveness and discoveries, and the software advances that emerge from innovation and new directions in thinking. We can call this R&D-driven business.
2. Businesses developed through R&D require parts or intermediate products that can be utilized by the IT industry as a whole. This gives us the second part of the classification, the components and intermediate-products business, which embraces products as diverse as semiconductors and personal computers.
3. Finally, there is a business area that combines all these different products, particularly those of the components and intermediate-products sector, to offer services and solutions to individual customers and corporate customers. This is the solutions business.

As any management executive can tell you, every one of these business areas presents unique difficulties. In my opinion, the second, the components and intermediate-products business, is particularly challenging, as its products tend to become commodities as they become widely used and mature. It is also a market where companies compete fiercely for small profit, and where even the companies that trailblaze new markets cannot be confident of sustained profits, as other companies soon follow their lead.

These three business areas are also difficult when looked at from the perspective of the corporate manager, as each throws up distinct management tasks. In the first area, research and development, there is a need to gather innovators and the wise, and they are few in number. There is also a need for the confidence to not be obsessed with immediate profit. In the components sector, the single most pressing need is to secure human resources able to achieve continuous improvements in cost and quality. Manufacturing also brings with it a requirement for large-scale equipment investment, which is particularly severe in the semiconductor business. In the third sector, solutions, it is necessary to attract a lot of people with street smarts.

It is interesting and useful to apply this three-fold classification to the U.S. and East Asian IT sectors. Doing so makes it very clear that the U.S. has focused on the first and third areas of the overall business, R&D and solutions. Put another way, the U.S. has created new business models and new product models. East Asia is different. It can be said to have shared in the IT industry primarily through its contributions in the area of components and intermediate products; through supplying high-quality parts, such as semiconductors, and intermediate products, such as PCs.

The crucial fact to bear in mind here is that it is the research-and-development business and the solutions business that play what we can characterize as the active role of generating new potential and creating markets. While the components and intermediate-products business plays a necessary supportive role between these sectors, it is a passive role, not an active one. To put this another way, the components and intermediate-products business is ultimately dependent on the research-and-development-based business and the solutions business.

While there is no argument that IT had definitely and successfully provided East Asia with an engine for growth, surely there can be little disagreement with the observation that it has been a rather passive engine. Within what I will call the conventional international division of labor, the IT revolution has brought development to East Asia, but only by making East Asia a factory that provides hardware to meet demand in the U.S. and Europe. While this may seem acceptable during periods of growth, a time such as we are experiencing now of severe global recession makes it clear just how vulnerable our situation is.

In the present situation, a chill in the U.S. IT market sees East Asia quickly reaching for the tissues, all because of its passive role in the international division of labor. Another consequence of this is a tendency to accelerate any downturn toward global recession, at a stroke. There are those who would argue that this situation is unavoidable, or even inevitable; that we live in a globalized age in which there is global linkage of all IT businesses at one level or another. However, if we look at the situation from an East Asian perspective, it is clear that it is necessary to promote and develop those parts of the IT industry that are less subject to economic shifts and conditions in other countries. That means that East Asia must increase its active role in contributing to global economic activities and achieve a new balance with the passive role in which it has traditionally excelled.

I believe that this change in emphasis is not only desirable, it is possible. And I want to make some concrete proposals on how we can turn on an active engine in East Asia, and achieve dual engines for growth.

The essential step for doing this is the creation of a new supply-and-demand relationship within the East Asian market itself. If we achieve this, we will greatly reduce the region's degree of dependence on other markets. And I propose that we do this together, because I truly believe our region as a whole is now ready and fully prepared to take this step. It is time for action. There are three areas where we must act.

1. First, we must assure the Internet-readiness of business.

By Internet-readiness, I mean reaching the point where all operations make full use of IT and the Internet. At the moment, East Asia lags behind the West in Internet-readiness and IT utilization. Seen from the global viewpoint, this is a definite handicap. However, viewed differently, we can see that this offers us a great opportunity to create an original Internet-readiness system that best suits East Asia's business environment. We can also see that now is the time to do so.

Success here is a matter of commitment and implementation. We need a strong leadership that aligns the nations of East Asia, and industry, government and academia within each nation, and that then promotes the development of a model East Asian system with its own characteristics and features. I have no doubt that the realization of an IT-based Internet-readiness system that suits East Asia will vitalize the region's own IT market. And if this know-how or any part of it is adopted in other regions of the world, it will also contribute to vitalizing the global market.

2. Further to this, we must promote e-government in the East Asian nations.

This will also be a decisive factor in supporting advancement of the IT industry in East Asia. Here, we can look forward to the development of communications infrastructure, of dedicated software, and more.

3. The third area where we must act is mobile connectivity.

Japan offers us a glimpse of the potential of mobile connectivity. With "i-mode," NTT DoCoMo not only established the world's most advanced model for bringing the Internet to mobile phones, it created a highly popular platform for personal mail and a whole range of new services. Building on this example, East Asia can lead the world market in devising new ways of using next-generation equipment in applications as diverse as mobile connectivity machines, interactive digital TV combined with the Internet, and Internet-connected in-vehicle equipment. If we look at population distribution and the current rate of mobile-phone penetration, it is very clear that East Asia is an enormous market. And if we look at the well-known phenomenon of leap-frogging that has appeared in some countries, we can see that it is possible to generate new markets, attract millions of new customers and achieve significant advances in a very short time. Here again, a strategic alignment of industry and government, and alliances among East Asian countries, will be the key for success.

Needless to say, in these fields IT can play a significant role in bettering lifestyles by enabling efficient and easy access to necessary information and by bringing useful and easy-to-use communications tools into people's lives.

There are a few more conditions that East Asia has to satisfy in order to appear attractive when looked at from other regions. These include abundant and capable human resources; all necessary infrastructure, including communications; and clear support for compliance with global standards. More effort is required in all three of these areas, and achieving full compliance with global standards is particularly important. There is a need to attach more importance to strengthening respect for rules of intellectual-property rights.

I want to conclude by going back to the question I asked at the beginning of these remarks: "Will IT drive future growth in East Asia?" And I want to reiterate my positive response: "Yes". If I did not believe that was the right response, I would not be here talking to you today. However, there is much we must do to achieve the future I envisage for this region. We must turn a new page in East Asia's IT history and must move beyond our present dependence on business and product models devised in Europe and the U.S.

Fortunately, the nations of East Asia enjoy excellent human resources with a high level of education. This is a resource that will be a decisive factor in stimulating new industries, creating new operation models and defining new and fulfilling lifestyles in this information age. We have the people, we have the vision, and we can do it. And I close with an appeal to you all: let us do it together.

A Perspective on the Asian IT Industry

Chen Wen-Chi
President and Chief Executive Officer, VIA Technologies, Inc., Taiwan

 Every business needs a fair wind to speed it on its way, but captaining a boat also implies a recognition that sometimes the sea will get rough and conditions become adverse. Navigating through stormy seas requires fine judgment as well as an ability to take advantage of those conditions that may at first seem hazardous but will help steer a merchant ship into a safe harbor.

Despite apparently difficult world economic conditions, I see many ways in which we can take advantage of our strengths and even turn our weaknesses into a sound platform to move ahead in the next two or three decades. Asia and, in particular, what we at VIA call the Greater China region will inevitably have a major role in both assisting growth and building a solid basis for that growth worldwide, even if times seem to be tougher than they've been for quite a while.

2001 saw business confidence apparently at an all-time low, with the U.S. particularly hard hit by what was eventually acknowledged as a recession at the end of the year, and with hundreds of thousands of job losses. The tragic events of September 11 served to further weaken the economy, increase despondency and threaten future growth. The U.S. Federal Reserve cut interest rates 11 times during 2001 and in early December it appeared that Japan was experiencing its fourth recession in 10 years.

Much of this economic misery appeared to be prompted by a collapse in high-tech and telecommunications stocks, underlined by the bursting of the artificial bubble of the dot-com companies and further exacerbated by the debt burdens many telecommunications companies were carrying.

The gloom has had its effect on our Asian Pacific region. Before the economic storms began to be detected in the U.S., and long before the atrocities of September 11, 2001, analysts estimated that our gross domestic product was likely to be cut in half, from nearly 4% in 2000 to 1.8% in 2001.

The economies of Greater China and other countries in the East Asian region have, in fact, been particularly hard hit, largely because they were responsible for manufacturing, with some countries' economies being built almost entirely on exporting products abroad. In 2001, we saw the major combines in Japan, such as Mitsubishi, Fujitsu and others, bite the bullet and start to lay off workers in the tens of thousands. The layoffs affected not just the islands of Japan, but because these combines had outsourced many of their production facilities to other Asian companies, we saw practically every other tiger and cub economy hit.

These layoffs have caused pain to many families' lives, but the underlying trends are even more serious. Many of the IT manufacturers in the Far East need to anticipate future growth and have done so in the past by investing in new factories and pouring money into research and development to ensure that they are ready to surf the next wave before it hits the shore.

Japanese companies, in particular, have traditionally invested in new IT technologies and have accepted the debt burdens that adopting or foreseeing the future might bring them. An analysis of the GDP for the region shows that Japan — the second-biggest economy in the world — still accounts for more than half of the Asia Pacific economy. Japanese companies have reached the limit of their borrowing abilities as a result of both corporate and government debt, and no doubt that is why we have seen all sectors of the country's economy slide. It would take a major rebound in the world economy to put Japan where it was two, six, eight or 10 years ago and it appears unlikely that that will happen.

If all of the above sounds gloomy, then it is not meant to be. There are bright spots in Asia, particularly the Chinese economic miracle, which continues to attract attention worldwide. At the same time, economists' eyes are also watching Australia, which looked like it might sink without trace towards the end of 2000. Both India and Indonesia are also showing signs of becoming lion economies in the future. The latter — its back almost broken by the troubles of the mid-to-late 1990s — is showing clear signs of recovering its former poise, while the Indian subcontinent is quite clearly on a growth curve.

Japan appears to offer fewer optimistic signs for the future. Its economy contracted by an annualized 3.2% in the second quarter of 2001 while the previous quarter only showed a positive growth of 0.5%. The reason for this downturn is a complex mix of corporate debt, itself slowing down business investment and deflationary pressures that prompt consumers to wait before buying in the hope that prices will sink even lower.

As the world economy slowed down during 2001, Japan began to suffer as its traditionally buoyant export business, which was particularly strong in the high-tech sphere, also showed signs of decline. Prime Minister Koizumi made a public pledge to bring order to the previous chaos and the Japanese people seemed ready to accept the harsh reality of an unemployment rate of 5% that might well rise higher than that.

The corporate restructuring that is under way and will likely continue throughout 2001 will further depress demand in the domestic market for at least two years. A swift recovery in the Japanese economy is possible, but would depend on a big upswing in the global economy. At the time of writing, interest rates stand at 0% while the world economy is showing every indication of more months of decline.

Japan's difficulties have had their inevitable effect on other East Asian companies, some of which have suffered more than others, but nearly all of which depended on a high level of exports to both Japan and the United States. Singapore exhibited a vigorous GDP growth of nearly 10% in 2000, which made its contraction by 10.7% in the second quarter of 2001 all the more surprising. Taiwan, which had shown unprecedented growth during the 1990s, is also experiencing difficulties and the unemployment rate is steadily rising, while the IT-centric and export-based nature of its economy makes it vulnerable to the slowdowns in both the U.S. and Japan.

The Malaysian economy also showed a precipitous slowdown in the second quarter of 2001, by 6%, with private investment slowing and exports falling steeply. Meanwhile, Hong Kong, which only 18 months back had aspirations to become the hi-tech hub of the region, has also made interest-rate cuts while demand for consumer products fell as companies cut staff levels and private investment declined. Its GDP shrank by 6.6% during the second quarter of 2001 — like Singapore, showing a clear reversal from the 10.5% growth in GDP it showed the previous year.

South Korea started to take steps to reverse its position as early as 1999 and so has not suffered as much as the other countries, with its economy growing by 2% in the second quarter of 2001, aided by cuts in interest rates, currency depreciation — which is continuing at the time of writing — and help from the government.

As I mentioned earlier, Indonesia and the Philippines have shown signs of bouncing back during this otherwise gloomy period for most of the East Asian economies. President Megawati Sukarnoputri has stemmed the flow of capital out of Indonesia and measures her government has taken since she was elected have helped her country gain a new respect from the International Monetary Fund (IMF). In the second quarter of 2001, rather to many economists' surprise, Indonesia bucked the East Asian trend by showing positive GDP growth of 10%.

The Philippines also managed to grow its GDP by 6% during the same period, largely due to sound performance in the agricultural sector, and that, in turn, has boosted the standard of living as well as spurring additional spending on consumer goods.

TOTAL CONNECTIVITY ERA

Despite the gloomy economic picture that I have just painted, I still remain very optimistic about the medium and long-term future, and cannot help thinking that we are experiencing early growing pains in what we at VIA call the Total Connectivity Era and that the adventure and the opportunities are very much there for the future. The early overconfidence in the Internet may have caused foolish investments and the speedy decline of the resulting businesses which did not conform to any realistic profit-and-loss models, but that does not mean that huge opportunities for growth do not exist, even in the next few years.

Worldwide figures for IT spending growth all show there are considerable opportunities to grow the marketplace between now and 2005, according to IDC forecasts released in September 2001. Globally, it is only 2001 which sees a significant drop in spending, but the median figure — again worldwide between 2002 and 2005 — is a steady 10–11%. When the figures are broken down by region, Asia Pacific shows the strongest opportunities for IT spending, with figures closer to 11%, but every other region, including Western Europe, North America, Latin America and the Middle East/Africa, shows strong growth. Some countries, such as India, China, Turkey, Egypt, the Philippines and others, show extraordinary growth rates, in some cases nearing 30% increases in spending, during the next few years.

Despite the early dot-com stumblings, it will be the Internet that is the real engine for this steady growth in both business and e-entertainment.

Morgan Stanley Dean Witter estimates that global Internet-user compound annual growth between now and 2003 will be 23%. In addition, growth in fixed and wireless broadband services is also healthy. Jupiter Media Metrix figures for the year 2000 showed penetration in Korea standing at 30%, Singapore 11%, Canada 8%, Hong Kong 8%, and the U.S. 5%.

Broadband growth is accelerating and it is the Asia-Pacific region that is the engine for it, with a population of 3.363 billion, aggregated gross domestic product of US$8,396 billion, and IT spending of US$183 billion. The population of the Asia-Pacific region represents 55.5% of the global population.

Fixed and wireless broadband services, delivered by a variety of technologies such as cable, ADSL and 802.11, are estimated to be worth hundreds of billions of US dollars in this decade, and while entertainment is said to be the key market driver for this growth, part of that cake will also consist of network access, giving opportunities for a variety of technology vendors and resellers, carrier companies, operators and service and content providers.

e-entertainment, in this Total Connectivity Era, takes the shape of Internet music and video, interactive digital TV, online gambling and gaming services, software platforms, syndication of content globally, so-called content on demand, and home and lifestyle management and tools.

That also means opportunities for hardware manufacturers and for component suppliers to those manufacturers, with home PCs, set-top boxes, broadband modems, home networking, game consoles, DVD devices, Internet appliances, personal digital appliances (PDAs), mobile telephones and a number of other devices all benefiting from the accelerated growth of e-entertainment.

There will also be accelerated demand in the software market, which many people had thought would become a re-usable commodity and was set to spend time in the doldrums. Streaming-media working over broadband, video-on-demand, video Internet commercials, news and breaking-news feeds, advertising tailored to an individual's needs and based on his or her preferences, and other applications based on peer-to-peer Internet broadband systems will also fuel that growth.

In 2000, according to Taiwan's Institute of Information Industry (III), information appliances (IA) only represented 3% of the hardware made on the island, worth around $220 million in value. But by 2005, according to U.S. market research company In Stat, that figure will have grown by 40% each year, accounting for 25 million products or one-third of the global output. And that figure, some observers believe, is very a conservative estimate.

The gadgets that people will tote around on their person will connect to vast server farms. These will service the burgeoning number of e-commerce applications, including streaming video and music for consumers, but will also provide backbone facilities for broadband, handle increased business-to-business traffic on the Internet, and soak up the terabytes of space required by the most successful Total Connectivity application of all: e-mail.

The impact of technology on all aspects of human life in the Total Connectivity Era will be both widespread and surprising. Because we are reaching the stage where the technology that enables us to connect is becoming so powerful and small, we are likely to see inexpensive, wireless-powered devices attached in unexpected ways.

If you mislay your keys, you'll be able to find them because they're connected to your own personal area network; you're unlikely to lose or have your cell phone stolen because it will also be part of your personal area network and won't be able to leave your vicinity unless expressly permitted to. Similar devices will safeguard credit cards, notebook computers, PDAs and a whole gamut of household and other paraphernalia. And the developments of broadband we've spoken of earlier will help the technology to reach every corner of the globe, including those nations and peoples who have been disenfranchised by a combination of a lack of access and price of entry.

Asia, and the business leaders of Asia, will clearly play an important part in this Total Connectivity future, and there are important recent developments that underline the responsible role we will take in the coming decades.

Towards the end of 2001, China and Taiwan were admitted into the World Trade Organization (WTO) in a move that will ease trade across nations and over previous boundaries. Membership of the WTO prevents small, self-interested cartels — whether prompted by business interests or because of political exigencies — from pursuing narrow goals that exclude competition and trade from what is clearly one of the most important marketplaces in our global village. Free-trade agreements, policed by the WTO if necessary, mean that contracts will be made on the basis of what is the best value for the best service and that will promote cultural diversity and prevent global monopoly.

Entrance to the WTO is not a one-way street for either China or Taiwan. It means that both entities have accepted the general agreements on tariffs, trade-related investment measures, trade on services, the rules relating to intellectual property (IP), and also a complex set of rules about how disputes are settled.

Both entities have accepted these binding agreements and will be expected to abide by them. Other agreements mean that members will have to apply tax laws fairly. Even though China opened its market up three or four years ago to telecommunications firms like Nokia, it may have to extend the agreement to other firms that have similar agreements with the European Union and the U.S., two of the major trading blocs in the WTO. In another landmark move, the admission of China and Taiwan into the WTO means an open market as far as organizations are concerned — countries can't tie investment measures to exports.

While there will inevitably be a measure of give and take between other countries and China during these early days of its accession to the WTO, telecommunications ventures, in particular, are likely to be opened up to direct foreign investment and possibly far fewer joint ventures very quickly. This bears out the IDC figures given above — as foreign investment moves into the country, one of the priorities will be to open up these markets which are themselves a catalyst for further IT change.

While no one can foresee precisely how these developments will affect business, we expect free and fair trade to greatly benefit countries in Asia, with barriers to entry being lifted and an equitable exchange of goods and ideas, allowing us to compete on an equal footing with others. This also implies that because of its geographic size, its vast population, as well as its cultural heritage, Asia will almost certainly have a leading and responsible role for the world in the decades ahead.

VIA intends to play a leading role in these new developments and we also believe that we can work together with other companies to create an equitable new model for IT growth. That model is based on a cooperative rather than a viciously competitive basis, and we have already begun implementing it through the development of close partnerships with various other companies in the industry. The traditional IT industry model of aggressive competition slows innovation rather than encourages it and, given the nature of future growth in the next 10 years, cooperation will not only be the most desirable way forward from the point of view of people using the technology, but also the most logical for all the companies and businesses involved in the industry.

I believe that the IT industry has begun to realize that, like the rest of our planet, it is part of an ecosystem in which all parts depend on, nurture and help each other. The Internet will be a broadband-based ecosystem in which no single company can dominate because of the diverse nature of the appliances, the software, and the network — both business and domestic — that make up the organic whole.

The all-encompassing nature of the Web means that the people who access the Internet via fixed and wireless broadband networks stand in a different position to consumers who are merely sold a product. People, and the way they interact with each other, will be involved in the development of the Total Connectivity Era in a manner they never have been before. The invention of moveable type and even the invention of radio and telegraphy over 100 years ago, while playing their part in vastly expanding communications, bear the same relationship to the Net and to Internet communications as a mustard seed to a mountain.

The growth of peer-to-peer networks like Napster, for example, was an organic application made up of hundreds of thousands, if not millions, of individual human beings who gave birth to a new type of application before most large corporations noticed the phenomenon. The speedy growth of broadband services worldwide and the number of people joining this Total Connectivity Era also mean that companies will have to cooperate more closely to help explore new frontiers, establish easier and perhaps quite different hardware, and give people the confidence to move in new directions.

We shouldn't forget, either, that the Internet offers the possibility of bridging divides and crossing frontiers as never before, and has cultural, social and other dimensions that will open fresh opportunities that perhaps we can only dream of now. This will be particularly important in the area of education, where people in even the remotest areas of China should, for example, be able to access online classes and curriculum materials from the world's greatest universities.

At VIA we are strongly committed to both understanding and evangelizing the importance of bridging the so-called digital divide so that people of every class and in every country may share the benefits that are bound to accrue as a result. We have already begun working with a number of leading universities in China to support projects in this area and will be expanding the scope of our activities not just in China but also other countries in the coming year.

We also believe that from a business point of view it is most important that all companies in every sector of the IT business work together to help achieve this goal, which is of benefit not only to people in those businesses and to shareholders, but also as a driver of technology.

The reason is easy to understand. Connected devices with the ability to communicate anywhere and at anytime will be in every office, every school and every home — not in decades, but a matter of years.

From a business perspective, this rapid roll-out of Total Connectivity will require tapping the fountain of creativity and allowing employees more free space in which to develop ideas, foster innovation and have a clear, joint vision of where a company is going.

As a company begins to grow, it is inevitable that it will, to some extent, become stratified, and one of the biggest challenges entrepreneurs face is to avoid fossilization and to keep new ideas coming. We've all seen examples of companies that failed to notice trends or in some other respect fell behind and thereby fell by the wayside. This danger is particularly great in the technology sector, where product cycles are so fast.

The vision for the overall company will be guided by a firm's top management but, at the same time, the structure of a company needs to be flexible enough to allow new ideas to bubble up from anywhere inside the superstructure, with those ideas being taken seriously and suitably rewarded. Many firms claim to have schemes like this in place but vested interests and perhaps empire-building within the organization can stifle innovation and prevent the best ideas from becoming reality or of even coming to the notice of those who can help make them happen. Best practice for large organizations in these early years of the 21st century will require that middle and senior management also show sufficient flexibility to adopt new ways quickly. Close and constant communication through Total Connectivity devices over the network will be the most effective means of ensuring this.

The shakedown in East Asia during the last decade of the 20th century and the early years of this century demands similar flexibility towards new markets and, therefore, additional opportunities. Sometimes this means that entrepreneurs need to brave what could turn out to be politically choppy waters. Making alliances or starting businesses in other countries can be challenging but should also bring out the best in a company.

Governments can play a strong role in the development of their own countries by helping to make trade easier between nations, and by facilitating links at the highest level. 2001 saw some very significant moves that illustrate how this process can help individual nations and also assist the commonwealth of countries.

One of the ironies of 2001 was that despite the downturns, recessions and political uncertainty that plagued the economy during the year, nations across the world met to agree on future directions and decided to take greater steps towards dissolving global protectionism and move towards free trade worldwide. Harvard University professor Jeffrey D. Sachs, who heads the prestigious Center for International Development, said towards the close of the year that the award of the Nobel Peace Prize to the United Nations and to its secretary-general,

Kofi Annan, was a recognition of the importance of globalization to the peaceful future of the world.

The participation of all the nations in the world in this type of dialogue has many positive features for stability and prosperity. For one thing, it spells the end for vested interests and monopolies with narrow interests. While governments seem ready to participate in conferences aimed at bridging differences, there are other major trends that aid the concepts of cooperation and growth. Participation in the world economy is assisted by technology, as shown by the growth of the Internet in crossing frontiers and helping to close the digital divide, and also allows populations in other nations to be exposed to other cultures, to other political systems, and to concepts of sound governance, as well as giving minorities a voice that perhaps they have never had before.

The acceptance of China and Taiwan into the WTO in November 2001 reflects more liberalization in China. All people have a tendency to show some resistance to change but we must embrace such changes, knowing that they are certain to bring, in the medium and in the long term, more prosperity for all.

In anticipation of China's entry into the WTO, foreign capital has flowed into the country to the tune of tens of billions of U.S. dollars, and a far bigger amount in personal savings, which some estimate to be to the tune of six or seven trillion U.S. dollars. This capital will aid not just growth in China's infrastructure, but will provide better opportunities for all of its important traditional markets, including agriculture. The sheer size of the population, the amount of foreign capital being invested, and the opportunities for growth after the liberalization of its telecommunications, financial and insurance markets will cause massive changes both in East Asia and in the global markets. It is clear, too, that China has the political will and vision to embrace such change wholeheartedly.

Naturally, there are conservative voices that will continue to be heard. It is sensible not to discount such influences but, rather, to listen carefully to such words, bearing in mind the cultural legacy of the years of wisdom embodied there. Even if the current economic slowdown means that China's GDP does not grow as much as expected during 2002, it is only a matter of time before it takes its rightful position on the world stage.

In fact, businesses in Taiwan, one of the three global powerhouses of technological growth during the last decade, have already embraced the opportunities inherent in the Greater China region, with many of them being the first to make alliances and to create the foundations and infrastructure for future expansion. There are many, many examples of such alliances, with leading companies such as motherboard manufacturers Microstar, Asus and many others now having factories on the mainland, together with the logistics systems necessary to deliver their products worldwide. We at VIA have also made substantial investments in China to boost our engineering and local sales and marketing capabilities.

Some outside observers have suggested that Taiwan, being far smaller than China, is likely to suffer because, as capital and manufacturing moves to the mainland, its traditional base will be eroded. That, I believe, is a short-sighted view of the future. It also does not take into account the innate resilience of Taiwan and the ability of its people and its business leaders to adapt to different circumstances and times. In fact, Taiwanese companies have shown that they look further ahead than perhaps other Asian, European and U.S. companies do themselves.

Using a model that relies on cooperation and not competition, many of us realized some years ago that rather than supplying bare-bones systems to global brand names, we needed to develop specialized expertise in design. This was especially necessary as Japanese companies shut down factories supplying memory and other components, unable to continue to invest in future technology that will be absolutely necessary to fuel the growth in the global IT market.

Our own company, VIA, realized the trends in the microprocessor and chipset businesses were altering rapidly, with information appliances and lower-priced value PCs becoming necessary to help growth in the Asian and other new markets. Fabrication plants, the factories that turn raw silicon into microprocessors, memory devices and other high-tech components, require a high degree of capital investment. But there are third-party foundries that bear the strain of these costs and that are willing to partner with designers to produce leading-edge products. VIA is a so-called fabless company and, in June 2001, became the first company to create a leading-edge CPU for this particular marketplace, ahead of Intel, the industry giant.

Other well-known companies which also follow this fabless model are Broadcom and Qualcomm, and this gives them the ability to be more nimble players than their factory-bound competitors. We believe that a cooperative model, where companies work together to make products which are the best of their type and do not restrict users on price or on performance, are the best vehicles to satisfy the demand for technology over the coming decade. While other companies have been slashing jobs and shutting factories, Taiwanese and Chinese companies have been investing billions in ensuring that there will be sufficient capacity in the future to feed ever-growing demand.

At VIA we have been, and continue to be, highly active in making alliances with other high-tech industry players and, indeed, with other companies that share our vision. We believe that this cooperative model serves the interests of the world and humankind better than any narrow, proprietary or otherwise restrictive approach.

The coming advances in Internet broadband speed, the much lower cost of entry to technology, together with the increasing number of individuals from every corner of the world with access to this technology, mean that the digital divide is rapidly narrowing and we are committed to playing our part to help usher in this next phase in our world. Economically priced digital devices that are connected to the big broadband pipe will play their part in breaking down the barriers and bridging the divide.

While the figures for GDP and growth represent to some people a cautionary and perhaps even pessimistic note for the future, we would do well to remember that the IT industry is one of the first to recover from recession and downturn. Indeed, at the time of writing, the semiconductor industry is, after a very hard and storm-tossed year, beginning to see prospects of recovery on the horizon, perhaps as early as the third quarter of 2002. This first glimmer of light on the horizon represents real hope for the world against all the negative trends and the storms that have rocked our own and other industries over the last two years. Globalization has been founded on the IT industry and this industry will continue to help bridge the differences and bring together the world in the future.

At VIA, we hope to play an important part in this new phase of growth and look forward with well-founded optimism to a future where economic storms, poor trade winds and false starts are consigned to history.

Asia's Changing Telecommunications Landscape

Keiji Tachikawa
President and Chief Executive Officer, NTT DoCoMo, Japan

MOBILE COMMUNICATIONS SERVICES IN THE LATE 20TH CENTURY

The three key technological trends that propelled major technical innovations in the latter half of the 20th century are widely perceived to be digitization, networking and personalization. These technologies facilitated the convergence between the telecommunications networks and computers, and contributed to the rapid spread of the Internet among the public. Diversification in people's lifestyles accelerated the trend of personalization, with users migrating from fixed telephones to mobile phones and from mainframe to personal computers. These innovations generated a tide of change in various corners of the society, including economic activities and politics. The use of information technology (IT) has penetrated deeper and closer into our daily lives while rapidly transforming its own format from conventional voice service to new multimedia services.

The mobile-communications industry, in particular, achieved a remarkable growth against this backdrop. At the end of November 2001, the aggregate number of mobile subscribers in Japan exceeded 70 million. In fact, it had taken only 13 years when, in March 2000, mobile subscribers outnumbered the user base of landline telephones, which had been developed over a period of 110 years. With a mobile penetration rate of over 50%, Japan has become one of the most advanced mobile-communications markets in the world today. However, this should not be construed as a phenomenon unique to Japan. There are many countries in Asia with a cellular penetration rate higher than Japan's, and the region itself is establishing its position as an advanced region in the use of mobile-communications services.

ELEMENTS LEADING TO MOBILE DIFFUSION IN JAPAN

Mobilephone services were introduced in Japan in 1987, but it was only after 1994 that the market started to show a full-fledged expansion. The number of mobile-phone subscribers doubled every year in the three-year period from 1994 with a net growth of more than 10 million in each subsequent year to date. The revenues of cellular operators increased in parallel during this period. In the case of NTT DoCoMo, our operating revenues grew at a compound annual growth rate of 24.3% during fiscal years 1997 through 2000.

The three major reasons for this remarkable growth were the expansion of service coverage, continuous tariff reductions, and improvements in the handset performance. As a result of our meticulous efforts to expand our service areas, NTT DoCoMo currently provides coverage to 99.9% of the populated areas in Japan. The number of base stations operated by the company today is 50-times higher than the capacity provided in 1987, enabling users to communicate virtually anywhere throughout Japan. By successfully responding to customers' requests to enable the use of cell phones no matter where they are, be it on the top of Mount Fuji or on a golf course or even in an underground shopping mall, we laid the groundwork for the rapid development of the cellular-phone market.

In the meantime, NTT DoCoMo aggressively reduced its prices ahead of the competition from time to time. Back in 1987, a customer had to pay a total of about US$1,400 to join the service (approximately US$600 for subscription and about US$800 as a guarantee deposit for rental handsets). Today, the total initial cost of becoming a cell-phone user has been reduced to a mere US$25 handling commission, while other recurring costs, such as the monthly subscription fee and communication tariff, have also been slashed to about only one-fifth of the 1987 level. These price discounts lowered the entry barrier and boosted the demand for cell phones. Thanks to the price-elasticity effect from the discounts, both our customer base and revenues have grown constantly over the last several years.

Additionally, huge advances were made in the performance of mobile handsets. In 1987, it was impossible to carry handsets in a jacket pocket, given their size of 500cc and weight of about 750 grams. Today, the handsets are miniaturized to around 58cc and 57 grams, eliminating such concerns while making substantial improvements in the features and functionality the handsets offer. For instance, in 1987, the battery life of the handsets provided a standby time of only six hours and continuous talk time of 60 minutes. Currently, these have been improved to 350 hours and 125 minutes, respectively, while supporting more complicated specifications and larger color displays.

These elements have contributed to the expansion of the Japanese cellular-phone market, and more than half of the population now owns a mobile phone. Although there were concerns earlier that the market might be saturated as the take-up rate increased, such worries have been wiped out with the emergence of various non-voice services, including mobile Internet, which are now widely accepted by the general public.

MOBILE INTERNET-ACCESS SERVICE

Landline Internet was first introduced in Japan in 1993 and gradually took root in society. NTT DoCoMo launched its mobile Internet-access service, "i-mode", in February 1999, and this later became an unprecedented success, acquiring more than 30 million subscribers by the end of December 2001. The aggregate number of mobile-Internet users for all mobile carriers in Japan had grown to approximately 47 million as at the end of November 2001, igniting a rapid increase in Japan's Net population. The primary reasons why mobile Internet was able to accommodate a user base that was about 2.5-times larger than the landline Internet service are threefold: 1) its ease of access, 2) its low price structure arising from the use of packet technology, and 3) the abundance of accessible sites. Unlike a PC-based connection, wireless Internet users can enjoy the luxury of an always-on environment without the need to go through the usual ritual of turning on the PC, waiting for the operating system to start up, and establishing a connection to the Internet service provider. Wireless users do not face any constraints as to when or where to establish a connection; they can have access anywhere and at anytime they like with a simple touch of the buttons on the handset. i-mode was widely accepted, especially by first-time Internet users, because of this simplified human interface and its low cost. The basic monthly fee to subscribe to i-mode is kept low, at ¥300, and the communication tariff is billed not by the connection time but by the amount of data actually sent and received (¥0.3 per packet), allowing the users to take as much time as they need to search for information. Furthermore, in an effort to enrich the number of sites accessible, NTT DoCoMo adopted the standard

Internet mark-up language, HTML, for i-mode, which allowed information providers (IPs) to easily reuse the home pages originally developed for landline Internet as i-mode content. Currently, the total number of sites accessible from i-mode stands at more than 50,000, providing a diversified content portfolio that ranges from entertainment (horoscopes, ringing tones and cartoon characters) to more serious sites (news, banking services, stock quotes and directory service to name but a few). The adoption of HTML helped us create a positive feedback loop among the parties concerned, in which the increase in the number of subscribers motivates the IPs to provide more information sites, and the upgraded and enriched site offerings lure more customers. This was a major element that accelerated the take-up of mobile Internet in Japan, where both mobile operators, such as NTT DoCoMo, and content providers have benefited from the service.

The success of mobile Internet transformed mobile handsets from a mere telephone into a much more sophisticated tool that supports various forms of communication. Being able to transmit mail and access the Internet from cell phones has become the norm for Japanese users, as more than 75% of our total cellular-phone customers have already signed up for i-mode.

PROJECTED DEVELOPMENT SCENARIO IN THE 21ST CENTURY

The mobile communications industry is expected to develop further and deliver more value for the economy and society in the 21st century. NTT DoCoMo has set ubiquitous, multimedia and global services as the three major pillars in its corporate strategy to drive the growth of mobile communications in this new era.

By pursuing multimedia services, NTT DoCoMo intends to expand non-voice services such as data and image communications in addition to the conventional voice services. According to our analysis, non-voice traffic is projected to account for about 50% of the total in 2005, and rise further to occupy 70–80% in 2010. "Ubiquitous service" means expanding the size of the market by equipping anything movable or portable with a communication capability. In other words, this aims to support not only human-to-human but also human-to-machine and machine-to-machine communications. Even today, mobile technology is already applied to check the inventory of vending machines, to monitor the operation of public-transport vehicles, and to help improve business efficiency in various industries. In our calculation for the Japanese market, the potential user base of mobile services could increase dramatically when cars, PCs, bicycles, vending machines, refrigerators, parcels, digital cameras and even pets are included as potential users. The sum of such devices used in Japan by 2010 is expected to amount to 570 million, which is roughly five-times greater than the human population of 120 million. The "global service" pillar is designed to enable users to communicate with a single handset, no matter where they are in the world. This is not only about voice-roaming; users who are traveling abroad will be able to enjoy the same environment as they do at home, so that they can access the same voice, e-mail and other sophisticated multimedia services even when they are out of the country. For example, Japanese customers traveling overseas should be able to receive voice calls and e-mail, and access Japanese information in Japanese language and local content in English or the native language of their destination.

If we are able to turn these visions above into reality, the mobile-communications market should be able to grow further without facing saturation. When this is achieved, our lives will become much more convenient and affluent, and mobile-communications services of the 21st century will be characterized by the slogan "communicate anywhere, anytime, and with anyone and anything".

THIRD-GENERATION MOBILE SYSTEM, IMT-2000

To realize these visions as soon as possible will require innovative enabling technologies and collaboration on a global scale. Advancements in nano-technologies and battery or other energy techniques are expected to help in miniaturizing handsets even further. Video and language-coding technologies will enable the terminals to behave in a more "human" manner and store more knowledge. Progress in network technologies will offer faster transmission speeds and a larger capacity, allowing us to offer seamless services between fixed and mobile networks to enhance the convenience offered to the users.

However, the benefits from innovation may diminish unless a certain level of compatibility is guaranteed. The world failed to create a unified standard for second-generation mobile networks and, thus, failed to ensure global connectivity. There are mounting requests to standardize the techniques used for distributing information on the networks, too. The WAP language, for instance, used for mobile Internet in Europe is incompatible with HTML, making it difficult to use the content originally developed for landline Internet on wireless networks.

In this context, the IMT-2000 standard, completed in December 1999, is viewed as a significant paradigm for such global collaboration, involving as it did the joint efforts of researchers, engineers, manufacturers, operators, standards institutes, and government authorities of various countries. In Japan, 3G service was launched on a fully commercialized basis in October 2001. An early launch of 3G service in other parts of the world is eagerly awaited, in order to allow users to travel and communicate across borders with a single handset, and to enable the benefits from collaboration to be enjoyed by the entire world.

The most significant feature of 3G is its fast-speed and wide-bandwidth transmission capability. The wide-band code-division multiple-access (W-CDMA) technology, for instance, can send information at 384 kilo bits per second, which is about 40-times faster than the speed offered by 2G systems. Users will therefore be able to access data, visual information and other multimedia services comfortably, without stress. Various new services are likely to be developed for 3G, including music and game distribution, live TV broadcasts, cinema previews, remote-control and remote-monitoring applications, locating services and other new services utilizing agent functions. 3G is expected to create new business opportunities and provide productivity gains in various industries. Office environments can be created outdoors instantly, allowing sales representatives to obtain customer information from the headquarters via intranets, for instance. The scene of Ichiro Suzuki slamming a homer into the stands can be distributed on cell phones, and parents at work will be able to check how their children are doing in nurseries through real-time video. Furthermore, as electronic commerce will eventually be handled on mobile networks, handsets may replace wallets in the near future. People will be able to go through station gates or purchase drinks from vending machines without spending cash, just by showing their mobile terminal, and making reservations for concert tickets could also be done easily with just a few touches on the phone. The mobile handsets can even function as a remote controller for home appliances. Users may someday be able to use their cell phones to check what is left in the refrigerator, and buy necessary food items before going home.

ACTIONS REQUIRED FOR SUSTAINABLE CORPORATE GROWTH

With the arrival of an era of a truly global economy, businesses now have to compete on the basis that the world is a single market. Under such circumstances, the two keywords that are expected to lead corporations to a stable growth are "efficiency" and "creativity", and untiring efforts should be made to achieve improvements in these areas.

To boost efficiency, it is important to make the best use of IT and maximize the benefits from partnerships with others. Traditionally, businesses have concentrated highly capable human resources in administrative jobs for the management of corporate information, such as finance and customer-related information. We should try to replace this manual practice with IT, so that computers can handle the procedures up to the point where individual data are processed into valuable managerial information. Precious human resources should therefore be spared for the activities that can be handled only by people, such as the development of corporate strategies and the cultivation of new markets, or sales and marketing. Labor productivity will certainly be enhanced if IT is properly used in these areas.

To develop and market value-added products and services in a timely manner, collaboration with leading partners with expertise is indispensable. i-mode is a successful model of such a partnership, in which the collaboration between the telecom operator and content providers functions very well. Collaborative relationships are expected to be formed and go forward on a global scale, which in turn will bring greater economies of scale. That is why we have such huge expectations of the globally standardized third-generation system, which will help us maximize the synergies from our global partnerships through the provision of common services in different markets, while slashing operation costs through joint procurement with our overseas partners.

On the other hand, creativity is also important to facilitate the development of society through creating new values. Given the level of maturity we enjoy today, there is a limit to what we can deliver to existing customers as value-added services. In other words, an industry cannot expect further growth unless new demands are successfully cultivated. For this reason, each industry should employ key technologies such as IT, nano-technology and biotechnology in order to create new global values ahead of the competition

What is important for Japan and other economies in East Asia that have achieved a high rate of economic growth in the past is the transition from a capital-intensive industrial structure, predicated upon mass production and mass consumption, to a more knowledge-oriented one.

CONCLUSION

We are now living in an age of change that can be witnessed only once in centuries. Going forward, individual demands are expected to become more diverse and personal, while businesses will have to provide more value-added services to survive in an increasingly globalized economy. On the other hand, trans-boundary social problems, including environmental concerns and crime, are likely to become a pressing issue in many countries and regions across the world. For Asia to achieve a stable growth in this new era, corporations must not fear change but should, rather, respond quickly to the rapid shift in socio-economic trends by employing new methodologies and technologies. We believe mobile communications has a role to play in this new age of change, and we are committed to make every endeavor to meet the requirements of users. Under the slogan "Think drastically, and implement steadily", I would like to lead NTT DoCoMo to continue creating new values through the use of 3G and other mobile-communications technologies, making contributions to enhance the level of safety, and transforming our society into a more knowledge-based, environmentally oriented one. By so doing, NTT DoCoMo should also be able to grow further and contribute to economic development in Asia.

Building Broadband Internet Service: The Korean Experience

Y.T. Lee
Chairman, Trigem Computer Inc, Republic of Korea

OVERVIEW

The wide acceptance and utilization of broadband Internet service in Korea has caught the attention of the world. It has created a consensus that broadband Internet service in Korea is the best in the world, and this is backed by a number of key indicators. As of the end of November 2001, there were more than seven million broadband Internet subscribers out of 14 million households in Korea. This 50% penetration rate is roughly five times that of the United States, where there are estimated to be eight million. Moreover, among the 10 largest broadband Internet providers there are three Korean companies.

The Korean Internet market also leads the world in the intensity of individual usage, when considering both the narrowband and the broadband together. AC Nielson/Net Rating reported that an average Korean Internet user accesses 2,164 web pages per month, or almost twice that of the immediate follower, Hong Kong (1,123 pages per user). An average Korean Internet user spends over 16 hours per month on the Internet, far ahead of the second-ranked country in this category, Canada, at around 10 hours; even in the U.S. users spend only nine hours and 57 minutes online per month. These figures imply that a high broadband penetration rate in Korea has enabled the average Korean Internet user to spend more time on the Internet, due to the convenience, consistent availability, and rich multimedia experience.

One of the favorite Internet applications in Korea is online stock trading, which accounts for over 69% in monetary value and for 80% of the volume of all transactions. This dramatic shift to a reliance on online trading signifies a fundamental change in doing business in the Korean securities industry. The proliferation of the online trading is also making the physical presence of financial institutions obsolete. A majority of securities companies in Korea are maintaining hundreds of branch offices, which exist to serve about 3% of individual investors, whereas institutional and foreign investors do not rely at all on branch offices. Eventually, many of these offices will no longer be needed. This is just one example of how broadband service has fundamentally transformed the ways of doing business.

THE EVOLUTION OF BROADBAND INTERNET TECHNOLOGY

For the past several years, global traffic on the Internet has grown exponentially and currently the total number of Internet users is estimated at over 400 million. Such a widespread usage of the Internet signifies that the Internet is penetrating and becoming an essential part of many people's daily lives.

Despite the benefits that the Internet has already brought, many people are still not able to utilize its full potential because of the less-than-ideal quality and capacity (often termed "Quality of Service" — QoS) of the current Internet infrastructure. The most frequently heard complaint among Internet users is the limit on speed and response time for various online services and contents. Narrowband Internet service, using ordinary copper-wire lines originally built for the telephone network, can transmit 56K bits of data per second, which can barely support basic online applications such as text-based e-mail. For activities that consume more bandwidth, such as downloading multimedia files, the time and network resources required make it prohibitively costly for users.

This limitation of access speed for the narrowband Internet infrastructure has called for an upgraded network infrastructure. In response to this need, an interim solution called Integrated Services Digital Network (ISDN) technology emerged to become the next standard in networking infrastructure. Several countries, including Japan and Germany, invested heavily in deploying the ISDN infrastructure even though the increase in access speed obtained by an ISDN network is marginal at best. The ISDN technology can provide bandwidth for up to 140K bits per second, or only about twice the speed of the narrowband network.

Today, the term "broadband Internet" refers to a network with speeds far exceeding ISDN. Among the ways to provide broadband Internet service, the most popular is a cable-network-based approach, which provides advantages in speed and expandability compared to other means. A cable modem on top of a cable TV network can transmit digital data at the speed of 10 to 30 million bits per second, which uses only 6Mhz out of total spectrum resources of 750Mhz. Moreover, data streams on the CATV network can be combined to provide even higher data-transfer rates. This expandability up to 30, 60 or even 90Mbps can be achieved merely by upgrading the end-user's cable modem equipment, signifying a distinct advantage over other technologies such as the Asynchronous Digital Subscriber Line (ADSL).

ADSL requires upgrading existing telephone lines to reach speeds of up to 8Mbps. Wireless broadband, on the other hand, is not yet mature enough for widespread deployment, but will eventually play a critical role in complementing cable and ADSL technologies as it can distribute broadband network to isolated rural regions and islands. For the future, the billions invested to build the infrastructure for Third Generation (3G) wireless network are looking to support both voice communications and high-speed wireless Internet services.

Another advantage of the cable modem is its ability to realize online broadcasting efficiently. The cable modem requires only minor equipment upgrades to accommodate so-called multi-casting, which is destined to become one of the most popular Internet applications. By contrast, the ADSL network requires much more investment to achieve this. The difference results from the fact that the CATV network was originally designed for broadcasting, whereas ADSL networks were designed for point-to-point communications. The World Cup Soccer tournament in 2002, jointly hosted by Korea and Japan, could help to trigger widespread acceptance of this multi-casting technology as another major form of mass media. In light of the convergence of broadcasting and the Internet industries, investment in and the use of cable-modem technology will provide a much larger return on investment than ADSL technology.

THE ORIGINS OF BROADBAND INTERNET SERVICE IN KOREA

Broadband Internet service in Korea began in an interesting fashion. Korea Electric Power Company (KEPCO), which held the monopoly on ownership and operation of power generation and transmission, inserted optical communication wires inside ground wires wherever they laid electric power lines. Thus, high-speed optical communication networks and a nationwide backbone network were constructed by incurring only a minimal incremental cost.

To provide Internet services to end-users, this backbone network required connection to a local access network. In 1996, KEPCO was awarded the license to deploy CATV infrastructure to provide this connection with CATV television services. Although the initial purpose of this network was to support broadcasting, which requires one-way communication, KEPCO constructed the network as a bi-directional communication system. This forward-looking strategy made possible both broadband Internet services and CATV broadcasting and, furthermore, endowed KEPCO with nationwide network coverage. In order to utilize this versatile infrastructure, Trigem Computer and KEPCO and a number of other shareholders jointly established Thrunet to offer the very first broadband Internet service in Korea. When the service was launched in November 1997, the market reaction was enthusiastic.

Another company, Hanaro, won a license to offer local telephony service in 1997. Unfortunately, Hanaro's initial business plan of competing directly with Korea Telecom (KT) in local telephony service was disastrous. Not only did it require a huge investment to construct the network infrastructure and telephone exchange systems all over the country, but it also needed to penetrate KT's monopoly on the local telephone market. After its initial struggle, Hanaro turned its attention to the broadband Internet service market, targeting multi-dwelling units such as apartments and condominiums. It began constructing the optical-fiber network and deployed ADSL modems to households and eventually began operating ADSL-based Internet service.

Although it began its broadband service later than other providers, KT has captured almost half the market. This is due to its dominance of local and long-distance telephone services, its rich financial resources and its network infrastructure. One result of the fierce competition between Thrunet, KT and Hanaro is that broadband Internet service in Korea has rapidly penetrated the home market.

SUCCESS FACTORS OF THE KOREAN MARKET

The rapid and deep penetration of broadband Internet services in Korea is remarkable when compared to other countries in the world. Identifying key reasons for this success could therefore be quite enlightening.

Low subscription fees are among the foremost reasons for the high broadband penetration rate. Whereas the local telephone monopoly, KT, charges calls based on usage without offering flat rates or discounted Internet service, the broadband Internet service-users pay a fixed fee for Internet access at much higher speeds. Therefore, broadband access becomes better value for heavy end-users (over 10 hours per month).

The second factor is the prevalence of multi-dwelling housing units in Korea, which enables efficient and economical network deployment.

The third contributing factor are cyber cafés known as 'PC Bangs', which have become widespread and very popular. It is estimated that there are 20,000 PC Bangs around the country, thus providing an excellent Internet infrastructure used most heavily by teenagers. One interesting contrast in gaming preferences and patterns between Japanese and Korean youths is worth mentioning. Whereas Japanese kids usually tend to favor playing single-user games on the dedicated game console machines, Korean kids prefer to play multi-user games, which have spawned a number of network-based, multi-user game-development companies.

The prevalence of the Internet infrastructure extends to educational institutes in Korea. All the primary and secondary schools are connected to broadband Internet and it is common for primary students to submit homework via the Internet. After experiencing broadband at school, students frequently ask for the same service at home.

People's willingness to try out new technologies has also helped Korea to embrace broadband Internet service. This can be compared to the mid 1990s when penetration of paging services in Korea was among the highest in the world. The same intense adoption is now seen with mobile-phone services and already two million users subscribe to 3G wireless services.

Looking back through Korean history we can see a more fundamental reason for the wide adoption of broadband service. Throughout the Korea and Chosun dynasties, civilians with middle and noble lineages qualified to become government officers by passing an examination and, as a result, for the past 1,000 years study has become one way of moving up for many young Korean men. This emphasis on education has created an "education fever" among Korean parents. The advent of the information age has extended this high value for quality education to a strong drive towards entrepreneurship. These rapid adaptations to the knowledge-based economy and burgeoning venture businesses in Korea can be better understood in these contexts.

BROADBAND: THE BUSINESS MODEL

In the aftermath of the bursting of the dot-com bubble, it is widely believed that the Internet-service business is not profitable and this has made the IT industry reluctant to invest in it, despite potentially huge demand. This fear of unprofitability is misplaced. The broadband Internet-service market provides a good counter-example.

The business model of the broadband provider Thrunet is marked by partnerships at every level of its value chain: for network infrastructure, parts of the backbone network and the subscriber network are leased from KEPCO, and local CATV system operators (SO) act as sales agents. Digital contents are serviced by a subsidiary, Korea.com, which itself has a large number of affiliated content providers. By contrast, Korea Telecom provides all resources for its broadband Internet service by itself, with the exception of content.

For Thrunet, 88% of revenue comes from the subscription fee, whereas modem rental fee and installation fees account for 8% and 3.8%, respectively. Other categories of revenue streams such as content, e-commerce and advertising are counted as revenue for Korea.com, the portal subsidiary of Thrunet. On the cost side, major costs for Thrunet are network infrastructure, commissions for CATV operators, sales agents, installation, customer support and maintenance. Under current efforts to improve efficiency of operations, the ratio of operating costs to revenue is expected to improve to 72% in 2001, from 99% in 2000. The rental cost of the network facility, international bandwidth leasing and installation are expected to increase in line with the strong growth in the number of subscribers, whereas costs in relation to revenue are expected to continuously decrease. As a result, Thrunet is expected to record positive net income in the near future.

Understanding the environment of the broadband Internet industry is critical for success in this market. The group of narrowband Internet users is a potential customer base for whom the subscription price is the key purchase driver. We have also found that the churn rate (the rate at which old subscribers drop out and new subscribers are added) is relatively low in this market and, therefore, being the first mover carries many advantages. Obtaining a wide coverage is the key to capturing these markets. Another condition to keep in mind is that since both ADSL and cable-modem services are utilizing existing networks and facilities, many chronic problems can occur. The natural next step for this industry is to improve the network quality and to provide more comprehensive services. When narrowband users switch to broadband, they want to enjoy both the faster speed and rich multimedia contents. Therefore, a wide range of broadband portals and multimedia content must be delivered to meet the high expectations of the users. To prepare for a mature stage of business, when competition between providers will get intense and the customer churn rate may increase, Thrunet has been redoubling its efforts in the areas of customer retention and satisfaction. Also, bundled and value-added services such as video-on-demand (VOD), voice-over-IP (VOIP) and virtual private network (VPN) services are becoming essential parts of product and service portfolios.

BROADBAND PORTAL

Ideally high-speed broadband Internet service should be accompanied by a collection of high-quality contents. Thrunet opened the first broadband-focused portal service in Korea with Korea.com, which has been specifically designed to support multimedia content and broadband services. The business strategy of Korea.com can be summarized by the four Cs: communications, community, contents and commerce.

The next generation of portals will become successful by learning from the experiences of established portals such as Yahoo, Lycos and AOL. Since its inception just a year ago, Korea.com has attracted over 5.6 million subscribers, of which 1.2 million are paying. As broadband portals develop new and diverse revenue streams, billing information on customers will enable the portal to deliver vastly more effective and seamless services. Because its customers represent a diverse cross-section of Korean society, Korea.com must offer very diversified content and, to this end, has established more than 13 program channels, interactive e-commerce solutions and communication functionality. By the end of 2001, the Korean content market will be worth approximately US$500 million, and Merrill Lynch has estimated that the revenue generated by the commercial content will be US$3.5 billion by the year 2005. This signifies a new era for the commercialization of Internet content.

MULTIMEDIA CONTENTS SERVICE

Of various digital content-market segments, the leading paid-content service is VOD, which comprises 40% of all content-service offerings. The second-most popular content-service category is online gaming, which occupies 32%, followed by animation, at 23%. Educational broadcasting and stock trading occupy the remainder. Korea.com offers over 1,000 VOD movie titles and currently has 30,000 VOD subscribers, with over 70% of them each purchasing one or two titles a week for US$0.80 to US$3 per title. The quality of online VOD is comparable to the quality of the VCR systems on the television set.

The broadband network's high-capacity infrastructure can enable upgraded and enhanced versions of existing applications such as e-mail. For instance, every Thrunet subscriber can enjoy e-mail service and even access many addresses scattered around different portals through a unique address on Thrunet's mail system. Korea.com also offers a Unified Messaging System (UMS) service, which enables a user to access various forms of communication streams coming in by telephone, facsimile and the Internet in one channel. For instance, graphic facsimile messages can be received in the e-mail box, and e-mail messages can be accessed by the telephone terminal and also directed to a mobile phone. This versatility of access to various forms of communications data is one of the advantages of broadband service.

Communities offer some of the most captivating services for many online users and there are over 25,000 communities at Korea.com. Each benefits tremendously from faster and better facilities for communicating with others in their special-interest group.

The broadband-based content services are very effective because the high capacity of the underlying infrastructure is capable of supporting rich multimedia contents. One very interesting development enabled by broadband-based content services is online education. Although the Korean government decided to teach oral English in the nation's primary schools, there were not enough capable teachers. To remedy this, many schools decided to use the broadband network connection and online video instructions as a substitute; as a result, there are now many online English education-service providers available. Some are even providing individual language-education sessions with teachers in the United States.

Another motivating example of broadband's implications for education is the HAJA school in Korea, which uses project-based teaching. Students work together in groups on specific projects, emphasizing teamwork, cooperation and problem-solving skills. At the HAJA school, knowledge-based education is supported and aided by the Internet. Each student acquires appropriate knowledge through computer terminals, based upon ability, knowledge of the subject and personal interest. Clearly, then, broadband Internet service has a huge potential to change the fundamentals of education systems.

CONCLUSION

Korea has been fortunate in preparing for the knowledge-based economy early by deploying broadband Internet infrastructure. The current level of development can be attributed to a number of favorable conditions, including a unique cultural background that has emphasized education, the rapid embracing of new technologies, MDUs and PC Bangs. However, much remains to be done if we are to make full use of these advantages to further develop the national economy to be more flexible and competitive.

First, the national backbone network needs to be redesigned. Up until now, there has been strong competition for building the national backbone infrastructure, and this has resulted in asymmetric development. Some regions are covered by redundant infrastructures while others are not equipped at all. In addition, there are few links between competing networks, which results in an inefficient utilization of network resources.

Second, the service offerings of Korea Telecom need to be changed because KT's practice of offering monopolized service bundled with competing services in a single entity will eventually undermine the healthy development of the telecommunication industries. For example, KT provides broadband Internet connection to primary and secondary schools free of charge. Since this was a national project, the costs should have been provided by the government and construction should have been open to competitive bidding. Economic efficiency demands that rights for the network deployment and cost recovery should be distributed in a transparent and competitive process.

Third, the major supporters of broadband Internet services in Korea are individuals, while small and medium-sized firms do not yet use broadband service effectively. In order to rectify this situation, both the government and industry associations must support their adoption of broadband infrastructure. In addition, there is not enough broadband content to justify higher-speed Internet and, therefore, serious efforts must be put into developing software and multimedia content. The quantity and quality of software must be increased at least in line with the increase in the network capacity.

To achieve this goal, I'd like to propose a few important policy initiatives. The first is to double the number of college graduates in IT-related areas, which currently stands at 100,000 IT graduates a year. My recommendation is to encourage 100,000 more students majoring in other areas to take IT training as a second major. In addition, I recommend that the government and industry accumulate 300,000 hours of experience in five years by providing college graduates with extensive internship and on-the-job-training programs.

Finally, it is necessary to share our experiences of the broadband Internet market with the world. Strategic alliances that provide synergies between various countries will be beneficial to all parties. Such international cooperation will also help in narrowing the gap between the haves and have-nots in the information infrastructure. Sharing human, knowledge and financial resources among various countries will also accelerate the infrastructure-deployment process across national borders. The globalization of the world economy in the 21st century calls for a smart and efficient utilization of all resources in order to bring the true information age to a full realization.

The Telecom Revolution, Round Two: The Bumpy Road to 3G

Manuel V. Pangilinan
President and Chief Executive Officer, Philippine Long Distance
Telephone Company (PLDT), the Philippines

The town of San Miguel in the remote province of Catanduanes in the Philippines does not appear on many maps. It has no bank, no movie house, no gasoline station. A grocery and a *sari-sari* store make up its commercial center; its market is a table with a few vegetables on display.

But in January 2001, Philippine Long Distance Telephone Company (PLDT), the largest telecommunications company in the country, through its subsidiary, Smart ACeS, inaugurated a new satellite-based public calling station (PCO). The owner of the only store in town, Aling Soling, was invited to place a call to anywhere in the world. She chose to call a number in Chicago, Illinois, and the call was broadcast for the entire street to hear.

Everyone was there — all the residents and the local officials — and when her daughter answered, her voice coming crisp and clear from Chicago, the entire street erupted in applause. In that electrifying moment, the small town knew its future would be different; its life would be changed forever.

Given the vast capabilities of current technology, that first phone call may have been more a modest step than a giant leap. Nonetheless, the town of San Miguel has, in a small way, joined what has been described as the "informationally empowered" global community. It is now indeed connected to the world.

Telecommunications is an enabling technology. It helps people to help themselves. Going by past experience, deploying satellite PCOs in rural communities will help stimulate local businesses and improve the quality of people's lives.

However, there are times when telecom operators need to put themselves at arm's length from technology.

Operators in Asia have seen, for example, the excessively expensive outcomes of the license auctions in Europe. That was the product of the "irrational exuberance" that accompanied the rush to 3G.

For telecom companies in general, it is sometimes useful to take an agnostic attitude towards technology. That means being technologically savvy but not technology-driven. We must be mindful of this basic tenet: technology is to be used as a means to two basic ends — customer satisfaction and shareholders' returns.

CONVERGENCE STRATEGY: THE BROAD VIEW

Convergence has been talked about by many telecoms and multimedia groups. Many others dream about it because a convergent network is the shape of the future.

Telephone companies that have opted to use data-capable, Internet-based technologies as the platform for future operations have the flexibility to choose not just one but many transport systems — whether it is fixed line, mobile, cable or satellite — and choose which one will prove to be the most effective and cost-efficient in meeting customers' requirements.

The key to convergence strategy is a single core network that can handle voice, video and data simultaneously.

Asymmetric Digital Subscriber Line (ADSL) technology is being introduced into the traditional copper-wire network so that it can be broadbanded to handle high-speed data and even video transmissions. Cable-TV subscribers in parts of a major city in the Philippines can make telephone calls using their cable-TV wiring and many others are able to access their Internet with high-speed modems using the same network.

Convergence is not just an issue for the network engineers — it also applies as an interface with customers' operational support and with the content and applications that are now being developed and offered.

With respect to customers, the convergent opportunities can be identified in call centers, Internet data centers, and bundled services involving fixed-line, cellular, satellite, and cable-TV products.

With regard to operational integration, the convergent issues revolve around integrating the cable-TV, satellite, cellular, and fixed-line networks (including international facilities) and managing them as one; for example, integrating customer-care services and integrating the business offices of the various subsidiaries.

With regard to content and applications, the convergent opportunities lie in tie-ups with telecoms abroad for the cellular business, linkage with the banks for payment facilities on the phone, cooperation with a host of content providers that supply information, and the use of the Yellow Pages.

Apart from the explosive growth of the wireless business, telecoms have taken the lead in bringing a comprehensive range of Internet, e-commerce and multimedia services to the Philippines.

To take advantage of these new convergent opportunities, PLDT has created a single corporate vehicle. Initially, this will serve as the holding company that will house PLDT's interest in a number of existing businesses, including the cable-television operator (Home Cable) and the Internet service provider (Infocom). A number of other investments and businesses, including a new e-procurement joint venture, has also been integrated into this vehicle.

The Group's call-center business will be part of it. This will be an important part of PLDT's consolidated business and revenue moving forward.

Finally, included in this portfolio is the new P1.6 billion Internet Data Center ("VITRO") whose fit-out has recently been completed. VITRO will host, co-locate and/or manage the computer servers, applications and bandwidth needed by its customers for their Internet and multimedia operations.

The convergence strategy has, without doubt, been one of PLDT's most exciting and challenging projects as the industry itself, on a global basis, is going through such fundamental changes. The results are starting to come through and there is no end to the excitement in the years to come.

CELLULAR STRATEGY

It is within the context outlined above that the cellular strategy of PLDT has been crafted.

Take the case of PLDT's mobile-phone company, Smart. It started out with a 1G platform — ETACS, a mature analog system developed in Europe — even if the conventional wisdom then was to go GSM (Global System for Mobile Communications). Digital technology at that time was still developing and digital handset prices were high. ETACS, in contrast, was technically proven and inexpensive. Handsets were markedly more affordable. ETACS enabled us to roll out our network rapidly and thus meet the pent-up demand of the mass market for dial tone. To win subscribers, unheard-of tariffs were offered, with monthly service fees as low as US$5 per month. In three years, Smart overtook the incumbent.

It was only after four years and more than a million subscribers that Smart switched to a 2G platform. By then, GSM technology had matured and terminals were affordable and available to the mass market. Thus, history affirms the axiom that "We are not the first by whom the new is tried, nor yet the last to lay the old aside".

But with respect to products, services and solutions, Smart is the market innovator. It has pioneered a rich portal of personalized mobile-data services in Smart zed. It has also developed a world-first in the award-winning Smart Money, the only electronic-payments card linked to a cellular phone. These are examples of compelling wireless services on the 2G platform.

In fact, 2G has gained new respectability over the past year. There was some degree of backsliding in the mobile-data world because some operators retreated from their early efforts to build their wireless-data business on Wireless Access Protocol (WAP). WAP, sadly, has turned out to be a wimp. Disappointed, some operators have chosen to go back to SMS as their mobile-data platform.

For the Philippines, the choice of technology has been a no-brainer. Filipinos are the most prolific users of SMS or text messaging. The Philippines, with only 10 million GSM subscribers, produces approximately 100 million messages a day. The global total for text messages was about 750 million daily late last year. With this level of SMS usage, the Philippines has embraced text messaging as the technology platform for wireless services.

But why SMS? Why retreat to a system that relies on transporting packets of information containing no more than 160 characters in an age when data is measured in gigabits?

First, 2G handsets that feature SMS are already a widely available mass product. This gives operators a huge, ready-made market for SMS services. This spares them from the frustrating experience of waiting for high-priced handsets that support new-fangled services.

Second, billing SMS is a straightforward proposition. The low tariff of two U.S. cents per message and higher rates of five to 25 U.S. cents per message for value-added services are within easy reach of the average Filipino.

Third, SMS is easy to use and remarkably adaptable as a platform for low-bandwidth services. It is always online. It can handle a wide range of interactive services. It can also be made secure enough to handle safely m-commerce applications.

The net result is this: operators can make money on SMS-based services today, and not have to wait till some indefinite point in the future.

This stands in sharp contrast to the huge uncertainties that cloud prospects for turning 3G and even 2.5G into profitable businesses.

Moreover, SMS has become more flexible and powerful in the past year because of advances in SIM toolkit or STK technology. The memory capacities of these tiny chips that fit into GSM mobile phones have leapt from 4K to 64K. Makers of SIM have, at the behest of many operators, packed increasingly sophisticated programs into these chips.

The use of these advanced 64K SIMs to create menu-driven SMS services has resulted in cell phones that are easier for subscribers to use. This is akin to upgrading from DOS to Windows, and the bigger memories of these chips has put in place advanced security features for mobile banking and m-commerce services.

Over the past two years, more than 130 wireless services — including messaging and communications, news and information, games and entertainment, vehicle and package tracking, location-based services, mobile banking and electronics payments — have been introduced to customers.

Using cutting-edge 2G technology, SMS traffic rose from less than 100 million messages in January 2000 to over 600 million messages in December 2000. By December 2001, the figure was 1.6 billion messages. On New Year's Eve, Smart's network alone handled 85 million messages for that single day.

The bulk of that traffic — about 80% — consisted of basic text or person-to-person messages. But revenue derived from SMS value-added services as a percentage of total GSM revenues has grown from zero two years ago to 20% of the rapidly growing text-messaging pie.

In December 2000, total SMS revenues accounted for one-third of the outbound revenues generated from each Smart GSM subscriber. By October 2001, 50% of revenues per subscriber came from text messaging.

In terms of the contribution of SMS revenues to total cellular revenues, major international mobile operators have attained rates ranging from 3 to 17%.

To attain these results, the technology strategy is clearly defined. The focus is on providing immediate, low-cost access to the Internet and the abundance of low-bandwidth applications available from it. The premium is on programs that are simple, quick to make, easily deployed and affordable to customers.

Creating these services has become increasingly akin to producing films or entertainment programs. Operators — on their own or through partners — need to keep supplying a steady stream of new service offerings, realizing that many will be just so-so products, but that some will become monster hits or killer applications.

In fact, entertainment content has become increasingly prominent in SMS-based services. These include such staples as ring tones and logos, chat services and a wide range of text games and contests. One of the biggest hits has been a text quiz game where subscribers who answer three quiz questions correctly over SMS get a chance to win millions of pesos in a lotto series.

As these services are launched, we accomplish three major objectives vital to the future of mobile-data services.

First, we build the market for mobile-data services. The rich portfolio of SMS-based wireless services makes possible a mass experience of creating, sending, receiving and manipulating data. Mobile-phone users are introduced to a world where handsets are multi-purpose terminals. This ensures that there will be content for higher technologies such as 2.5 and 3G and that the market will be receptive to such services.

Second, we build and develop a network of partnerships with content providers. This requires a mutually beneficial business relationship between operators and content developers. Building these partnerships has been fraught with more difficulties than technology challenges.

Third, we test various business models for mobile data. Given the rapid progress of technology — even on 2G — it is abundantly clear that mobile operators will be able to offer many new and interesting wireless services. The question is, will these make money for both operators and developers and at prices that are affordable and attractive for customers?

There are several sources of content. Some come from portals for mobile-data services, others are m-commerce based and the operator himself generates some content. But the most important and largest content providers are the subscribers themselves.

In the Philippines, jokes make up a disproportionately large part of the total SMS traffic. Political jokes, green jokes, brown jokes — they come in all colors. Some wonder if operators keep a bunch of gag-writers in some dark, smoke-filled room and make them churn out a steady supply of jokes that are then pumped into the SMS traffic. The honest and interesting answer is "No". The truth is, subscribers create all these jokes — and then circulate these among themselves.

Sometimes, these jokes produce unintended results. Last October, Philippine newspapers reported that a Filipino immigrant was detained for 12 hours upon entering Belgium because of a text message that he received on his mobile phone. The person was stopped for routine questioning, during which immigration police checked his cell phone. They found a message that read as follows:

"I was wondering if I can stay with you for a couple of days. Everybody's so angry at me. And I really need a friend. Yours truly, Osama."

This is the substance of what a recent survey on the mobile Internet referred to as "person-to-person communication" or "user-generated content". There are many opportunities offered by the emerging location-based services, advertising and mobile commerce. But the bulk of the traffic — and thus operators' revenues — will come from the users themselves.

In that light, operators must thus exert every effort to make it easier for subscribers to generate that content. Progress through the introduction of mobile e-mail and group texting services has been made. Soon, multimedia messaging will be available. This will be helped by the introduction of handsets with built-in cameras. One interesting area is interactive-TV text services. Aside from answering TV opinion polls and on-air quiz games, these text services give mobile-phone users the chance to post their text messages and see them flashed onscreen during popular TV programs.

What does all this activity mean to the pursuit of 3G? Although our basic commitment to 3G remains, the price tag, the delayed commercial roll-out, the availability of handsets, and the desire to see the existing networks substantially depreciated first, tell us to be cautious.

The key challenge ahead is to discover fresh applications based on existing technologies, and on applications that are appropriate to the mass-market consumer whose disposable income is modest.

Some analysts have expressed fears that such a gradualist approach will undermine the growth of 3G. Operators aiming for 3G may end up cutting off their own legs by pushing 2G or 2.5G services. There is the real danger of cannibalization. On the other hand, promoting the mobile Internet on 2G and 2.5G platforms helps ensure that there will be a wealth of wireless services that will run on 3G.

Operators have to make up their own minds based on the competitive and regulatory conditions that prevail in their own markets. I think it would help if they maintained a certain amount of agnosticism when it comes to technology platforms. They must keep their eyes focused on services that customers are willing to pay for. They must strive to make these services available now, using existing technologies. And they must not wait for 3G before creating a rich wireless-services environment. That way, operators will be able to take full advantage of more powerful technologies as these come onstream and make possible an even richer user experience.

In these uncertain times, this makes business sense. And that, in the end, is the real role of operators in driving innovation: to make business sense out of the dazzling possibilities created by massive leaps of technology.

While such inroads into SMS-based value-adding services have been achieved by a mobile-phone company like Smart, PLDT, a telecom company, has also benefited by transplanting this business model to its landline operations. The landline phone units, for example, have been given the capability to send SMS messages. Soon, the same units will be capable of two-way "texting" via adjunct boxes, enabling the same popular content on mobile phones to be more household pervasive. As the family becomes dependent over time on information pushed or pulled via the landline unit, the cost of technology to implement broadband setup boxes for the ubiquitous TV set will have decreased — opening up a whole new experience in streaming content such as movies, live webcasts and interactive shopping. The need for bigger data-pipes into the household will be driven by content.

To manage this content diversity properly, other Internet-focused teams such as ISP and Cable TV have set up parallel, but complementary, initiatives on other access platforms. Cable TV, for example, now offers a UHF channel where SMS-users can join public chat rooms. The same TV experience could thereafter be a launch pad for online commerce. A new offering from our ISP, Infocom, on the other hand, pushes the same narrowband content onto its ISP subscribers with a choice of prepaid or postpaid Internet accounts. Prior to this, both the ISP and CATV launched broadband gaming, in coordination with content providers, to address a separate market community hungry for DSL and/or cable-Internet services.

The approach is quite simple. Build a community on a sustainable and popular content platform, such as SMS; provide a choice of affordable access-device choices to the community; and ensure that the most popular content is available regardless of access choice or geography. This is what convergence strategy hopes to achieve.

Convergence strategy's ultimate beneficiaries should not only be the employees, customers or shareholders. It should reach out to all of society, recognizing that often its less-fortunate members must have more of these amenities.

Thus viewed, a telecom company like PLDT should make a difference in the lives of everyone. Let us then go back to the little town of San Miguel in the province of Catanduanes.

The Philippines still has thousands of communities that, like the town of San Miguel, entered the 21st century with no communication links to the outside world. The country cannot truly be one nation, cannot honestly claim to be one community, as long as it remains fragmented.

The town of San Miguel, Catanduanes, is just the beginning. Like PLDT, the mission of all telecom companies is to enable people to get in touch, to listen, to be informed, to understand and to make intelligent choices.

PART
3

Managing Political and Corporate-Governance Challenges

Introduction

Pre-crisis Asia was often mentioned in one breath with authoritarianism, corruption, and a lack of institutions to ensure political and corporate governance. Investors and potential contractors had to pay "tea money" (the Thai expression) to pursue their goals in top-down systems where currying favor with fickle officials preceded competence for a project. Japanese *yakusa* — the local equivalents of the Italian mafia — regularly disturbed the shareholder meetings of even the most high-profile Japanese companies to guarantee their preferred outcomes. Political hopefuls had to have deep pockets to obtain the blessing of the right parties, and then sought to replenish their coffers once in office. The cycle of advancement and enrichment through patronage was ubiquitous and self-reinforcing, and voices for change were left shouting on the outskirts.

The Asian economic crisis induced many changes in the political system, at least at first glance: Indonesian President Suharto, South Korean President Kim Young-Sam, Thai Premier Chavalit Yongchaiyudh and Japanese Premier Ryutaro Hashimoto had to step down. New governments promised more democracy and responsiveness to the needs of the citizenry. The corporate sector vowed to implement significant reforms into their way of doing business and to be more mindful of their duties to shareholders.

However, in many cases, the initial momentum was only a passing fancy. When East Asia was lucky enough to drag itself out of crisis by piggy-backing on the strengths of the U.S. economy, the zest for reform retreated noticeably. A return of confidence in the economy brought a return in old methodology. Only the second Asian crisis, caused by the shrinking of U.S. corporate and consumer demand, especially around the aftermath of the terrorist attacks, has forced Asians to recall their lost reform agendas from the wilderness.

Again, there are hopeful signals in the region. Above all, China's drive to implement legal reforms, to clarify investment structures and to fight corruption are all important and landmark steps towards the establishment of modern governance systems. The obvious challenge is to link economic progress and political stability with the need for a vibrant civil society. Likewise, Hong Kong under Chief Executive Tung Chee-Hwa is further upgrading its institutions, trying to tame the tycoons who frequently undermined the government's authority in the past. Japan, finally, is slowly taking its leave from the inherited governmental feudalism, triggering long-awaited reforms under Junichiro Koizumi.

For many East Asian societies with feudal traditions, the strengthening of institutions and the rule of law will have a long-lasting impact on the region's competitiveness. However, the challenge is clearly how to maintain momentum and to get beyond the initial transition and euphoria to achieve sustainable solutions.

In a similar vein, corporate governance became not only a buzzword, but also a nucleus for survival in most of East Asia. Still, some degree of caution is recommended. Universal theories meant to explain and steer economic processes across cultures are almost certain to mislead. The structure and patriarchal thrust of many Asian companies, including those listed on the stock exchanges, are distinct from most in Western economies. In Asia, the founder or founding family may still retain a controlling interest, and may be indifferent to so-called international (read "Western") governance practices. Now, the globalization of corporate finance and the need to restructure corporate debts have combined to force Asian companies to distinguish between local or Asian governance traditions and worldwide best practices. A combination of these will provide the foundations of sustainable corporate governance for the region.

The lingering question is how far is Asia from reaching this watermark in establishing its own brand of good governance that will endure through prosperity and strife? There is no unanimity on this. If one believes social activists such as Tunku Abdul Aziz, that day is far off indeed, and will not come without a thorough overhauling and undoing of the political and business power points. On the other hand, Christine Loh, no stranger to critiquing Hong Kong's political system and outputs, is more confident that the fundamentals exist to bring the former colony back on track. To Hong Kong's Chief Executive, this must come as good news, especially since he has been re-elected to another five years.

For those looking for signs of change in governance practices in Asia's business sector, the alignment of views between regulators and newly emerged companies may come as a relief. In countries that have relatively short "clean governance" records, one finds congruence in beliefs that good governance is fundamental to corporate recovery and growth, even in countries with relatively short histories of corporate-governance reform. Lilia Bautista and Felipe Yap from the Philippines capital markets, and Saifuddien Hasan and E.C.W. Neloe from the Indonesian banking sector, are all lining up against tradition in speaking out for more transparency and accountability.

Whether one regards the following chapters as indicators of real change or just more hot air is, of course, up to the reader. However, we would counsel that in Asia, when the majority speaks, it is more often than not an indication that a change has already occurred. Thus, leaders in government and business speak mostly in retrospect. This is nothing new. So, reading well: in this case, the majority has spoken, and good governance is here to stay.

Laying the Ground for Hong Kong's Competitiveness

Tung Chee-Hwa
Chief Executive, Hong Kong SAR

 Like other economies in Asia, Hong Kong faces a range of challenges that will impact on our short- and long-term prospects. Hong Kong's greatest challenge is how to ensure that we remain relevant, competitive and capable of sustainable growth.

Short-term problems caused by a downturn in the global economy have been exacerbated by the fallout from the heinous terrorist attacks in the United States on September 11, 2001. As one of the world's most externally oriented economies, Hong Kong will be affected by any global downturn. But the effects are potentially more severe when the world's largest economy — the United States — is in a slowdown.

For the second time in three years, Asian economies are grappling with negative GDP, shrinking exports and rising unemployment. As Asian governments devise domestic solutions to a global problem, a number of other factors also warrant close attention.

Successive interest-rate cuts and additional tax cuts in the United States will, hopefully, help the American economy eventually rebound strongly and vibrantly. But a key factor will be how to restore the confidence of the American people so that consumers will begin to spend again, people will begin to travel again and business will begin to invest again. The fight against terrorism is helping to restore that confidence. It is important that every country joins in this effort to counter international terrorism.

A weak Japanese economy continues to be a concern to the region and the global economy. An early recovery of the Japanese economy would have had tremendous benefits for the rest of the global economy and most likely lifted Asia out of the doldrums. Recent sharp declines in the value of the Yen are adding to the uncertainty. Regional economies are rightly worried about the ripple effect that cheaper Japanese exports will have on their own export-oriented economies. A stable Yen, means a stable Asia.

Bearing these points in mind, it is my assessment, however, that a repeat of the 1997–98 Asian financial crisis is unlikely. One important reason for this is that the economic fundamentals of Asian economies have improved since 1998. These include:

- Improvements in the external positions of Asian economies. Between the end of 1997 and the end of 2000, foreign-exchange reserves of Asian countries (excluding Japan) increased by 35%, to US$651 billion. The current-account surpluses of these economies increased from 1.2% of GDP in 1997 to 4.2% in 2000.
- Leverage in Asian financial systems has reduced. Between mid 1997 and the end of 2000, about US$341 billion in international bank credit was withdrawn from Asia, and the trend is continuing. Short-term debts have been reduced dramatically. Asset prices have fallen substantially, greatly reducing the risk of a crisis caused by another asset price bubble.
- The self-defense mechanisms of many Asian economies have been strengthened with reforms to financial markets and improvements in risk management. At the same time, the threat of disruptions to financial markets by highly leveraged institutions has greatly reduced.

Nonetheless, we must remain on alert. Near-term difficulties faced by APEC economies may be aggravated by corporate failures in hard-hit sectors, a further decline in the stock markets and a sharp fall in consumer spending. Difficulties in the trade and real-estate sectors may further weaken the banking sector and thus increase financial vulnerability.

The risk of financial contagion in the region is presently not high, but this may change if the global and, by extension, the Asian economic environment worsens. We must remain on high alert.

The one big positive is the continued opening up of the Chinese economy, which has been described as the "island of growth". China's accession to the World Trade Organization in 2001, and further liberalization as a result of that accession, will surely continue to boost the global economy and regional economies.

China's continued opening up and its entry into the WTO will have enormous ramifications for Hong Kong, which returned to Chinese sovereignty on July 1, 1997. On that day, 156 years of colonial administration drew to a close and the Hong Kong Special Administrative Region was born, ushering in a new era for Hong Kong to move forward under the concept of "One Country, Two Systems". Hong Kong's historic mission is to turn this innovative concept into an everyday reality.

Over the past four years, with the firm support of the Central Government and the determination of the Hong Kong people, this mission has been achieved. The successful implementation of "One Country, Two Systems" is perhaps best illustrated by the significant inflows of capital into Hong Kong as well as the return of many, many Hong Kong residents who migrated overseas before July 1, 1997. Emigration is also at a 20-year low. International companies are establishing regional operations in Hong Kong in record numbers. And the influential Heritage Foundation of the U.S. has, once again, for the eighth consecutive year, assessed Hong Kong as the world's freest economy. Clearly, there is confidence in the long-term future of Hong Kong.

However, like other economies in the region, Hong Kong needs to restructure its economy as a result of globalization and the rapid development of information technology. The rise of economic China has thrown up new opportunities, as well as new challenges.

While undertaking necessary structural reforms, our economy has also been affected by a cyclical downturn. Earlier forecasts have had to be significantly revised. More jobs will disappear before they reappear. Government revenue will fall short of its target, whereas expenditure will rise, in part because we need to spend more to help those caught up in the economic downdraft.

In such a situation, a good government does two things: first, it responds quickly to the vagaries of the moment and deploys resources in a timely manner to solve the problems of the day; secondly, and perhaps more importantly, it does not lose sight of the bigger picture, of the trends and driving forces that will shape economic development in the long run.

In the short term, and faced with a serious cyclical downturn, we devised some short-term fiscal measures (rates rebates, tax deduction for mortgage interest, a freeze on government charges, etc) to relieve the financial burden of our citizens. Additionally, public-works projects and much-needed social-services programs have been accelerated which, in turn, will create over 30,000 new jobs over a short period of time to alleviate rising unemployment.

However, the government's main efforts are concentrated on a number of longer-term challenges. Central to our policy thinking and activities is how best to make the transition to a knowledge-based economy in the shortest time possible, ride the wave of China's progress with the greatest success and least economic and human dislocation, and adapt to the era of globalized competition to nurture an economy that can perform brilliantly in the most demanding and competitive situations.

In this regard, Hong Kong's government has set itself five major tasks:

- First, we must invest in human capital in a sustained manner and on a vast scale, sufficient to form a deep, strong base of brainpower to support a knowledge economy with high value-added economic activities.
- Second, we must enhance hard and soft infrastructure and generally make Hong Kong even more business-friendly and efficient.
- Third, we must improve our environment to make Hong Kong a better place in which to work and live and enjoy life.
- Fourth, we must strive to make life easier, hardship more bearable and jobs more accessible for the less-fortunate members of our society who find it difficult to weather the process of economic restructuring.
- Fifth, we must make government more efficient, more accountable and responsive to the needs of the community.

We have already been working hard on education reform and investing heavily in education for several years, despite the economic situation. Government spending on education has increased by 46% in the four years since 1997 and will continue to increase in the foreseeable future. We have a three-fold objective: to greatly improve the quality of teaching and learning in our basic education system; to further enhance our tertiary education with systemic reforms to make it available to many more of our young people — our goal is 60% within 10 years; and to make lifelong education the norm of an adult workforce poised to enter the knowledge economy.

Besides enhancing and upgrading our human capital, we need to work hard to continue improving our hard and soft infrastructure and make Hong Kong even more business-friendly.

We have committed to spend up to US$75 billion over the next 12 or so years on transportation and other infrastructure projects. There are currently six railway-construction projects due for completion by 2007, and several more are planned for completion by 2016. In order to maintain our position as the world's busiest and most-efficient container port, work has started on a new Container Terminal Number 9 that will gradually come on stream from 2002 until completion in 2004. Phase 1 of Hong Kong Disneyland, which lies at the heart of our tourism development program, is due to be completed by 2005. In order to meet the growing need for world-class convention and exhibition activities, a second convention and exhibition center will be built adjacent to the Hong Kong International Airport. For telecommunications, broadband connections to homes and office buildings are among the best you will find anywhere. Liberalization of the telecommunications market over the past six years has also provided consumers with far greater choice and cheaper prices.

Some infrastructure projects are geared to facilitate a closer economic cooperation with our hinterland in the Pearl River Delta, a market of 40 million people that we cannot afford to ignore. These projects will enhance the development of Hong Kong as a regional transport and logistics hub. Projects would include an express rail link to Guangzhou, a port rail link from our container port feeding into the mainland's railway network, and additional road and railway crossings to the mainland.

In 10 years from now Hong Kong will be a very different — and a vastly superior — city in terms of physical infrastructure.

But to make Hong Kong a truly business-friendly city, concrete steps are being taken that will bear results quickly. Business-relevant bureaucratic procedures will be simplified. Assistance to small and medium-sized enterprises will be greatly increased, including financial assistance through various loan programs. It is being made easier for foreign and mainland companies to come to Hong Kong to set up offices and headquarters. And more is being done to enhance the quality of life for those coming from overseas to work and live here. We will also make it easier and faster for multinationals and local companies to import foreign and mainland talent into Hong Kong.

On the environment front, concerted efforts over the past two years have achieved good initial results. Most diesel taxis have been put off the road, and we are working with the transport sector to clean up the emissions of other diesel vehicles. As a result of these initiatives, the air in Hong Kong these days is much cleaner. We are also working closely with our counterparts across the border to treat regional air pollution. Hong Kong and adjoining Guangdong Province have agreed to reach a consensus by April 2002 on a joint plan to implement long-term measures to improve the air quality of the entire region. In addition, the first stage of a major sewerage system was recently completed, which will greatly improve the quality of water in our greatest natural asset, the beautiful Victoria Harbour.

Urban renewal is also being given a shot in the arm with the setting up of a more powerful Urban Renewal Authority. The Authority will push ahead with urban redevelopment while, at the same time, striving to preserve important cultural-heritage sites.

On the social-policy side, our commitments to the elderly, the handicapped and other less-fortunate members of our community continue unabated. In good times, we want people to be able to share in that prosperity. In trying times, we want to lessen the pain. A strong tripartite partnership — the coming together of government, business and the volunteer or "third" sector — is essential for the effective development of our social programs. To foster this partnership, a Community Investment and Inclusion Fund will be established with an initial injection of US$40 million of government money. The fund will also accept private and corporate donations, and will support grassroots activities that aim to spur volunteerism, empower individuals and groups, strengthen families and promote healthy lifestyles for all.

We are developing a more accountable system of government, which is especially important during difficult times when the administration needs to respond better to changing times and evolving community needs.

There are other dimensions of good governance on which we are working hard to improve: a government that delivers better service at lower cost and a smaller government that does not stand in the way of the market and the individual; a government that promotes citizen participation and democracy, in full accordance with the letter and spirit of our constitution — the Basic Law; and a government that stresses the rule of law, safeguarding the freedoms that its citizens enjoy, as well as public security, especially in times that demand heightened vigilance.

Hong Kong is once again facing many uncertainties and challenges. This is nothing new. In every decade over the past 60 years, Hong Kong has faced and overcome many difficulties. Each time we have emerged stronger and more competitive.

There is good reason to be confident about the future at this juncture. We have a clear vision and a targeted strategy. We are endowed with distinct advantages — our unique geographical position and strengths as an international center for finance, trade, transport and logistics, and tourism. We can draw upon the hard work, creativity, entrepreneurial spirit and self-reliance of the Hong Kong people. And finally, we can leverage the support of the Central Government and the huge potential and opportunities made available by the rapid expansion of the mainland economy, particularly in the Pearl River Delta.

We are confident that Hong Kong can not only become one of the most important cities in China but also the world city of Asia — a community that is progressive, stable and free; where opportunity abounds and quality is premium.

Japan Takes on Challenges of Structural Reform

Heizo Takenaka
Minister of State for Economic and Fiscal Policy, Japan

STRUCTURAL PROBLEMS UNDERLYING THE PERSISTENT ECONOMIC WEAKNESS

In 2001, the global economy suffered the impacts of the terrorist attacks in the U.S. as well as the spread of the recession in IT throughout the rest of the economy. The global economy has not as yet reached the stage where we can firmly anticipate its complete recovery.

The Japanese economy began recovering from early 1999. But that recovery was lackluster and was, in fact, the shortest-lived recovery ever in the post-war period. Since the end of 2000, the Japanese economy has been in yet another recession.

This persistent weakness of the Japanese economy can be largely ascribed to structural problems, especially the problem of non-performing loans (NPLs). The NPLs of banks and the excessive debts of the corporate sector have been dragging down the Japanese economy. The disposal of non-performing loans is necessary to reallocate the resources, such as labor and capital, from inefficient, unprofitable companies and sectors to more productive uses.

For the Japanese economy to get back on a growth path, it is also necessary to promote structural reform, such as deregulation, fiscal reform, and reform of the pension and medical-insurance systems.

On top of its structural problems, the Japanese economy suffers from cyclical downturn due mainly to the slowdown of the global economy. Industrial production and business investment, especially in the IT-related sector, have declined significantly. The unemployment rate reached a post-war record of 5.5% in November 2001.

To cope with the worsening economic conditions, the government has formulated two economic-policy packages that are backed by two supplementary budgets for fiscal year 2001. The first is the "Advanced Reform Program", launched in October, which includes new job-creation measures, the formation of a safety net for job security and small and medium enterprises (SMEs), and measures addressing the NPL problems. In December 2001, the government adopted the second package, the "Emergency Action Program for Structural Reform", in order to accelerate structural reforms. The Action Program is accompanied by the second draft supplementary budget, which is to be debated in the Diet at the beginning of February 2002. An allocation of ¥4.1 trillion (US$34 billion) to social infrastructures will facilitate structural reforms. It is estimated that this increase will lift GDP by 0.9% over a year.

In line with the government's structural-reform measures, it is hoped that the Bank of Japan (BOJ) will continue to adopt appropriate and flexible monetary policies to stem deflation, and that the government and the BOJ will work together in fighting deflation.

With such combined efforts, the government expects that the Japanese economy will start a recovery driven by private demand some time in the second half of financial year 2002. However, economic growth in that period will likely be as low as zero.

The much-hoped-for recovery will likely be fragile, unless economic fundamentals are strengthened. Structural reform is fundamental to solving the problems besetting the Japanese economy.

THE KOIZUMI REFORM UNDER WAY

Japan's Policy-Making Process Has Changed

Since its inauguration in spring 2001, the administration of Prime Minister Junichiro Koizumi has been living up to its pledge to push through reform, buoyed by strong public support.

In understanding the Koizumi Reform, it is very important to realize that the policy-making process in Japan has changed to a considerable degree. In order to implement the structural reform, strong political leadership is essential to fight against vested interests. Before Mr. Koizumi took office, no one could have imagined that the Japan Highway Public Corporation would be privatized, that the Government Housing Loan Corporation could be discontinued, and that expenditure on public corporations could be reduced by over ¥1 trillion in a year. The Koizumi Reform has progressed under the Prime Minister's strong leadership.

His strong leadership is, fortunately, supported by the administrative reorganization introduced a year ago. The Council on Economic and Fiscal Policy (CEFP) was then created in the Cabinet Office, and has taken a key role in the formulation of economic and fiscal policies. The CEFP has provided Mr. Koizumi with the machinery for his leadership. The CEFP, presided over by the Prime Minister, comprises economic ministers and 'wise men' from the private sector. I am in charge of steering the CEFP to make sure that the Council underpins the Prime Minister's leadership.

Moving Forward on Structural Reform

In June 2001, the government adopted a key document setting out all the basic directions of the Koizumi reform program. Drafted by the CEFP, the document — Basic Policies for Macroeconomic Management — has as its basic concept "no growth without reform". To take these policies forward, a Reform Schedule was formulated in September. The Schedule is a road map for reform, putting in place a clear timetable for the implementation of policy specifics.

The CEFP submitted another key document addressing economic and fiscal management over the medium term — Reform and Prospects — to the Prime Minister in the middle of January 2002. This lays out targets for fiscal consolidation and the medium-term policy framework focusing on structural reforms. It also includes a likely scenario for economic growth over the next decade.

The period of intensive adjustment over the next few years will be an important preparation for achieving private-demand-driven economic growth. During this phase, overcoming deflation will be of great importance. The government and the BOJ will need to work in unison in fighting deflation. It is expected that economic growth will stay low for the next two years or so, but subsequently the economy will pick up and approach a 2% growth for the rest of the next decade.

Non-Performing Loans

The NPL problem has been a drag on the Japanese economy. The Reform Schedule includes a set of measures for accelerating the disposal of NPLs and revitalizing the financial sector. The Financial Service Agency (FSA) has introduced special inspections, the purpose of which is to ensure adequate loan classification and secure sufficient loan-loss provisions. The Resolution and Collection Corporation (RCC) will purchase NPLs more actively because, unlike before, the RCC is now allowed to purchase NPLs at market prices. The RCC and the

Development Bank of Japan will support private investors in establishing deleveraging funds, which will facilitate the restructuring of debt-ridden companies. As a result of these efforts, the resolution of the NPL problem will be steadily attained.

Deregulation and Reform of Public Corporations

Creating demand by fostering competition and innovation is crucial for revitalizing the economy. In particular, the Japanese government has been undertaking deregulation in health care, social welfare, childcare, education and other fields directly linked to people's daily lives. While it has long been considered that the market mechanism cannot work well in these areas, the Koizumi administration thinks differently.

In December 2001, the government also announced a plan for the rationalization of public corporations. Under this plan, 62 public corporations (40% of the total) will be, in principle, privatized or abolished. In particular, seven public corporations — which have been dependent on substantial government expenditures — are now slated to be privatized or prioritized ahead of other public corporations. In the next fiscal year's budget, the government is set to cut spending for public corporations by as much as ¥1 trillion, a cut of 20%.

Fiscal Reform

The draft budget for the 2002 financial year is formulated on the principle of limiting the issuance of government bonds to no more than ¥30 trillion. Under this principle, the draft budget prioritizes spending, allocating greater funds to priority areas such as measures to meet the demands of an ageing society; the promotion of science, technology and education; the revitalization of the metropolitan region; and revitalization of the regions, taking account of environmental considerations. On the other hand, expenditure on public works is to be reduced by more than 10% while prioritizing projects. The draft budget also reduces ODA expenditure by 10%, and introduces cut-backs in medical service compensations for hospitals and doctors. Total expenditures by local governments will be reduced as well.

Furthermore, the Reform and Prospects presently being deliberated will set the stage for improving the quality of government expenditures over the medium term, through better prioritization of budget allocations and the active use of private-finance initiatives (PFIs). The government will keep government expenditures in check. Implementation of these policies will enable the Japanese government to achieve surplus in the "primary balance" of the central and local governments combined shortly after the year 2010. The ratio of government debts to GDP will start to decline at around the same time.

Eight months have passed since Mr. Koizumi took office. Over this relatively short period, his administration has taken some powerful steps for structural reform. Yet, this journey of structural reform has only just begun. To move forward on these structural reforms, the CEFP will focus particularly on tax reform, new policies to rejuvenate Japanese industries and reform of public financial institutions.

JAPAN'S ROLE FOR THE FUTURE OF ASIA

While Asian economies are now facing difficulties amid economic stagnation, they have by no means lost their economic dynamism. Many IT products are produced in the region and IT literacy is very high in Asia. With the advance of globalization, goods, services, people, capital and technologies actively transcend national borders, resulting in higher levels of economic interdependence in this region. China's entry to the WTO will further accelerate the progress of globalization.

Asia's economic dynamism will continue to be a driving force for the global economy. Japan's solid recovery can contribute to the long-term growth of Asian economies.

As the Asian crisis in 1997 has highlighted, Asian economies must reinforce their economic fundamentals and improve their financial systems in order to achieve the best possible performance in the new era of globalization. Japan is ready to play an important role in global economic management by helping to reinforce Asian economies in a number of ways.

Firstly, Japan's foreign direct investment (FDI) in other Asian economies is conducive to promoting their growth through transferring capital and technologies. Japan's FDI in Asia has been expanding rapidly, and it will contribute to promoting growth. While there are concerns in Japan about industrial hollowing out, Japan must overcome such concerns by promoting domestic investment through its own structural adjustments.

Secondly, Japan is prepared to promote bilateral or regional arrangements for investment and trade liberalization in tandem with multilateral liberalization. The Japan-Singapore Economic Partnership Agreement is a case in point. Another case is a meeting of IT ministers in the Asian region. I took the lead in organizing a first get-together of Asian IT ministers to share best practices and stave off the digital divide. We are of the view that bilateral and regional arrangements will complement multilateral frameworks such as the WTO, enhancing the prosperity of this region.

Thirdly, the Asian crisis highlighted the importance of structural adjustment in each economy and Asian economies need to implement structural reforms. We are hoping that the Japanese economy will set a new model for growth by creating a market-friendly economy through structural reforms in which the private sector, not the government, takes the lead.

Heir to Capitalism with Chinese Characteristics

Christine Loh
Founder and Chief Executive Officer,
Civic Exchange, Hong Kong SAR

It is easy to be pessimistic, especially when it involves someone else's misfortune. It is fashionable for supposedly knowledgeable people around the world to suggest that Hong Kong is "finished" — that it will end up playing second fiddle to rising Shanghai. It is particularly easy to have such doubts when Hong Kong folks are wallowing in the winter of discontent.

Yet, the Hong Kong story is far from over. Arguably, Hong Kong is the face of capitalism with Chinese characteristics. The southern Chinese were already enormously successful traders and entrepreneurs in the 19th century, expanding their bamboo network all over the world. Despite the collapse of the state, businessmen did well. Although the Chinese state reasserted itself with the founding of the People's Republic of China, its experiment with Soviet-style socialism essentially killed market activities. Hong Kong has always been a critical part of the bamboo network and, with the closing of China's door to the world in the 1950s, Hong Kong became the undisputed crossroads for the Chinese-speaking world. Capitalism with Chinese characteristics took root and prospered.

When China reopened for business in 1979, Hong Kong played an essential role in revitalizing the private sector in South China. State policy enabled Hong Kong's manufacturing sector to move across the border, thereby expanding its scale significantly over the years. Today, Hong Kong is the most impressive light-manufacturing powerhouse in the world. The problem is that most people have forgotten about it because manufacturing does not physically take place here anymore. Out of sight is out of mind. However, Hong Kong remains a production giant because its companies are the world's most impressive managers of global manufacturing in areas such as electronics, toys and garments. Hong Kong has become a services center providing producer services to support its manufacturing prowess.

Hong Kong remains a city with a mission. As a Special Administrative Region, it is pushing market mechanisms deeper into China. Its services sector is supporting the further opening of Chinese markets as the nation opens up as a member of the World Trade Organization (WTO). A China without Hong Kong would have found it harder to achieve what it has since 1979.

HONG KONG'S IMPORTANCE

Hong Kong remains the place to watch for many reasons. First, it is a barometer of Beijing's temperatures. The return of Hong Kong to Chinese sovereignty was an important step in the evolution of China's political identity vis-à-vis the international community. Indeed, 1997 provided a special opportunity for China to adapt to greater openness and tolerance and, since then, Beijing has shown the world that it has basically left Hong Kong to administer itself. That relaxed attitude demonstrated the capacity of Chinese leaders to understand how capitalist Hong Kong works.

Second, Hong Kong companies are China's best-managed companies. The manufacturers transformed South China into the world's most competitive production region. Hong Kong is now part of a strong metropolitan economy with the Pearl River Delta (PRD). Hong Kong companies are investing in other parts of the country, including in Eastern China and Shanghai. With a "home" market at last, within the next decade Hong Kong-based companies may grow dramatically in size as they develop brand name products.

Third, Hong Kong's solid regulatory environment has produced institutions of real strengths. For example, the banks are sound, unlike their counterparts in many countries around the region. Its legal system is also an enormous asset as the city transforms itself to a full service economy ahead of any other city in the region. The Hong Kong Trade Development Council noted in 1999 that: "Hong Kong's competitiveness has depended on its dynamism and its ability to evolve and change under pressure of market forces. As in other major, successful metropolitan economies, low valued-added activities have been crowded out by high value-added activities. This is a sign of progress, not decline."

FIRE THE IMAGINATION

Despite their undoubted strengths, Hong Kong people are suffering from collective depression. Indeed, we are overdoing it. There is actually much cause for optimism. Hong Kong's most serious problem is a failure of the imagination. In order to climb out of the dark hole in which we seem to be trapped, we need to help ourselves to see new opportunities.

These opportunities rely on Hong Kong's ability to retain its status as a superlative trader. Hong Kong must collaborate with Guangdong Province to develop the PRD into the world's most flexible and efficient processing area and ensure that it is capable of rapid delivery and quick adaptation to new global demands. Hong Kong must also adopt sustainable development practices to transform the PRD into the preferred investment area for multinationals and into preferred living areas for the growing middle class. Moreover, as more people in emerging economies enjoy middle-class status, the demand for products and services will continue to grow. Hong Kong companies are well equipped to provide high-quality products and services to meet these new demands.

Hong Kong traders and manufacturers are already extremely efficient in using PRD resources for global processing and are likely to outpace future competitors in other parts of the world as a result of technological upgrades. These facts have been obscured by seemingly more exciting technical advances, such as those in biotechnology and information technology. It would be a mistake, however, to ignore the continuous and incremental success of Hong Kong businesses in making basic improvements to a range of essentials, such as technologically sophisticated textiles, well-designed garments and innovative day-to-day electronics, all sold at good prices.

THE GOOD OLD DAYS

Much of the uncertainty that Hong Kong people are now experiencing is due to the collapse of the old economic franchise, which was based on a property bubble, during the 1997 Asian financial crisis. For more than a decade, Hong Kong had enjoyed an easy ride as property prices shot through the roof and large numbers of people made money by speculating on housing for a quick buck. The stock market was another easy route for making money as everyone took advantage of the inflated property market and bought stocks in property companies. Hong Kong people accumulated wealth and felt good. At the height of the economic boom, many ordinary people earned more from these activities than from their regular jobs. This meant that a large number of people had additional sources of income to fuel consumption, prompting heavy spending in shops and restaurants. With the decline in the property market, people have begun to feel poor and prefer to hold onto money. As a result, retail has suffered. Disinflation has set in. There is no mood for spending.

The political transition from British to Chinese rule in 1997 was relatively calm; Hong Kong's economic transition, on the other hand, has been turbulent and prolonged. In effect, the Asian financial crisis was like a whirlwind that brought many regional economies to their knees. Hong Kong survived, but not before asset prices fell by more than 50%. The Hong Kong Monetary Authority estimated that 60,000 homeowners bought at the height of the market in the run-up to 1997 and are now experiencing "negative equity", meaning that the value of the mortgage exceeds the value of the property. Even those in more fortunate circumstances have experienced a drop in asset values and are feeling much poorer in consequence. Stocks have also taken a beating and the bust of the dot-com industry has not helped to improve sentiments.

Starting in early 2000, Hong Kong's economy seemed to show signs of recovery, but any progress was set back by the events of September 11, 2001. The Hong Kong Special Administrative Region (HKSAR) Government has a sizable budget deficit for 2001–2002 and has warned that jobs will continue to disappear before they reappear. A quick rebound in the U.S. economy will help but the pain will not disappear overnight.

A major cause of collective depression in Hong Kong is uncertainty about the possibilities for a new economic franchise. Whatever the formula for the new franchise, it will require more brains and brawn than simply speculating for a windfall. There are fears that Hong Kong people have gotten soft — perhaps they have forgotten what it is like to work hard and move fast to make a buck. Hong Kong's education system is another source of concern. Whatever the basis for a new franchise, Hong Kong will require well-educated people expert at adapting to continuous change and competing in the "new economy" of a globalized world. Employers often complain that the abilities of the Hong Kong workforce are not up to scratch. They prefer to recruit on the mainland and elsewhere.

THE MAINLAND: FRIEND OR FOE?

Prior to 1997, conventional wisdom held that Hong Kong could assist with the economic modernization of China. Hong Kong people saw mainlanders as country bumpkins and poor cousins. Today, the poor cousins are catching up at a furious — some would even say breathless

— pace. With its huge population, China is even capable of supplying Hong Kong's entire workforce. And given the economic beating that Hong Kongers have taken over the last few years, the mainland is now a formidable competitor. As increasing numbers of low-end, white-collar jobs move across the border, Hong Kong workers feel increasingly threatened by their compatriots.

Moreover, the leadership in the central government and in some local governments, such as Shanghai, appears to be very competent, and even better than that in Hong Kong. After all, despite dire predictions of civil unrest in China during the post-Tianamen period, China has enjoyed a decade of political stability and has continued to push its reform agenda. Furthermore, China's international status has improved as a result of its pragmatic and relatively restrained approach to foreign affairs, including its post-1997 handling of Hong Kong. The combination of these factors has resulted in a gradual improvement in morale among Chinese people, most of whom feel good about China's position in the world. This is particularly true at a moment when the Chinese economy is chugging along and China is the new flavor of the month, even though the world economy is still sluggish. Overall, this situation is good news for Hong Kong, but many Hong Kong people have reacted negatively because of doubts about their own ability to stay ahead.

The perceived lack of political leadership in Hong Kong only exacerbates the general lack of self-confidence. The HKSAR has only been self-governing since 1997 and had no professional politicians while under British rule. Leading members of society were co-opted to help run Hong Kong by filling relatively minor positions and had no real power in the decision-making process. Those who were "helpful" were appointed to higher positions on various committees and councils, but the agenda was controlled by the colonial administration. There were no direct elections for the legislature until 1991 and even the post-1991 elections opened only a minority of seats to general vote. Today, only 24 out of 60 seats are elected directly. The majority of the current legislature was elected indirectly by an 800-member election committee and various functional constituencies, made up mainly of business and professional interests.

Today, top decision-makers are learning on the job — literally — which is tough on them and tough on Hong Kong people. While many of Hong Kong's new leaders are long-time civil servants, they function more like glorified administrators than like politicians. Leaders have not acquired the skills for devising policies and selling them to the public that are necessary in a modern government. This inability to articulate and market a compelling vision for the future is felt keenly at a time when Hong Kong needs to outline a new economic franchise and social contract and has led to a lackluster view of the current leadership. The situation is complicated by the fact that those who hold power cannot claim political legitimacy, as they were not elected by the Hong Kong people. Thus, the collective depression about Hong Kong's future is caused by a confluence of external events, the resultant need for domestic restructuring and a common belief that the current leadership is not up to scratch.

THINGS ARE NOT SO BAD

It is useful to examine Hong Kong's performance immediately prior to the terrorist attacks in the United States because it provides a snapshot of Hong Kong's response to the fallout from the Asian financial crisis. Even before September 11, world interest in Hong Kong markets was declining. Hong Kong's exports had dropped, although the drop was relatively modest. Yet its export of services grew 6.2% in the first quarter of 2001 and by 5.3% in the second quarter. While the quantity of cargo declined, transport services actually improved. Overall, Hong Kong was able to maintain its margin in re-export trade. What does this tell us?

This information suggests that the Asian financial crisis may turn out to be a blessing in disguise. The need for quick restructuring in Hong Kong companies was a shock to the system. Weaker interests were eliminated. Some are barely hanging on and may not weather the crisis. Others, however, improved efficiency by improving productivity, reducing debt and improving liquidity. As rentals dropped, those who signed new leases enjoyed lower accommodation costs. The cost of hiring was also much cheaper. Unlike other regional economies, Hong Kong had to adjust to economic change through price deflation rather than currency deflation as its exchange rate is fixed to the U.S. dollar. The adjustment was sharp and painful but enabled the economy to head in the right direction relatively quickly. Hong Kong was able to regain price competitiveness with its neighbors in a short time. However, people remember only the pain of the adjustment period and remain depressed about the situation. After tough times, people continue to be cautious, even when they may have gained a more favorable position.

For example, while it remains fashionable to complain about local costs, the truth is that costs are now quite competitive in relation to the level of services available in Hong Kong. It would be misleading to compare Hong Kong prices with those of cities that are still unable to compete on the same scale. Rents have dropped substantially. At least in the private sector, salaries have decreased by a large margin. No decent employer would fire its entire staff to re-hire at lower rates. Therefore, businesses that are still living out old tenancies and have kept original staff face lower overall costs, although the cost base has not improved.

THE NEW FRANCHISE

It would be a mistake to see property as the sole basis of Hong Kong's previous economic franchise. The older franchise was based on trade and Hong Kong today is still a superlative trader. But trade lost its appeal as a sexy story some time ago. It seemed too "old economy" for anyone to get too excited about it. Yet manufacturing, processing and trade are the lifeblood of daily business. While Hong Kong manufacturers have not developed many retail brands, a few brands have become regional and even global names, including Giordano, G2000, Esprit and Episode. Many more Hong Kong brand names carry solid weight in the wholesale retail industry. These companies produce retail goods for the world market and own a large number of factories across the border in South China, particularly in the PRD. They represent a steady business opportunity and many of the better companies have upgraded over the years and are now quite sophisticated. During the 1980s and 1990s, however, steady income from retail trading seemed much less exciting than the fast buck generated by property deals or the dot-com industry, both of which are now in the dust heap.

These companies combine manufacturing capability across the border with higher-end service providers in Hong Kong and serve as a model for Hong Kong's new economic franchise. The formula for this new franchise is economic integration with the PRD. Through integration, this area has the potential to become the world's most efficient and flexible processing zone with the ability to adapt quickly to changing world demands. The fact that mainland China is price-competitive for almost all products is to Hong Kong's advantage. The mainland is not a competitor but a collaborator. It needs the expertise developed by Hong Kong companies over the years in order to work the supply-and-demand chain more efficiently.

The challenge for policy-makers in Hong Kong is to ensure good communication with the Guangdong authorities so that both sides receive maximum benefits from collaboration. If Guangdong implements policies designed to undercut Hong Kong, both sides stand to lose. If, on the other hand, the Guangdong authorities recognize the long-term benefits of improving efficiency in the area, then policies should reinforce this vision.

Construction of the physical infrastructure needed to promote efficiency should begin only when a clear understanding between Hong Kong and Guangdong authorities has been reached. At present, too many people in Hong Kong see Guangdong as a competitor only and are attempting to concentrate hub economic activities in tiny Hong Kong by prioritizing road and bridge construction.

HIGH-END SERVICES

In addition to the tremendous possibilities for economic development in the PRD, Hong Kong itself has a number of potential growth areas. This is true even in traditional areas of growth, such as the property-development sector, which needs to reject Third World standards of building and make Hong Kong a center for the design and construction of a new generation of sustainable buildings that are user-friendly and comfortable, that have good internal air circulation and lighting, and that are energy-efficient. There is sufficient expertise in Hong Kong to achieve this goal and property-development groups only need to be nudged forward by new government policies that reward innovation rather than speed in putting up concrete.

Another area with growth potential is the environmental sector. Given the mainland's growing interest in "cleaning up", Hong Kong could become a major center for environmental business. This sector is very broad and includes consultants, academics and scientists, and retail groups. Growth potential in this area is best demonstrated by the business opportunities associated with air-quality control. Besides various technologies for emission reduction, there is an exciting future for other aspects of air-quality management, including collaboration with the mainland to reduce cross-border pollution. If Hong Kong wakes up to these opportunities, it can work with Guangdong Province to improve air quality in the entire South China region. A similar strategy could be adopted for improving water quality. Staking a claim in the environmental sector is forward-looking and has the added advantage of enabling Hong Kong and mainland cooperation in a way that is mutually beneficial and addresses top government priorities regarding pollution control.

Education is already a growth area in Hong Kong, although it is now dominated by the public sector, which has failed to provide a system that is sufficiently flexible in helping young people to adapt to today's fast-changing world. The HKSAR Government seems to have recognized this fact and is willing to allow more private-sector involvement in education. A greater variety of education services at all levels will be necessary for

Hong Kong to upgrade its human resources. Many of the new and innovative ideas must come from the private sector, which should view investment in education as a new line of business.

If decision-makers can outline a plan for economic recovery that not only results in higher productivity but is also sustainable in environmental and social terms then this will provide Hong Kong people with an important boost in confidence. This plan would allow Hong Kong to be something bigger than it has been in the past. Seizing the opportunity to act on it will take a positive act of the imagination. Even if the public sector is slow to catch on, there is no reason why the private sector cannot take the lead as many of the local and regional opportunities for growth can be privately funded. Hong Kong needs to fire up its imagination and look ahead in order to recreate itself and enjoy a new lease on life.

CONCLUSION

Hong Kong remains the city to watch as a barometer of China's development. It also provides a fascinating window into how a city transforms itself into a full-service economy at breakneck speed. As the center of the Pearl River Delta region, it is a world-scale competitor in light industries and, with China probably becoming the world's factory, Hong Kong companies are best placed to manage that production capability. Furthermore, Hong Kong companies, already used to meeting the needs of multinational clients, will probably lead the pack in bringing better occupational safety and environmental standards to the mainland. Finally, it remains a free city, open to the world, where mainland visitors are going in increasing numbers and coming into contact with ideas that are still sensitive on the mainland. Just reading Hong Kong newspapers, with their more critical reporting of Chinese affairs, must already be quite an experience.

Ensuring Good Corporate Governance in Asia

Lilia R. Bautista
Chairperson, Securities and Exchange Commission,
The Philippines

 The globalization of the marketplace has ushered in an era in which traditional dimensions of corporate governance are being challenged by circumstances and events that are having an international impact. Inadequate corporate governance and standards of transparency were considered to be among the factors that weakened investor confidence and contributed to the Asian economic crisis and its aftermath.

With growing global competition for capital, investment funds will follow the path to those markets that have adopted efficient governance standards, such as acceptable levels of investor protection and board practices, as well as satisfactory accounting and disclosure standards. Investor confidence stems in part from a country's or market's reputation for good corporate governance. If investors are not confident with the level of disclosure, or if a country's accounting and reporting standards are perceived as lax, funds will flow elsewhere. Thus, the ability of the market to raise capital in this highly competitive environment is prejudiced.

Good corporate governance is imperative for strengthening the financial system. The appropriate reforms can help to lower the risks of loan defaults through a system of legal compliance and oversight over key and critical corporate operations under the care of a diligent and independent board of directors. It would be simplistic for anyone to presume that independent directors in an autonomous board can make all the difference. But a proposition can be advanced that directors who place their primary loyalty with the corporation, all of its shareholders and other stakeholders, and are made accountable for doing so, can lower the risks of abuse. Among these are DOSRI accounts (directors, officers and stockholders and related interests), behest loans, insider trading and self-dealing.

Good corporate governance is imperative for a globally competitive corporate sector. As globalization continues to impact on the ease and cost of moving goods, services and capital across markets, firms need to continually find new sources of competitive advantage. Assessing a firm's competitive position within this environment must take into account its capability to sustain growth and add value to all stakeholders. Developing this capability takes more than just good business strategy. It requires a corporate culture and policy that respects the independence of directors, promotes long-term shareholder value, and recognizes accountability to stakeholders beyond its shareholders. Furthermore, this may seem a paradox where strong and efficient markets need strong and efficient regulatory regimes.

THE STRUCTURE OF ASIAN COMPANIES

Close family ties in Asia resulted in closed family businesses. Historically and sociologically, Asian firms are principally family-owned and/or controlled. As businesses grew and required public listing, control by families remained significant. Based on a study made of 2,980 public companies in nine East Asian countries – Hong Kong, Indonesia, Japan, Korea, Malaysia, the Philippines, Singapore, Taiwan and Thailand – more than half of publicly-listed companies continue to be controlled by families. Japanese corporations were more widely held than others in the region. Indonesian and Thai firms were mainly family-controlled. State control was significant in Singapore, Malaysia, Indonesia and Thailand. At the extreme are the Philippines and Indonesia, where 17.1% and 16.7% respectively of the total value of listed corporate assets could be traced to the ultimate control of a single family. The 10 largest family-controlled businesses in these countries, as well as in Thailand, control half of the corporate assets surveyed. In Hong Kong and Korea, the 10 largest family-controlled businesses control one-third of the corporate sectors.

The result of such sociology is that voting rights exceeded fund cash-flow rights (ownership rights), creating a lack of transparency in board action and management since families do not feel the need for public disclosure. As a result, minority shareholders are pretty much kept in the dark as to the actual status of the corporations of which they are part-owners precisely because the large shareholders dominate decision-making activities involving the company. There is therefore a clamor for building the necessary structures for governance and the adoption of the appropriate governance behavior, especially in jurisdictions where ownership is family-concentrated.

Although corporate governance received much attention in East Asia as a result of the 1997–1999 Asian financial crises, it is now widely regarded as essential for sustained economic recovery. Corporate governance is important not only because we want to avert another crisis but because corporate governance principles, when strictly applied, bring about efficiency in operations and improved profitability.

In terms of ownership and control, it is desirable to have companies that are broadly owned. Not only must they be broadly owned, but they must also protect the interest of minority shareholders and ensure that shareholders are treated equitably. Family-owned companies must open up more shares to the public, as most regulators in the region are advocating.

In managing the corporation, it is imperative for the governance function (which is the responsibility of the board of directors) to be separate from the management function (which is the responsibility of the CEO and operating officers). The board of directors must be able to function in an independent and competent manner, with oversight over management. Corporate boards can be made more independent with the election of independent or external directors and the creation of board committees. For family-owned companies in Asia, this has been a difficult process.

Ample mechanisms for disclosure, transparency, and external audits must be in place, comprising professional accounting and auditing standards, strong disclosure requirements and active monitoring by both regulators and independent entities. Family-owned companies are naturally reluctant to disclose their business to the public.

Corporations must have access to broad capital, provided by highly developed and professionally regulated financial markets. In Asia, there has been too much dependence on bank loans. Accessing capital in the financial markets to most family-owned companies might mean loss of control. One notes that the public float in listed companies is rather small in Asia; hence, the move to require a higher percentage of total shares for public offerings.

DEFINING CORPORATE GOVERNANCE

There are several ways to define corporate governance. According to Stilpon Nestor of the OECD, we can think of corporate governance as being made up of two aspects.

On the one hand, corporate governance encompasses the relationships and ensuing patterns of behavior between different agents in a limited-liability corporation. These patterns of behavior define the manner in which managers, shareholders, employees, creditors and key customers interact with each other and shape a company's strategy. This is the behavioral side of corporate governance.

On the other hand, corporate governance also entails the set of rules, laws and requirements that frame private behavior. These include the overarching regulatory framework governing corporations, as well as voluntary private codes of conduct and standards. This is the normative side of corporate governance and is also called political governance.

The Asian Development Bank has defined a corporate-governance system as consisting of a set of rules that define the relationships between shareholders, managers, creditors, the government and other stakeholders and a set of mechanisms that help, directly and indirectly, enforce these rules.

It is not enough, therefore, to ensure that managers, officers, employees, creditors and key customers practice good governance because the state and its policies establish the basic foundation by which all corporations and their stakeholders are to be held accountable.

These two aspects are not mutually exclusive; rather, they define each other through an iterative process. The normative side helps define the behavioral side, while the behavioral side will cause the normative side to evolve in response to new needs.

Thus, the institution of corporate-governance reforms must begin from two sources: the state, through political governance in enacting reforms in line with changes in the global environment; and the corporate stakeholders, through corporate governance, by admitting that changes can only occur by policing themselves.

Having defined corporate governance, we now try to establish why corporate governance is fundamental to development. Corporate governance has four major benefits which are vital to any country's development agenda.

First, it strengthens corporate fundamentals so as to promote and maintain investor confidence. After all, people can only be persuaded to invest if they are assured that a company's fundamentals are sound. By promoting investor confidence, corporate governance generates the second benefit of creating an investment climate that attracts capital, allowing a country to broaden and deepen its financial and capital base.

Third, corporate governance promotes efficiency and improves profitability. By promoting a culture of transparency and accountability, corporate governance forces management to allocate resources in a way that will maximize gains. Finally, corporate governance promotes social responsibility, by taking into account the interests of a wide range of stakeholders.

Ultimately, these immediate benefits will reduce the vulnerability of the economy to external shocks, which will in turn bring broader welfare gains to society.

PILLARS OF CORPORATE GOVERNANCE

To be able to reap the benefits of corporate governance, however, certain critical elements must be present. We can conceive of these elements as influencing the four pillars of corporate governance, namely: 1) corporate ownership and control; 2) corporate management; 3) disclosure, transparency and external audits; and 4) corporate financing.

Corporate ownership and control play a major role in shaping the system of corporate governance. In Asia, because of concentrated ownership, the owners have a direct hand in controlling the company. They decide who will sit as members of the board, who will be named as executive officers and managers, what policies will be adopted and how they will be implemented. Presumably they are likely to act in their own best interests, leaving the minority shareholders subject to prejudicial actions. In the alternative of diluted ownership, the control and management will be directly proportionate to the degree of activism of shareholders. The more aware the shareholders are, the greater the monitoring of corporate conduct. Thus, more and more governments are promoting programs on shareholder rights.

In either case, the second pillar of corporate management comes to the fore and, with it, the requirement that corporate directors be made aware of and accept their powers and responsibilities, their rights and duties. Directors in corporate boards need to know what is expected of them and the legal and regulatory ways in which they are accountable. Director education is an important step in this regard.

The most important function of the board of directors is to monitor and oversee the management of the company. Admittedly, although the authority of the corporation to act devolves upon its board, the actual management and implementation of corporate policies and decisions are vested in persons other than the board members. Many of the problems that corporate-governance reforms are seeking to address came about as a result of mismanagement by corporate officers. Chief executive officers were, at one point in time in the corporate world, untouchable, for as long as they delivered what the board of directors wanted — profits. The trust vested in them by the board was absolute and their actions were not questioned, until it dawned upon the board that the profits could have been even bigger, if only the manner of management had been less pompous or frivolous. Recent events in the corporate world have shown that these CEOs were not indispensable and their removal from their positions could only evidence the active engagement of the board in monitoring executive actions.

In Philippine culture, because of the family-concentrated ownership, executive officers generally are people who are either relatives or good friends of the board members or shareholders. Sons, daughters, nephews, nieces or cousins are brought in to manage the family corporation. They are taught and learn the ropes during the course of their employment. However, the trend has been changing. Following international standards of corporate governance, a law has been enacted which requires the appointment of independent directors in publicly-listed corporations. As this is a relatively new law, it remains to be seen how it is implemented and what advantages will accrue to the corporation.

Directly related to the corporate monitoring of management are the requirements of full disclosure, transparency and external audits. The information necessary for the board and the corporate stakeholders to make an intelligent decision with respect to their corporations depends to a large extent on the legal and internal systems of disclosure and audit.

Corporate financing, in its most ideal sense and as a pillar of corporate governance, should equalize the relationship between the management and its shareholders because the manner by which financing is acquired and how it is used ultimately affects the financial situation of the corporation.

Financing in family-owned corporations used to be mainly internal. With the growth of business opportunities and the internationalization of business activities, external financing became more prevalent. In most Asian countries, including the Philippines, bank loans are the most accessible forms of external financing because of the lack of a well-developed capital market. As a form of external control, banks have the resources to monitor company performance. Necessarily, this resulted in the need for more extensive monitoring and internal controls within the corporation to safeguard its credit rating. Thus, the effectiveness of any corporate financing model will largely depend on the realization that financial plans must be a concerted and unified activity of management and the shareholders.

EXTERNAL FORCES FOR CORPORATE GOVERNANCE

Corporate-governance reforms need to be broad-based and wide-ranging. They need to support financial-sector strengthening, proper macroeconomic management, changes in laws and attitudes, as well as regulatory reforms. However, responsibility for the reform process does not rest on corporate directors alone, although they have direct responsibility. We need outside drivers — external pressure — from other stakeholders and the public to shape a regime of good corporate governance.

We need independent watchdogs that understand corporate governance, such as NGOs, consumer and special interest groups, and media, to be vigilant against non-compliance to discourage undesirable corporate practices.

The assessment and rankings of corporations made on the basis of their adoption of and compliance with governance practices can also be an important external driver to encourage compliance.

Corporations are accountable to the public they serve. But the public must know, be made aware of and ensure this accountability.

It is in this aspect that some countries in the region have been remiss. Present legal systems can be said to have within their respective frameworks sufficient bases to implement good governance, but there is not enough incentive for stakeholders to actively participate in monitoring management. For one, while the legal structure allows the suits by shareholders, the entire judicial process is at times prohibitively costly or time- or effort-consuming. Two, while there have been cases filed against erring directors and corporate officers, very few have been punished. Three, investor and shareholder activism, while already a reality in other jurisdictions, has not fully developed in some areas.

There is, therefore, a need to acknowledge that if strong corporate governance is to filter through the marketplace, its practice must extend beyond merely prescribed mandates, responsibilities and obligations.

REGIONAL INITIATIVES

Recently, APEC countries adopted guidelines on corporate governance patterned after the OECD Guidelines. Such a move indicates an acceptance that standards of good corporate governance are universal and that cultural differences or the family-owned structures of Asian companies can not preclude their implementation. There may be differences in the implementation but, overall, the Code of Corporate Governance adopted by countries in the region recognizes that there are other stakeholders in a corporation aside from owners and majority stockholders. Minority shareholders as well as the general public, as another stakeholder, must be protected.

Certainly, the institution and implementation of corporate governance reforms require an understanding of the cultural, economic and political history of a nation. The corporate-governance system of one country may or may not work for another. In the United States, for example, corporate governance became prominent with the active participation of institutional investors in the decision-making of companies where their funds are invested. With the huge investment portfolio of these institutional investors in big corporations, corporate governance was necessary to protect their members' investments. In fact, the managers of these institutional funds have shifted from being mere monitors to being owners of companies where their funds are invested. In the Philippines, such investment portfolios are still in the making.

Regardless of the nature of the investments involved, no country can be excused from instituting and implementing reforms on corporate governance. Non-practice of good governance can be a death sentence for any economy. The OECD, the World Bank and the International Monetary Fund have established the principles and guidelines for good governance. They have taken the initiative to fund activities towards implementation of governance reforms, and they have sent representatives to monitor each country's compliance with these reforms. The message has been sent and received loud and clear.

Countries with no or few corporate-governance reforms and policies must sit up and take notice. They can do well by looking into other advanced jurisdictions which have implemented good governance practices and adopt the same, taking into consideration the differences in cultural, economic and political backgrounds of each country.

Under the Philippine Corporate Governance Program, a Code of Corporate Governance for Companies has been drafted and is set for implementation. For full disclosure and transparency, adherence to international accounting standards, which have been vigorously advocated, has been fully adopted. Amendments to the Corporation Code are under consideration to move for more independent directors in the corporate boards. To protect minority shareholders, proposals have been made to create an organization composed mostly of minority shareholders and to develop comprehensive investor-education programs. Additional reforms include the codification of rules that specify the fit and proper conduct of directors, and the implementation of a corporate-governance program which includes not only accounting and auditing, but also legal and judicial reforms.

THE IMPORTANCE OF CORPORATE GOVERNANCE

Corporations are indispensable to a country's economy. As Monks and Minnows have said, "Corporations determine far more than any other institution the air we breathe, the quality of water we drink, even where we live. Yet they are not accountable to anyone." That is how much power a corporation has.

With the coming of the corporate-governance era, corporations are now made to realize that with that power is attached accountability — not only to its owners, but also to all people whose lives may be affected by it. Where before it did not matter what a corporation, through its board and corporate officers, did to attain its profit-oriented ends, now it will and has to answer for its actions that do not rebound to the benefit of the general public. It will have to answer for the industrial wastes it disposes of in the streams and rivers of the community and for acquiring raw materials from a company that paid below-minimum wages and salaries. The extent of its accountability goes far in scope and breadth.

The challenge of managing governance, both political and corporate, must come from a recognition of the fact that both kinds of governance are essential for a country's economic growth. The problem lies not in its conceptualization, for the concept of governance is by itself multifarious. Its complexity is, however, made easily understandable by the principles it advocates. As Sir Adrian Cadbury has said, "the principles on which it is based — transparency, accountability, fairness and responsibility — are universal in their application. The way they are put to practice has to be determined by those with the responsibility of implementing them." In other words, the problem lies in how much care and concern the stakeholders have in practicing good governance from within the corporate structure. It is imperative that all stakeholders practice self-governance and assume responsibility for their actions. Once they have done that, the remaining challenge will lie in making good governance the most important underlying principle for the economic success of a nation.

Accountability and Good Corporate Governance in a New Environment

E.C.W. Neloe
President and Chief Executive Officer,
PT Bank Mandiri (Persero), Indonesia

BACKGROUND

The economic crisis in mid-1997 sent massive shockwaves through every sector in the Indonesian economy. Prices skyrocketed and interest rates soared while the Rupiah plunged. Many businesses and major financial institutions failed or suffered significant financial distress, resulting in major dislocation for many Indonesians.

At the same time, Indonesia experienced a major political transformation, which gave more voice to the people after more than 30 years of authoritarian rule. People took their dissatisfaction to the streets and there were massive riots. The transfer of power took place in May 1998 and a general election in the following year brought in a new government. Indonesia, the largest country in Southeast Asia, was going through a dramatic change.

Many reasons have been expounded for why the crisis erupted and why it was so deep and pervasive. Was it failure in economic policy? Was globalization of capital the main culprit? Was the absence of foreign-exchange controls at fault? This was more than an economic crisis; it was clearly a crisis of confidence. In hindsight, it can be seen that the economy was built on a very fragile foundation. Law enforcement was weak. Monopoly practices flourished. Corruption and irresponsible mark-up practices prevailed. These factors compounded the effect of the capital flight, which sent ripples throughout the economy.

The international view of Indonesia was, and continues to be, very negative. Indonesia's sovereign-debt ratings were lowered. Indonesian banks' letters of credit were not accepted in many foreign banks. McKinsey, in its Investor Opinion Poll of 1999–2000, stated that Indonesia had fallen to the bottom of the field in good corporate governance. The Hong Kong-based Political and Economic Risk Consultancy (PERC) named Indonesia as one of the most corrupt countries in the world. Indonesia was also one of the worst countries in its lack of prudent accounting practice, shareholder accountability, disclosure, transparency and corporate governance.

A NEW BEGINNING

In response to the banking crisis, the Indonesian government, with the support of international financial agencies — in particular, the International Monetary Fund (IMF), the World Bank and the Asian Development Bank (ADB) — initiated a massive bank-restructuring program. The restructuring program included the closure and consolidation of many Indonesian banks. The government also issued bonds to re-capitalize the balance sheets of selected banks after transferring bad loans to the Indonesia Bank Restructuring Agency (IBRA), thus preventing a total collapse of the banking sector. The government spent around IDR540 trillion (US$54 billion) to restructure the banking industry. The restructuring program restored the capital and profitability of many banks, which allowed them to gradually resume lending activity.

The restructuring took place in the midst of a changing business environment. As the result of the 1997–98 crises, large conglomerates were no longer the main driver of the economy. Small and medium enterprises (SMEs) were able to expand their domestic and international footprint, contributing to job creation in many parts of the country. The agriculture industry grew at a rapid rate because of currency depreciation. Domestic consumption became the backbone of the economy.

Bank Mandiri emerged from the merger of four state banks, namely Bank Bumi Daya, Bank Bapindo, Bank Dagang Negara and Bank Ekspor Impor, all of which were adversely affected by the financial crisis. Aside from the obvious tasks — recapitalization of the balance sheet, unification of the technology platform, the implementation of a much-improved system of risk management, and the rationalization of branches — one of the most important challenges facing Bank Mandiri has been to transform the corporate culture.

The most important question in the late 1990s was how to avoid similar crises in the future. A new culture was required for Indonesian banks to survive in the new environment: a culture where banks operate on principles of prudence and commercialism; a culture where the highest standards of governance and risk management are implemented thoroughly. The creation of a new culture requires commitment from the top and middle-level management. Management will be held accountable for their actions. Accountability and governance are two subjects that I would like to focus on in this chapter.

I am of the opinion that Bank Mandiri needs a common vision that can be shared throughout the institution. And, to this end, good corporate governance and the adoption of best industry practices have provided an excellent starting point. There are many definitions of good corporate governance. These all boil down to a process and structure to manage and lead an organization towards increasing its output and accountability with the objective of realizing long-term shareholder value while being responsive to other stakeholder interests. It is interesting to note that good corporate governance focuses on creating and maximizing the value of the corporation and not simply on following best practices for their own sake. Consistent implementation of good corporate governance will contribute to developing and sustaining the optimal operating platform for the bank. Therefore, it will not matter who manages the organization, as long as the system is in place.

Following the establishment of Bank Mandiri, we spent considerable efforts to institute governance and accountability measures based on international best practices. At this stage, we have a standard internal policy that is widely committed and continuously revised and improved over time. The policy is set in a framework of achieving the following vision and mission for the bank.

Vision   : [To be] the Trusted and Preferred Bank.
Mission : 1. Meeting the needs of the customer.
               2. Generating maximum return for the shareholder.
               3. Committing to transparency, accountability, and good corporate governance.
               4. Developing professional human resources.
               5. Caring for our community and environment.

POLITICAL CONSTRAINT

It is true that Indonesia is slowly emerging from the crisis. Indonesia recorded a 3.5% economic growth in 2001, which was better than its regional neighbors. Strong domestic consumption and the country's insulation from the global technology meltdown have contributed to steady growth. However, the recovery is not solid, as the country continues to face many challenges, especially on the political and security fronts. Legal uncertainty and corrupt behavior persist which, in turn, create major concerns among domestic and international investors. Growth derived from consumption alone is not sufficient for sustainable economic development. Further structural change is needed in the economy, as well as in social, political and other institutions, to stimulate higher levels of investment. In the past, insufficient attention was given to institutional development, and this has been a cause of our problems today. Better enforcement of the law, better supervision of the banking and capital market, better business ethics and greater professionalism are some of the areas of institutional development that need addressing. In view of this changing political environment, every organization operating in Indonesia must remain responsive and proactive.

THE ROLE OF GOOD CORPORATE GOVERNANCE

Indonesian people have demanded greater transparency and accountability of their government. Similar demands have been made of companies and businesses. There is still lots of work required to improve governance in Indonesia. In an increasingly globalized market, one cannot ignore the importance and the impact of good corporate governance to commercial entities.

I believe that Indonesian corporations have a responsibility to apply the principles of good corporate governance codified in international best practices. The implementation of good corporate governance not only applies to publicly-listed firms or major corporations. All firms must realize that it is essential to protect the interests of their shareholders, creditors and employees, as well as those of any other, external, stakeholders in the area in which they are located or in which they have a business interest.

Bank Mandiri has the responsibility to build a commercially sound institution that can perform its crucial intermediary function in the economy. The government invested IDR175 trillion to re-capitalize the bank, which created a very high expectation on the bank to perform and be accountable. Since its inception, management has acknowledged that the bank must operate on commercial principles supported by governance mechanisms in line with the best international practices. We have had to race against time. Without efficient financial intermediaries, the economy will stagnate. Economic recovery can be accelerated only if the nation's banks begin their lending activities again.

CORPORATE RESTRUCTURING

Bank Mandiri's management began the task of rebuilding the bank with a thorough organizational restructuring. When the merger took place, there were major overlaps in branches, employees, technology platforms and other operating systems. Management developed an organizational structure that could support the requirements of a world-class institution and serve its customers well. The bank consolidated branches, reduced numbers of employees and consolidated its technology platform. The bank also recruited outside professionals, including expatriates, to join the management team and bring new ideas and skills to the bank.

Management also improved communications with staff by adopting an "open-management" style and breaking from the strict top-down approach that had operated in the past. The greater involvement of staff in the decision-making process also led to greater sense of accountability.

ADVANTAGES OF GOOD CORPORATE GOVERNANCE

As the business environment changes, the players must be able to adapt quickly. The crisis of 1997–98 resulted in increased scrutiny of Indonesian corporate affairs. Stakeholders demanded more information from Indonesian companies. The capital market authority, BAPEPAM, revised a number of its disclosure requirements to bring them up to international standards. The Indonesian government, with the support of business associations and international institutions, set up a task force on Corporate Governance and Partnership for Governance Reform. Bank Mandiri was one of the founders of the Indonesian Institute of Good Corporate Governance. But there is still much to be done, especially on the law-enforcement side.

On a corporate level, the application of good corporate governance requires commitment and consistency in promoting transparency vis-à-vis various stakeholders. Many firms feel burdened by requirements with regard to governance and accountability. They view good corporate governance as an additional cost without a guaranteed return. Bank Mandiri, on the other hand, places high priority on good corporate governance. Bank Mandiri is committed to operating on strictly commercial principles, including the need to be accountable and responsive to its stakeholders. There were initial doubts that Bank Mandiri could escape its past and that the culture and business principles of the banks that came under its wing would not change. Following the restructuring and consolidation, the bank adapted a new Code of Conduct, and established a Compliance Group and an independent Audit

Committee. The central bank, Bank Indonesia, the Supreme Audit Agency and a firm of international public accountants (Ernst & Young) conduct regular audits on Bank Mandiri.

Bank Mandiri is currently the largest and one of the most profitable banks in Indonesia. As at the end of September 2001, our assets totaled IDR235.7 trillion (US$24.5 billion) or around 23% of the total assets of the Indonesian banking sector. Our net profit was IDR2.1 trillion (US$214 million). By that time, we had reduced our level of non-performing loans (NPL) from 70% in 1999 to 12.7%. Bank Mandiri has one of the most rigorous credit-restructuring programs, with a dedicated unit assigned to manage the 19-step procedure.

Following the financial crisis in 1997, international banks did not want to conduct business with Indonesian banks. Access to international capital markets was also limited. While it was critical to win the confidence of domestic customers, at the same time we had to regain the trust of our international partners. In this process, consistency, transparency and clear communications were essential.

In late 2001, Bank Mandiri issued its first Floating Rate Note (FRN), which was listed in Hong Kong. The objective of this was to test market sentiment and develop our access to a more diversified funds-base to manage our liabilities and support our growth plans. The size of the issue was planned for US$100 million. The transaction proved to be successful, with a 25% over-subscription. International investors made up 40% of the subscribers. More importantly, Standard & Poor's gave both the notes and Bank Mandiri, as the issuer, a B-rating, placing the bank two grades higher than Indonesia's sovereign rating. This was the first time such a rating had been achieved by a state-owned entity in Indonesia, indicating the high level of trust enjoyed by Bank Mandiri among the investment community. The success was also shared by Indonesia, as the transaction returned the country to the international capital market after a four-year absence. The challenge is to maintain the momentum and ensure that the bank continues to deliver consistently good performances.

CHANGING THE CULTURE

The bank still has to manage the ongoing internal cultural transformation. Efforts to institutionalize good corporate-governance principles will take time, but the bank has already taken several important steps.

First, we adapted a comprehensive Corporate Governance Policy with a Code of Conduct to which all bank officers must subscribe. New Board of Directors Guidelines and the Board of Commissioners Guidelines were also developed with the assistance of international consultants PricewaterhouseCoopers.

Second, we set up an Office of Compliance and adopted best practices with regard to risk, to the extent that Bank Mandiri has become a benchmark for other banks in Indonesia. The bank also has Internal Control and Compliance (ICC) units at the branch level that are accountable to the Office of Compliance at head office.

Third, the bank has set up various committees at the board level to provide strong oversight and ensure better and more accountable decisions. Board-level committees at Bank Mandiri include the Audit Committee, the Risk and Capital Committee, the Personnel Policy Committee and the IT Steering Committee.

Fourth, we have adopted international accounting standards alongside the Indonesian accounting standard and have greatly expanded our disclosures in our audited financial statement. To illustrate, the annual reports of the four legacy banks only had 15 to 20 notes to the consolidated financial statements. In its third-quarter report ending September 30, 2001, Bank Mandiri had 60 notes to the consolidated financial statements spread over 120 pages. This reflects the bank's commitment to promote transparency and conform to international standards.

Fifth, the bank has launched its new corporate principles. The principles, known as Three Nos — "No Delay", "No Error" and "No Special Payments" — are shared with customers, employees and other external stakeholders. The third principle, "No Special Payment", is of particular note in that it means employees are not allowed to accept bribes or gifts or put themselves into situations of conflict of interest. The bank has also publicized these principles through posters in branches and offices, newspaper advertisements and written communications to customers. We consider it important to inform the staff that they have the responsibility to deliver results as well as being held accountable for their actions. We want to embed such values into our corporate culture and to engage our customers and stakeholders in the process.

The bank has gone beyond organizational change in adopting a new credit culture. Credit approvals and monitoring are subject to a highly structured "four eyes" approval process, which separates credit decisions from marketing decisions. The separation reinforces the need to be accountable in making new credit decisions.

CORPORATE STRATEGY

The business landscape has changed radically in Indonesia. The public did not trust domestic banks following the crisis of 1997–98. Bank Mandiri had to regain public trust before it could perform its role as a financial intermediary. Our long-term strategy is to be a universal bank serving corporate and retail customers, including small and medium enterprises. We still have to address public skepticism with regard to our lending activities. We have conducted numerous events to inform the public of our governance mechanisms and the performance of the bank. We consider it our duty to inform the public better as to how the bank is managing the challenges in the changing business environment in Indonesia.

Part of our strategy is to leverage on our market dominance in Indonesia. Bank Mandiri will be a pillar of commercial and retail banking nationwide and its two subsidiaries will focus on niche markets: Mandiri Sekuritas on investment banking and Syariah Mandiri on Islamic banking. We have to be responsive to our customers' needs. And we have to be accountable. Ultimately, our vision is to be the "Trusted and Preferred Bank" for our customers and stakeholders.

Underlying our strategy is our comprehensive risk-management policy. There are three main risk categories that the bank has to monitor continuously: market risk, credit risk, and operational and legal risk. The bank's Risk Management and Control Group (RCMG) has to ensure that risks associated with market movements are comprehensively identified, accurately measured and effectively controlled. When it comes to credit risk, the bank follows the "four eyes" principle, where decisions on new credits have to be made by at least two independent officers — one from relationship management and one from risk management. The bank has set up comprehensive policies, systems and procedures, internal controls, management information systems, communication systems and fraud-detection mechanisms to address operational and legal risks. These policies are continuously updated in line with developments in the business environment. Ultimately, the risk-management system is absolutely crucial to gaining the trust of the bank's various stakeholders.

CONCLUSION

In a global economy, we have to play by international rules. Indonesia is no exception. The transformation of the country's political, social and economic environments has required companies, including state-owned firms, to be more transparent and accountable. Since its inception, Bank

Mandiri has been committed to the promotion of good corporate governance. While many argue that the implementation of good corporate governance will not be effective without an improvement in governance in all key institutions such as the public service, the judiciary, the law-and-order agencies and the central bank, we believe that in doing our part without delay or compromise we can do much to build trust among our various stakeholders. Good corporate governance will not bring results overnight, but it will contribute to improving the organization's performance over time. Bank Mandiri has benefited from increased transparency and accountability for the past three years. We have to encourage others to follow. I am convinced that consistent implementation of good corporate governance will strengthen the foundations for future growth for our bank and for Indonesia.

Corporate Behavior and Capital Markets in Asia

Felipe Yap
Chairman of the Philippine Stock Exchange, The Philippines

 As one of the emerging markets in the Asian region, the Philippines is thriving and becoming a significant player in the region's financial arena. Here are just some of the strategic initiatives being taken by the Philippine Stock Exchange (PSE) to address the challenges on corporate governance.

BEST PRACTICES PROMOTED BY THE INTERNATIONAL FEDERATION OF STOCK EXCHANGES.

In this era of globalization, the PSE recognizes the need to shape up in order to keep itself afloat in the keen competition for foreign funds being mounted by different emerging markets. For instance, as advances in technology have had significant impact on stock markets, the PSE has taken advantage of such state-of-the-art facilities to make its market more efficient.

Our market is now 85% scripless, using electronic entries in lieu of paper certificates. Brokers and investors are now required to convert their stock certificates to the Philippine Central Depository (PCD) credit-debit book-entry system before executing any trade. Actually, the PCD has been able to capture only about 85% of the stock certificates since there are still individuals or entities who choose to keep their share certificates in their possession.

The PSE is also moving to shorten the settlement period for stock transactions. We recognize the fact that the longer the settlement period, the bigger the settlement risks — such as loss of capital, market decline, liquidity pressures and the domino effect from failed trades.

Trade settlement in the PSE used to be at T+4, or four days after the actual trade, but this has now been reduced to T+3. Our long-term goal is to further reduce this to T+1.

STRENGTHENING GOVERNANCE AND SHAREHOLDER PROTECTION

I was elected chairman of the PSE at the time that the Exchange was reeling from a loss of confidence triggered by the worst stock-price manipulation scandal in its history. This involved gaming stock BW Resources Corp., whose share price skyrocketed phenomenally in 1999 only to collapse afterwards. Investigations by both the PSE and the Securities and Exchange Commission uncovered certain irregularities in the transactions of this stock.

The BW scandal became a wake-up call for the PSE and the government regulators. What followed next — after the investigations had been elevated to the level of the Philippine Senate — was a series of radical administrative and legislative reforms to prevent the recurrence of such a crisis. In 2000, the Philippine Congress passed the new Securities Regulation Code. The reforms include:

• **The reorganization by PSE of its 15-member board of directors to give non-brokers majority control of the highest policy-making body of the Exchange**

The PSE is now governed by a board of directors composed of eight non-broker and seven broker members. In the past, only three out of the 15 board seats were allotted for non-brokers.

By removing majority control of the PSE board from the brokers, the Exchange proved its commitment to getting fresh perspectives from key sectors outside its own ranks, to improving trading practices, to enhancing transparency and further professionalizing its management. It also dispelled accusations in the aftermath of the BW scandal of the old-boys-club mentality that protected the interests of its own members.

The Exchange has since elected to its Board well-respected business leaders — representing key sectors such as the investing community, the issuers or the listed companies, and academe — as non-broker directors. They have so far provided valuable inputs that have helped steer the PSE towards a path of better governance.

- **The incorporation in the new securities law of a specific provision to protect minority shareholders through the tender-offer rule**

This is in line with our belief that minority shareholders must not be left out during corporate buy-outs but, instead, enjoy the same benefits as the bigger shareholders will get from such market-moving deals.

The PSE, on its own, had recognized the importance of such a tender-offer rule even before any law was enacted, putting as a requirement in its listing rules that any group taking over majority of a listed company should offer to buy out minority shareholders at the same price at which the majority stake was bought.

The provision in the Securities Regulation Code has made the requirement for a tender offer more stringent. This law provides for a threshold of 15% or more for a single acquisition or 30% for creeping acquisition over a period of one year. However, this was recently amended by The Philippine Securities and Exchange Commission in a special resolution dated September 12, 2001, which established a single threshold at 35%.

- **The introduction of crucial reforms by the PSE to eliminate conflicts of interest between brokers and the investing public in the trading of stocks**

Heeding lessons from the BW scandal, in August 2001 the PSE started operating a new computer system to ensure 100% compliance by brokers with its "customer-first" policy. The system was designed to automatically prevent front-running, the practice whereby a brokerage firm gives priority to orders from dealers over the orders of its clients.

Under the new system, as soon as a client gives an order to his broker, the broker must give way to his own client even when the dealer has a pre-existing order in the computer system. This is also an important safeguard in view of the suspension by the Securities and Exchange Commission of the broker-dealer segregation rule in the Securities Regulation Code which for some time prevented member-brokers from trading their own accounts.

We have proven that the PSE is capable of policing its own ranks and that there are sufficient safeguards to allow its member-brokers to continue performing both broker and dealer functions.

- **The tightening of parameters in monitoring unusual stock-trading movements as part of efforts by PSE's compliance and surveillance division to detect anomalies in stocks trading**

Three new indicators were put in place to complement the existing price-trading band — the volume-movement alert, the cumulative-price alert and the significant cross-transaction alert. All of these are aimed at providing a more vigilant monitoring system, as these alerts represent signals that will require the issuer to provide any information that could trigger unusual trading movements.

The volume-movement alert activates when the trading volume of a certain issue for a particular day exceeds by a certain percentage the moving average within a specified number of days.

The cumulative-price movement alert is triggered when the daily percentage change in the closing price of an issue adds up to a cumulative increase or decrease of a certain percentage within a specified number of days. This has been put in place to monitor unusual changes in the price over a period of time which cannot be detected by the usual trading band (whereby the PSE allows the share price of any listed company to rise by a maximum of 50% upwards and 40% downwards within a single trading session).

Lastly, the significant cross-transaction alert is activated when such transactions for a single day amount to a certain percentage or more of a broker's aggregate transaction for the entire trading session.

DE-MUTUALIZATION OF THE PSE

Following the mandate to de-mutualize, the PSE was converted from a non-profit member organization to a for-profit stock corporation last August. We have shed our mutual status and have distributed shares of the Exchange to our 184 member-brokers, in preparation for becoming a publicly listed company in the near future.

The overall goal of the de-mutualization plan is to modify the organization and redirect the corporate culture of the exchange into a commercial and performance-oriented market-operator as a response to globalization, consolidation and technological advances.

One reason why the PSE was mandated to de-mutualize was to bring back confidence to the market in the post-BW period. We know that de-mutualization is not the ultimate cure to the confidence crisis but only the first in a series of reforms needed to rebuild investor confidence.

When the PSE took the big leap of converting itself into a stock corporation, it segregated at the same time the ownership of shares in the Exchange and the members' trading rights, which means that any member can now sell shares and still retain trading rights, and vice versa.

But the de-mutualization process has just begun. In a matter of time, we will see investors outside of the brokerage industry buying shares of PSE Inc. We will see our very own company's stock-trading symbol flashed through the trading terminal. In the future, we will be selling PSE shares to the public and these will be listed and traded in the Exchange like shares of other companies now listed in PSE.

Until that project is accomplished, we are faced with the task of continually restructuring and molding the Exchange into a cutting-edge company that the public will want to invest in. We are currently identifying various business units and profit centers within the organization to generate a healthy revenue stream.

AMENDMENT OF THE SECURITIES REGULATION CODE

While we generally welcome the new securities law, we feel that there are certain provisions — mostly an overreaction to the BW scandal — that must be amended for the stock market to flourish.

One of these measures is the broker-dealer rule I cited earlier. This provision has been relaxed at the urging of President Gloria Macapagal-Arroyo, who recognized that there is no need to prohibit brokers from trading their own accounts as long as there are safety measures against possible abuses.

However, despite the relaxation of the provision, it is clearly not enough. The PSE is pushing for no less than the repeal of this provision so that the policy will be consistent, irrespective of which administration is in power. Amidst the difficult global economic environment that is keeping investors away from the stock market, specifically those in emerging markets like ours, the additional volume from dealer accounts helps a lot in generating stock-market activities and, for each member-broker, in raising revenues to offset operating costs.

Another draconian provision that we are lobbying to repeal is the broker-director rule, which prohibits brokers from buying and selling securities of listed companies to which they are related by reason of their officers or directors holding officer positions in such companies, or where the officers/directors and employees of the brokerage firms are related to persons in listed companies within the fourth civil degree of consanguinity or affinity.

We believe that this rule is too stringent and should, instead, be replaced by tighter disclosure rules. Otherwise, it makes an all-encompassing assumption that insider-trading happens when you have a relative in a certain listed company and thus unnecessarily restricts even those people not holding positions of trust in said company, or not privy to sensitive information. People cannot choose their relatives. Why, therefore, should members of a brokerage firm be punished for simply having relatives in a listed company?

LISTING REQUIREMENTS IN THE FIRST, SECOND AND SMALL-AND-MEDIUM-ENTERPRISE BOARDS

We want to give a chance to more companies to raise funds for business expansion. However, the relaxation does not mean that the PSE will just allow any company to sell shares to the public.

In the case of listings on the first board, or for companies with a minimum authorized capital of P400 million, of which 25% must be paid up, the PSE agreed to waive the three-year profitability track record. The alternative requirement, though, is that the IPO candidate must have a market capitalization or net tangible assets of at least P500 million and a five-year operating history.

For the second board, the PSE retained the minimum capitalization requirement of at least P100 million, of which 25% must be paid up, but allowed companies to list even without a track record.

The PSE also dropped its list of preferred industries for listing in the second board in order to accommodate more companies, reduced the lock-up requirements for stockholdings and allowed secondary shares to be sold for IPO. The candidate, however, must have an operating history of at least one year and must not change its primary purpose for a period of five years.

Despite the poor stock-market conditions this year, the PSE, after years of conceptualization, was able to launch its SME board, which caters to companies with capitalization of P100 million and below. The very first SME to go public, software marketing firm SQL Wizard, had a very successful debut, making history not only as the first SME to list on the PSE but the first to hit the 50% share-price ceiling on the first day of trading. Its share price continued to gain sharply afterwards, indicating investor interest in small companies with high-growth potential.

The PSE has likewise recently revised its listing guidelines to allow certain leeway for legitimate "white knights" to buy shares of dormant companies at a discount. The new guidelines provide new investors with plans to resuscitate a dormant company with an exemption from the discount limit of 10% set by the Exchange vis-à-vis the market price or book value, whichever is higher.

The new guidelines, however, still contain strict safety nets against corporate raiders who will simply want to buy shares at rock-bottom prices and then dump them later at the expense of the investing public. In short, the exemption will open the door only to real, honest-to-goodness strategic investors.

INVESTMENT ALTERNATIVES TO INVESTORS

We recognize that in these difficult times, investors will not want to put all their eggs in one basket and the PSE must be able to diversify its products, too. In this regard, we are pursuing the listing of government securities.

When investors' interest in equities wanes, they usually shift their funds to fixed-income instruments. We therefore saw the need to list government securities to provide more investment products in our market. To date, the PSE has already listed the Philippine government's small-denominated treasury bonds with attractive annual yield of 13.625% and is looking towards the listing of other fixed-income instruments such as private corporate bonds

The PSE also plans to open a U.S. dollar-denominated trading board early next year. The new trading board aims to enhance the PSE's trading infrastructure by providing an extended off-floor trading session in the afternoon for trading of securities of Philippine companies that are also listed offshore. It also aims to prepare the local bourse for eventual cross-border trading.

We have now secured approval for this project from the Philippine Central Bank. With its help, we have mapped out certain safeguards to prevent the facility from being used for speculative attacks against the local currency.

ELECTRONIC CLEARING AND SETTLEMENT SYSTEM

By speeding up the clearing system, we are gearing up for a more efficient marketplace that could easily hook up to real-time cross-border trading with exchanges in the neighboring countries.

We know that the stock market, and the capital market in general, has a significant role to play in a country's economic progress. Our role is to provide alternative means of raising cheaper capital, particularly in our country where enterprises are heavily dependent on traditional bank loans. We in the PSE recognize the need for us to strive harder to continuously improve the regulatory structures, as well as our own corporate governance, to benefit the listed companies, the investing public and our domestic economy.

In closing, let me state our commitment to contribute our share in the effort to re-instill confidence in the region's financial markets and the drive to make Asia a dynamic international financial center.

A Strategy for Continuous Recovery in the Indonesian Banking Sector

Saifuddien Hasan
President Director of PT. Bank Negara Indonesia (Persero) Tbk.,
Indonesia

INTRODUCTION

This chapter starts with the assumption that the current crisis in Indonesia will come to an end as a natural process of the economic cycle. Therefore, only those players who can hold out and adjust will be able to survive and thus help create a better economy. Because of this, the topics covered in this paper include not only the crisis itself but also a basic survival process and adaptation, with "survival of the fittest" becoming the norm. Topics also cover who should implement the process, as well as how the process should be run in order to guarantee sustainable recovery by paying special attention to the costs that will arise. The focus throughout is on the Indonesian banking sector because of my conviction that the recovery of this sector is a prerequisite for the overall recovery of the Indonesian economic sector.

Ever since the collapse of the Thai Baht in mid 1997, the monetary crisis has assumed the form of a multi-dimensional crisis, particularly in Indonesia. This not only incapacitates economic principles but is also colored by political conflict, the threat of national disintegration and inter-group discords. The crisis should therefore, in fact, be viewed as a global correction process for the various forms of market inefficiencies that have occurred in the region, regardless of the source of these inefficiencies. It is to be hoped that the correction process will motivate new and better stability. It is also hoped that this correction process will bring an end to the crisis currently being experienced by Southeast Asia in general and by Indonesia specifically. What is most important is how these global correction steps are viewed while, at the same time, exploiting the momentum that is available within the recovery process.

In my opinion, the recovery process can be implemented by the running of two basic strategies that together constitute a series. The first of these is the **survival process**, where the aim is to save a system that is in mid-collapse as well as to set up a new economic platform. The second strategy is the **sustainability process**. Here, the aim is to guarantee the internal resistance of the economic system that has been set up.

SURVIVAL STRATEGY

A survival strategy that aims to save a system in mid-collapse and set up a new economic platform really requires strong government leadership (government-led restructuring and reform). It should be strong in the sense of having a clear future vision, consistent policies, sufficient skills and knowledge, as well as an administration that is not only clean but also has the full, legitimate authority of the people for all of its actions. The role of the government in this strategy is to be the initiator, the planner, and the motor of the recovery acceleration process as well as the executor. In certain cases, the government must be ready to take steps that are unpopular and very risky. In the case of Indonesia, for example, steps like this began even before the end of the Suharto administration. These included the setting up of the Indonesian Bank Restructuring Agency (IBRA), which has the twin goals of making the paralyzed banking sector healthy again and also revitalizing the real economy. Steps taken to date have included the liquidation or take over of several banks, followed by the separation of bad and good assets. Bad assets from the banking sector were transferred to IBRA and then the recapitalization program was implemented for banks that were considered to still have good prospects. This has resulted in the total number of banks, which stood at 237 in mid-1997, now dropping to only 149 and it is anticipated that this number will decrease even further as the consolidation process continues. At the very least, this first step provided the initial momentum for the recovery of the banking sector that was all but paralyzed. It was also the first step in the restructuring of the sector, which had not been properly organized previously and in which there had been a great deal of overlap. More than IDR653 trillion was allocated to this program and this recapitalization process was successful in repairing the capital structure of the banking sector. In March 1999, this had stood at a negative IDR244 trillion but by September 2001 had recovered to a positive IDR68 trillion.

Compared to the recapitalization costs that had already been spent, this amount in fact only reflects 10% of the total. In other words, there is a potential public loss amounting to 90%. Because of this, the next challenge will be how IBRA manages the banking sector's assets, which are valued at IDR541 trillion, in order to produce the optimum recovery rate. It has to be recognized, however, that the restructuring of such a large amount of assets is a hard task indeed. IBRA's success or failure in this regard will have significant implications from a fiscal point of view. In addition, the handling of these problem assets has already attracted the attention of the international community, through both the World Bank and the International Monetary Fund (IMF). Because of this, both nominal as well as intrinsic values resulting from the restructuring process are very much involved in the government's credibility and market trust.

By mid 2001, IBRA had, in fact, succeeded in meeting its revenue target of IDR27 trillion for the 2000/2001 budgetary year. This revenue came from the sale of assets as well as steps towards the privatization of transferred companies.

In addition to the restructuring of assets transferred to IBRA, the banking sector has also been active in carrying out internal restructuring (through the recapitalization program) as well as operational restructuring (covering assets, operational processes, IT and risk management, amongst others). These all formed part of a business plan that was part of a management contract between banks' management and the government (with IBRA for private banks and the Minister of Finance for government banks). There were many milestones in the management contract that had to be met in full by each bank. This was to ensure that after being restructured, every bank would be managed correctly, have fulfilled all necessary requirements, and be guided by the principles of good corporate governance in meeting business targets. IBRA and the Minister of Finance monitor the achievement of these targets, always in consultation with the IMF or the World Bank.

After the first nine months of banking recapitalization and restructuring, there were noticeable improvements within several of the banks in the recapitalization program. By the first quarter of 2001, for example, non-performing loans (NPLs) in the banking sector were down to 18.8%, much lower than the 1998 position of 48.6%. Bank Indonesia, in fact, targeted that NPLs be reduced to 5% by the end of 2001. It has to be pointed out that this was a very difficult target to achieve and, in my opinion, only a NPL level of 15% could in fact be achieved by the end of 2001.

There were also significant changes to be seen in the balance sheet. In terms of assets, for example, government bonds dominated banks' earning assets, accounting for more than 50%. As already mentioned above, capitalization had shifted from a negative to a positive position. The average banking capital adequacy ratio (CAR), targeted at 4% in the beginning, was then increased to a minimum target of 8%. It is anticipated that there will be more liquidations and the merging of seven private banks that were unable to meet the 8% CAR target in the 2001/2002 budgetary year.

On the other hand, the government realized that the banking crisis was systemic and that it was not enough for the restructuring process to be applied in the banking sector alone; it also had to embrace other, related sectors. Therefore, several legal reform steps were taken in conjunction with the House of Representatives (DPR) during Habibie's administration. In the economic sector, for instance, the DPR has already passed several new state decrees, including the anti-monopoly, bankruptcy and central bank laws. The latter guarantees the independence of Bank Indonesia and also repositions the main focus of the central bank to put the monetary sector in order. New state decrees relating to the social-political sector included the decentralization, consumer protection, and freedom of the press laws. Overall, the passing of these new state decrees was a progressive step, and one that produced a new economic platform and social order (that I refer to as the "Madani" system). Under this system, all controls — in the community, the government, and the private sector — run effectively and in harmony; so much so that one can move on to the next phase, that of sustainable strategy.

It has to be pointed out that several political agendas and the interests of certain groups impeded this survival strategy. Changes in political leadership, following the fall of both Habibie and Gus Dur, also hindered the recovery process. Now, President Megawati has to be able to show just how serious and consistent she is in pressing the recovery process, and at the same time ensure the return of market confidence.

SUSTAINABLE STRATEGY

A sustainable strategy is one that is oriented to create internal processes (built-in processes) within the economic platform that has been formed, so that the system has sufficiently high durability to face up to any possible crises in the future. This durability will be created as long as the economic players in the system have the ability to adapt quickly and precisely. This is, however, only possible if there are "early warning systems" in place as regards environmental and external working changes. In addition, the ability to carry out changes in production and mobilization factors must also run smoothly, so that adaptation can be implemented more efficiently.

Taking the above prerequisites as a starting point, steps need to be taken to bring the new economic system into the market mechanism (market-driven reform). This is based on the theory that market-mechanism economy activities will work better when driven by the private sector rather than by the bureaucratic and monopolistic systems usually run by governments. In addition, bureaucratic systems are often linked to practices such as collusion, corruption and nepotism or other market distortions that I am convinced are one of the main causes of the current crisis. What is fundamental to this strategy is that the function of the government has to shift from that of the initiator and the motor (leader) to that of the facilitator and the guide.

The success of this strategy is very much dependent on both the readiness and the maturity of the infrastructure created in the previous program. In several cases in Ecuador, Argentina, Russia, South Korea and even in Indonesia itself, governments have often assumed that the economic system infrastructure (the management of risks as well as good corporate and government governance) in place is in fact ready to enter a liberalization phase. However, what often happens is in fact the opposite and contrary to the market climate, resulting in governments being trapped in a new crisis. For example, a liberalization climate has forced the private sector in many crisis countries to experience increases in production costs as a result of rises in input costs (including currency devaluation, rises in fuel costs and higher workers' wages). These were in turn caused by the working of the global market mechanism that corrected domestic goods prices. These had initially been set by the government (administered prices) in the form of subsidies or monopolies so as to relate to international prices but this was not balanced in terms of supply activities. Without any real guarantee of safety, due to laws not being properly enforced, there has been no reduction in the illegal collection of levies. In addition, the bad state of transportation infrastructure — such as roads, bridges and warehousing — has meant that manufacturers have to pay higher costs and face greater risks. This will lead to short-term financial losses for economic players.

Because of this, it is best for the government to be very careful in applying the sustainable strategy, in the sense that it should not be applied to all sectors at the same time and in the same way. Rather, it should be applied selectively and be implemented gradually. One example of this relates to the efforts to delegate some of the central government's authority to regional governments. In some cases, however, this will lead to losses for certain regions. This is because of the lack of the necessary infrastructure, such as human resources, in several regions.

However, in the banking sector it seems that the implementation of the market mechanism is becoming stronger. Local banking players have now accepted as a given the lack of restrictions on foreign banks, which are now allowed to open branch offices throughout Indonesia, and other forms of global competition. Because of this, those involved in banking are more aware that risk management and good corporate governance, as well as compliance in terms of sufficient capitalization (CAR) and the legal lending limit, are essential in order to be able to compete. Certain banks (including BNI) have even realized that CAR compliance is, in itself, not enough because this does not take into account potential risks that a bank has to face. For this reason, the more advanced VaR (Value at Risk) calculation is deemed to be a superior approach. In addition, other international best-practice requirements are not yet regarded as mandatory, even though they are seen to be necessary in order to be competitive.

As a result the internalization of several international best practices, several of the top 15 Indonesian banks have succeeded in making improvements, as shown in the table below. This is particularly the case in meeting ROA, ROE and NIM ratios. Asset quality has also improved, as indicated by lower NPL ratios. Assuming the banking sector continues to become more sound, this will mean more banks being able to extend loans, thus leading to improvements in the real-estate sector.

In a national context, the government's steps as regards the divestment of several state-owned enterprises to foreign investors have highlighted the need for the internalization of international standards to be accelerated. This is reflected by the high expectations in corporate performance as indicated by the rise of share prices on the stock exchange. Therefore, the privatization program has an important role in this sustainable strategy.

BANK BNI CASE STUDY: CONTINUOUS RECOVERY THROUGH THE APPLICATION OF GOOD CORPORATE-GOVERNANCE PRINCIPLES

It is already common knowledge that prior to the crisis, corruption and collusion colored the Indonesian banking sector. This was because of abuse of authority by bankers as well as mismanagement arising from a lack of professionalism. This is indicated by the financial losses, totaling hundreds of trillions of IDR, in the banking sector during 1998. In general, between 50% and 60% of these losses were due to reserve costs (as a result of non-performing loans), 20–30% from net foreign exchange positions and the remainder because of negative spread. The situation was further aggravated by other violations of legal lending limits and several cases where loans were provided without going through the normal procedures. At that time, Bank BNI suffered financial losses of IDR43 trillion and its NPL ratio was 70%. It can certainly be concluded, therefore, that good corporate governance was still very rare then.

Bank BNI began implementing good corporate-governance principles in 1986 and these are included in the bank's corporate manual that covers the procedures of all banking activities. This manual was compiled in collaboration with the consultants Booz Allen and Hamilton as part of the bank's performance-improvement program. However, the standard de facto procedures were not implemented consistently, as shown by the many exceptions made in the provision of loans. In certain cases, exceptions are unavoidable within normal levels of tolerance, but an attitude and culture of "anything can be arranged" will lead to irregularities. This was not only prevalent throughout banking but also in all bank stakeholders, including the government, the monetary authority and even supervisory bodies. The IMF later referred to this attitude and culture as the systemic banking crisis.

Good corporate-governance principles were applied as an essential part of the banking financial and operational restructuring program run by the government with assistance from the IMF, as stated in the sixth, seventh and ninth letters of intent of 2000. Internally, Bank BNI has made the implementation of good corporate-governance principles one of the bank's milestones, which have to be met fully in the business plan.

The implementation of good corporate governance begins with the communication process at all levels in order to increase commitment and create culture. The aim of this is to develop an inner commitment to, together, apply good corporate governance principles. Commitment is required both internally and externally to include all stakeholders and the government specifically as the major shareholder. Good government governance is essential for the development of good corporate governance.

The development of corporate-culture pillars that relate to good corporate governance depend on the principles becoming an integral part of the attitude and behavior of every individual at Bank BNI. At the same time, this guarantees that good corporate governance is not just a formality but is, rather, reflected in every facet of the organization, on a voluntary and ethical basis. But it must be realized that this all takes a long time to achieve.

The next short-term step is the preparation of a managerial good corporate-governance manual. Once this has been completed, another manual detailing the code of conduct for all Bank BNI staff has to be prepared.

As is normal in any program carried out by Bank BNI, a measurement system has to be set up to confirm that good corporate governance is being implemented effectively. The first stage is direct measurement in the form of a scoring system to compare the internal practice of all documents and activities that relate to good corporate governance with international best practice. In this case, the management plans to use an independent auditor. The next stage is an indirect measurement system through which management can monitor the value-creation process through which success is to be achieved. The basic philosophy of the scaling is to start from the assumption that a company run in accordance with good corporate-governance principles will experience an increase in profits and a decrease in risks. In other words, good corporate-governance principles will affect the value-driver of the bank and the corporate bottom line.

In this case, management defines the value-driver as the achievement of both financial and non-financial targets in each business unit. However, the measurement has to be exact, as well as reflect the good corporate-governance principles of fairness, transparency, accountability and responsibility. This results in old parameters being enriched with more precise business parameters that are used to determine the amount of bonuses and rewards, including corporate, group and individual rewards. The measurements are then communicated to shareholders in the form of a more comprehensive reporting system. In the 2000 annual report, financial reporting was based on strategic business units as a follow-up to the previous consolidation report. In the next annual report, the quality will be further improved. This is considered important so that external evaluation of the company's performance will be fairer and social-control aspects will become more effective.

Through the implementation of the above stage, the management is convinced that the value-creation process will continue and, at the same time, confirm that Bank BNI is ready to face even-tighter global competition.

CONCLUSION

• From the above, it can be concluded that the commitment and capability of the government in terms of clarity of vision as well as consistency in implementation are prerequisites for recovery. Public figures should also have a clear vision and be consistent in order to avoid unnecessary political conflicts. It has already been proved that the lack of these not only impedes future progress but also proves counter-productive to the recovery results already achieved.

- The strategy of continuous recovery also requires the support of the international community. This is especially so with donor countries, the World Bank and the IMF providing support in the form of technical, consulting or financial assistance, as well as fair monitoring. Support also needs to be realized as regards the provision of both debt-rescheduling facilities and foreign-debt dispensations. While this may not be attractive to either party, it is very much needed by crisis countries. In addition, support is also needed in fostering better global relations for crisis countries in order to increase market confidence in the current recovery progress.

- Just as important, the global macro-economic situation is sufficient to be a serious threat to the recovery process in Asian countries. One effect of the tragedy could be the loss of the momentum already gained, bearing in mind that this has resulted in a decrease in the exchange value of the Rupiah, cancellation of several export orders and delays in foreign investment.

- However, from an overall point of view, I am optimistic regarding the steps being taken — in particular, as regards the result achieved by the banking sector — and anticipate that the recovery process in Indonesia will be continuous.

Prospects for Serious Reform of Corporate Governance in Asia

Tunku Abdul Aziz
Vice-Chairman, Transparency International, Malaysia

Negative perceptions continue to dog much of Asia. Both local and international investors, rightly or wrongly, view attempts at reforming corporate governance as half-hearted at best. Such attempts are apparently intended purely as a public-relations exercise to deflect criticisms of the way in which corporate Asia still conducts its business — in the time-honored tradition, or so it seems, of treating transparency and accountability in the management of company affairs with contempt. Who can blame potential investors when examples of less-than transparent and accountable corporate behavior pop up everywhere, all the time?

It does not help the regional cause much when, for instance, various government spokesmen say that the Transparency International Corruption Perceptions Index (TI-CPI) is "only the perception of the organization that developed it, and, therefore, should not be taken seriously". This is an extraordinary statement, especially given that the TI-CPI has become, since it was first published in 1995, the most authoritative international tool for assessing the perceived levels of corruption in selected countries. Countries in the region that ignore the red flags are at risk of being seen to be still stuck in denial, a situation they can least afford in the prevailing economic climate.

While it is true that the TI-CPI is based largely on the perceptions of the expatriate business community and may have no basis in fact, the point is that these perceptions help to form a reality. They exist, and they have an important bearing on the economic well-being of the countries concerned.

We need hardly be reminded that the countries perceived to be seriously corrupt, such as Indonesia, the Philippines, Thailand and South Korea, were among the worst hit by the Asian economic crisis. The Philippines escaped the eye of the economic storm, not so much by design but because it had not quite developed into a mainstream economy and did not, therefore, attract quite the same level of speculative interest. In any case, that country has been on the IMF/World Bank life-support system off and on — mostly on — for some four decades. The correlation between the findings of the TI-CPI and the severity of the suffering experienced by the countries perceived to have developed a high level of tolerance for unethical public and corporate behavior is, to say the least, uncanny.

We cannot even begin to discuss the role of the private sector in the battle for good governance without examining the part governments play in shaping the environment and setting the tone in which business is conducted. It is now widely recognized that the Asian economic crisis had, in a sense, less to do with economics and more with politics. No less a person than Singapore's senior minister, Lee Kuan Yew, came to that conclusion when addressing leading American businessmen at a Fortune 500 Forum in October 1997.

There is, of course, a great deal of truth in his observation because, at the end of the day, it is governments that set the moral and ethical tone, just as it is they that promote the incestuous relationships with favored corporate entities. It is an ethical aberration, and that is putting it kindly. These cosy, highly unethical arrangements have been dignified in the course of time as Japan Incorporated, Korea Incorporated and Malaysia Incorporated. Predictably, by their very nature, they spawn corruption and other forms of corporate and official abuses of power that have come to be associated with the Asian way of business.

To Asian leaders who have developed connections into an art form, any suggestion that this practice represents unadulterated cronyism is rejected out of hand as being utterly unfair. They treat such comments with the contempt that it does not deserve, citing envy on the part of the West and calling it a Western ploy to discredit, for instance, Malaysia's achievements. Among the more vocal in this way was Malaysian Prime Minister, Dr. Mahathir bin Mohamad.

By contrast, Asia's foremost liberal democrat and former Thai prime minister, Anand Panyarachun, the man who gave Thailand the world's first anti-corruption constitution, clearly understands the danger of exploiting connections. In his inaugural Asia-Europe Foundation speech in Bangkok in 1998, he deplored the fact that the Thais continued to retain their system of patronage networks, "a system based on connections" which could "become deadly because patronage is not based on merit, and, therefore, tends to breed inefficiency and corruption".

Targeting foreigners when things go wrong has become commonplace in many parts of Asia. A foreigner performs a useful function; he is there, in a manner of speaking, to be verbally savaged, especially if his name happens to be George Soros, who has been called "a moron". Soros returned the compliment by describing his detractor as "a liability to his own country". It is interesting to speculate just who would have been the favorite whipping boy if Soros had not been so devastatingly successful at what he does. If there were no Soros, it is said that he would have been invented.

Given that political will is crucial to the whole process of developing globally accepted standards of business integrity, its absence can only mean one thing. Unacceptable business behavior, often bordering on the criminal, is openly tolerated as a business or cultural norm. Governments of many Asian countries that have been used to complete freedom of action are not likely to submit voluntarily to the discipline and constraints of the new economy. For them, the first glimmer of recovery is a signal to return to the good old days of unbridled excess. Clearly, governments have a responsibility to develop and strengthen national integrity systems, and they ignore this obligation at their peril.

The corporate sector, too, has an important contribution to make to this process. It is, after all, the engine that provides the primary thrust for economic growth. No effective governance-reform program can be introduced, let alone sustained, against the rearguard action of the corporate community. It is no longer good enough for the business community to merely react to events; it must take the lead in promoting best practices to regulate transactions, both domestically and internationally. To this end, it should evolve a national code of business ethics that goes beyond a mere statement of intent; it should be a "wake-up" code that sets out clear guidelines and procedures for dealing with a wide range of everyday operational situations.

The corporate sector has frequently been an obstacle to good governance and part of the problem of corruption. It is totally opportunistic and will manipulate the often inadequately enforced laws and regulations in order to create an environment that encourages and promotes the sort of self-serving practices that even in colonial times would have made the notoriously unprincipled Cecil Rhodes blush. That does not say a great deal about the ethics of business in Asia.

The absence of effective, non-politicized and independent regulatory bodies in many of our countries appears almost as a gift from heaven itself to those bent on abusing the system. Equally, the absence of enforceable international compliance standards does not help matters. Opacity from all accounts remains an enduring feature of corporate life because disclosure, banking, investment, financial and other laws and regulations, for example, in several Asian countries are inadequately framed or, worse still, feebly enforced. It is said that Asia runs the danger of being over-regulated and under-enforced, with predictable consequences.

The rehabilitation of the Asian corporate community cannot begin until it takes a conscious decision to develop a sustainable business climate by finding ways of making it possible to conduct business ethically, without recourse to corrupt practices. It must put its house in order by developing and adopting enforceable rules of business engagement and conduct. Above all, it must accept the urgent need for reform in order to bring about greater transparency and accountability in both domestic and international business transactions. Such transparency and accountability have until now been totally absent in Asia. Asian corporations that are not prepared to make a complete break with their history of manipulating Asian values to justify political, social and economic excesses of the worst possible kind will only be postponing the evil day.

The globalized market will be much less forgiving, and the punishment meted out will be severe. Fortunately, Asian values have, like the Asian currencies, been devalued, and no self-respecting person will again resort to the once almost-sacrosanct mantra that "The Asian way of doing business is different" as a means of covering up inexplicable unethical business conduct.

An important challenge facing the corporate community is that it must understand that business is not just about managing risks, making sound investment decisions and coping with economic uncertainties. It is very much about what it can do to bring about the sort of change that will create a new ethical, and level, playing field on which business can take place fairly and transparently. In other words, it must close the windows of opportunity for corruption. It must institutionalize the system of checks and balances and encourage the government to review and, where necessary, strengthen the legal framework and to support corporate-sector reform initiatives. The government, after all, is responsible for developing a credible national integrity system that applies equally to the corporate community as it does the rest of the nation.

Viewed from the perspective of good governance, corporate Asia shares many undesirable features and practices. It, therefore, has its work cut out in rearranging its *post-crisis* governance priorities. Also, in preparing to meet the challenges of the global economy, the corporate sector clearly has to address the question of transparency and accountability in the formulation of national economic and financial policies. This is to ensure that these policies are not developed to provide even more opportunities for kickbacks to fill party coffers and benefit crony capitalists with impeccable political pedigrees. National economic and financial policies in Asia have tended to be used to legitimize public expenditure on overpriced projects. Corruption-watchers estimate, conservatively, that between 20% and 30% is routinely added to project costs.

The corporate sector, particularly corporations that are managed well enough to compete in an open system, clearly have an interest in ensuring that pressure is brought to bear on the authorities to put in place procurement policies that meet internationally recognized standards. A level playing field is the only guarantee of equity and justice in the award of contracts and, without it, investor and general business confidence goes out of the window, to the detriment of orderly and credible economic growth and social justice. Asian corporate-governance standards must be raised several ethical notches before business Asia can take full advantage of the opportunities and face squarely the challenges of the globalized economy, with its emphasis on much higher standards of corporate behavior than the region is accustomed to.

It is instructive to note what Andrew Sheng, Chairman of the Hong Kong Securities and Futures Commission, and a former advisor at the Malaysian Central Bank, had to say in a paper entitled "Global Financial Crisis: Implications for Financial Regulation", published in *Ekonomica* (Malaysia) in July 1999:

"Banking problems do not happen overnight, they have very complex roots. Many of the factors are country-specific and originate in defective structural or policy factors. Moreover, bank problems involve political, sectoral, legal, social, institutional and incentive dimensions. What was dynamite was the mixture of over-leverage, inadequate bank supervision, opacity and misunderstanding of risks in many markets, lack of sound bankruptcy laws and panic capital flight. Globalization, technology and financial innovation have created the conditions for large capital flows in the midst of weak corporate governance, outdated laws, policies and institutional structures. The outflow triggered the collapse."

Anyone seriously interested in, and concerned about, private-sector governance should go over very carefully the issues raised in the paragraph just quoted. It is quite clear that it was imprudent and irresponsible banking practices, aided and abetted by the authorities, that precipitated the meltdown of what had, only a few weeks before, been called the "miracle economies". Within hours of the devaluation of the Thai Baht, these apparently unassailable tigers disappeared without a trace from the world economic radar screen.

Corporate-governance practice in Asia remains, at best, patchy and uneven and, at worst, downright unwholesome in ethical terms. I shall illustrate my point by using one or two Malaysian cases. It is not because I particularly love or admire the Malaysian corporate-sector rope tricks, but I am more familiar with them, and they mirror much of the rest of business Asia in both form and substance.

Let us take the protection of minority-shareholder interests as an example. Several high profile Malaysian cases have underlined the very real possibility that the legitimate interests of minority shareholders may have been compromised through transactions which have conflicts between the interests of the company itself and its major shareholders:

- Recently, toll-road operator United Engineers (UEM) announced it was purchasing all the assets (except a 38% interest in itself) from its controlling shareholder, Renong. The share price took a tumble (a fall of 30%) when the shares resumed trading, before recovering.
- In 1999, UEM pledged its assets and cash flow to effectively enable its controlling shareholder, Renong, to restructure its loans.
- In 1997, UEM bought a 32% stake in Renong from unknown sources, with over RM2 billion in financing, which helped support Renong's share price for a while.
- Casino and resorts group Genting Bhd./Resorts World bought stakes in a Norwegian cruise operator. The value subsequently fell sharply. The stakes are being sold at a written down value to Star Cruises, a company controlled by the controlling shareholders of Genting/Resorts.
- The Genting/Resorts group is also subscribing to a large number of shares in Star Cruises for some RM1.7 billion, which will make the group move into a large net-debt position from the large net-cash situation it used to enjoy for many years previously. The share prices of both have been weak.
- Magnum, another gaming operator, had to write off RM140 million in loans made to an undisclosed borrower. The share price weakened on the announcement.
- Ekran Bhd. is trying to recover over RM700 million owed by a controlling shareholder.

This is by no means an exhaustive list. If laws and regulations are such that the interests of the minority shareholders are not given sufficient protection, then it is time to do so now. But one suspects that at least some of the problems arise from lack of enforcement.

If Malaysia is to be fair to its own investors and minority shareholders and become an internationally recognized and respected capital market, standards of corporate governance have to be nothing less than impeccable. There are strong arguments for capital controls and fixed exchange rates. But there are none whatsoever for poor corporate governance and insufficient protection of minority-shareholder interests.

Terence Mahoney, a private investor and former fund manager, has put it this way: "Malaysian investors are growing up. Because Malaysia's competitiveness as an equity market has declined relative to other Asian markets such as China, India and Taiwan, there is a realization that to attract foreign investors, companies have to clean up their act."

It is quite apparent from all this that effective supervision by the various regulatory bodies remains problematic. An important institution that underpins good corporate governance is the judiciary. The integrity of the judicial system in each of the countries coming under the purview of our discussion cannot be taken for granted. Can the courts be relied upon to dispense justice without fear or favor?

Corporate Asia is in a flurry of activity to reform governance, not, I might add, because of its natural preference for high ethical standards, but simply that it has little choice in the matter. Globalization is the great arbiter, and it is here to stay. Corporations that are slow to respond to calls for responsible corporate governance and do not see the need for putting transparency and accountability in the driving seat are unlikely to make it through the minefield of corruption in both domestic and international business transactions.

Reforms now being undertaken in the region cover, in varying degrees and intensity, areas of concern to the investing public as enumerated by Andrew Sheng and others. Our region as a whole is badly in need of these various reforms to promote better corporate governance and generate, in the process, investor confidence.

Like some other countries, after many years in the denial mode, Malaysia finally came clean with the following admission from the deputy prime minister, Ahmad Badawi:

"It is a fact, both you and I know, that the government engaged in many rescue operations during the crisis. A more laissez-faire government would have allowed many of our key companies to sink...I am well aware of the rumblings and discontent among the professional business community that the government should not continue to protect those who have blatantly mismanaged their corporate empires and have repeatedly come back crying for help."

We thought that the good old days of unfettered excesses were set to change. However, euphoria was short-lived. No sooner had the mighty roar of collective approval died down than reality struck with a vengeance. The government decided to use public funds, yet again, ostensibly this time to bail out the debt-ridden national flag carrier, Malaysia Airlines (MAS), by purchasing the 29% stake of its chairman at RM8.00 per share when these shares traded around RM3.60 each.

The perception, rightly or wrongly, is that it was not MAS being saved but, rather, that its chairman was being let off the hook with his original investment intact. It is mind-boggling that you should be rewarded for running a national airline into the ground. The fact that he was politically well connected lent credence to the suspicion that this was just another victory for cronyism. And yet, when it was suggested that it was a bailout with public funds, Daim, then Malaysian finance minister, was on record as saying, " No, it is not true, it is a wrong perception". He rationalized, as always, by suggesting that it was a deal done on a "willing buyer and willing seller" basis.

It is this sort of unaccountable official behavior that stops investors dead in their tracks. It is an Asian story with which we have all become only too familiar.

The question uppermost on every Asia-watcher's mind concerns not only the pace of change but also, more to the point, whether there is sufficient political will to ensure that the change in the pipeline is of such quality as to sustain long-term growth. In spite of protestations to the contrary by governments, the economic crisis is far from over, and it would be the height of folly and irresponsibility to delude the unsuspecting public. We are, of course, talking about sustainable growth, and not a mere flash in the pan.

There does not seem to be a great sense of urgency, and there is a danger that many companies may be reverting to type and revisiting the scene of earlier spoils and easy pickings on the back of corrupt governments. The challenge for corporate governance is real, and current reality leaves little room for complacency.

The corporate sector, ever opportunistic, circumscribes its business behavior by reference to what it perceives to be the official line on transparency and accountability, which, more often than not, falls far short of universal best practices. Few governments have the credibility, the moral authority, the political will, the inclination or the staying power to breast the tape in the good-governance race. It is not always in their interest to promote good governance, or so it seems, judging from their performance on this score to date.

Corporate governance cannot take root in the absence of a sustained effort to curb corruption in business transactions. Quoting his personal experience, one Western businessman claims to have delivered US$50,000 to a high-level government official as an inducement for approving a new project in Manila. Investors all over Asia, as recorded in the media many times, have similar stories to tell. Given the growing depth of corruption in many Asian countries, prospects for reforming corporate governance look positively bleak.

In Indonesia, the Indonesian Bank Restructuring Agency (IBRA) which has been set up, armed with special legal powers, to deal decisively with the growing mountain of non-performing loans has failed to live up to expectations. Vested political interests and a ramshackle and corrupt judicial system have combined to impede the recovery of the banking and other financial institutions.

In Korea, reform on a broad range of the corporate landscape is being attempted, but the results so far have been negligible. *Chaebols* continue to dominate the economy, and the pace of change is set by them, and it will be a while yet before their importance is reduced and the Fair Trade Commission really starts to implement tough measures against incestuous internal transactions and cross-subsidizing group companies and business affiliates.

On the banking front, foot-dragging seems to be the order of the day. While the basic direction of change is clear enough, there does not seem to be a sufficiently determined effort to remove resistance to reform by conservative elements bent on preserving the status quo. Korea's competitiveness in the global markets, as with all of Asia, will depend very much on how far it is prepared to go in putting in place the new governance regime.

However, all is not doom and gloom. The revamping of the securities commissions and other regulatory watchdogs now under way in the region has already resulted in many successful prosecutions of "big names" in several countries. This has clearly helped to drive home the point that it is not only the threat of a long prison term on which to concentrate the mind, but also the certainty of companies being exposed, and the consequent disgrace they face for rogue corporate behavior. The implications for such companies are far-reaching, and the risks are quite simply not worth the effort.

Corporate-governance reform in many Asian countries, particularly Malaysia and Hong Kong, is driven by the private sector, with governments playing an equally important role in facilitating important fundamental changes. Positive results are emerging that have put Malaysia ahead of Singapore and Hong Kong and other countries in East Asia, according to the Corporate Governance Survey released in July 2001 by the Political Economic Risk Consultancy (PERC). Malaysia's inherently strong economic fundamentals, together with a genuine desire to remain competitive, have helped in this process but, more to the point, the government in particular has at long last recognized that the excesses of the past must give way to greater transparency and accountability in the way the country conducts its business.

The challenges facing corporate governance in Asia stem from the somewhat relaxed cultural, social and political attitudes to stewardship, a concept that does not seem to have taken root in either the individual or national consciousness. How else would you explain a government secretly dipping into the national pension fund to support an undercover operation to corner the international tin market, which eventually proved to be an unmitigated disaster? How else would you explain a government using public funds to speculate on the international money markets?

It defies the imagination, to say the least. In a more open and democratic society, such unethical behavior would not only have attracted the most severe public censure but also brought the government down. We are, of course, talking about the past, but there is no certainty that these criminal adventures will not be repeated. Both the government and the corporate sector must embrace and absorb the culture of trusteeship and stewardship if business Asia is to succeed in meeting the new global challenges.

At the end of the day, no change or improvement in the way we manage our business operations can be sustained if our attitude to good governance is out of step with contemporary global trends. This applies both to government and the corporate sector. The principles of good governance, grounded as they are in trusteeship, stewardship, transparency, accountability and integrity, are as relevant to the governance of a state as they are to the management of a publicly-listed company. Good governance, like integrity itself, is no longer the luxury of the virtuous; it is a global business necessity.

PART

4

Exploring Regional Trade
and Business Links

Introduction

Asians have always been pragmatic in developing business and trade ties, and that pragmatism is as alive today as it was 10 years ago. This requires little further elaboration. Rather, much truth resides in the ways in which this pragmatism is evolving and pointing directions for the region's future.

Among the positive outcomes of the Asian financial crisis is the fact that Asian countries, having removed the rose-coloured lenses of high growth and international esteem, have become much more proactive about their development. Indeed, in the search for new principles of governance and, in some countries new governments altogether, those remaining in power seem more willing to step beyond the confines of established government agendas, especially in proposing areas for regional co-operation. They have realized, smartly, that their success will be judged domestically, but that many, and in some cases the principal drivers of that success, are in the regional or international realm. Certainly, regional interdependence as one of the principal drivers for regional economy and business is solidly in place.

As in other areas, when Asian governments decide that something is a good thing, they go for it "more than 100%", which has produced in the recent past strings of proposals for co-operation in every area from trade, sustainable development and environmental protection, to IT, health and the digital divide. While many of these olive branches are indeed worthwhile, one cannot help, and without cynicism, wonder whether the point is merely to co-operate on a (usually) non-threatening area or achieve real progress. Certainly there is no shortage of areas on which joint efforts could yield the latter, and among these are several proposed or discussed by the leaders in this section.

Judging from the number of free-trade proposals that have been mooted over the past two years, one has to imagine that regional trade is seen to be of paramount importance to the region's recovery. Indeed, the growth in exports to developed markets was a principal driver of the fledgling recovery seen in the region towards the beginning of 2001, as Supachai Panitchpakdi, Director-General Designate of the WTO, points out. In addition, it has been the main growth impetus in the expansion of Fujian into one of China's leading entrepôts, as outlined by Governor Xi Jinping in his persuasive case for open markets. More trade, and with greater product diversity, would be welcomed in other regions. Keat Chhon also writes a persuasive case for this with regard to the Greater Mekong Sub-region.

Monetary co-operation is another area on which there is agreement over the need to work more proactively together. Although frequently in public forums such as this leaders preach caution on the shape and timing of the creation of an Asian Monetary Fund, the idea of more information-sharing and co-operation towards the creation of an Asian lender of last resort is widely accepted. That both Oh Jong Nam and Governor Rafael Buenaventura of the Philippine Central Bank outline very strong arguments, from countries at different ends of the development spectrum of Asia, is indicative of its widespread support.

Action on the political front has been matched in the corporate sector; though, understandably, the business community has been much less vocal in this regard. Nevertheless, one merely has to look at the range of cross-border alliances and mergers that is gathering pace. Even given Asian companies' priorities towards domestic markets, the number of cross-border alliances is high. Capital market integration seems next on the agenda, almost as a precursor to market recovery. If Asia is to get back on the world's financial map, certainly its capital markets need to work more together instead of competing for the dwindling share of foreign portfolio investment. Georges Ugeux writes on this.

This is not to say that Asia's story is only about the nuts and bolts of economic recovery. Asians remain sympathetic neighbors, and are among the first to step back from strictly business or commercial demands to look around and be thankful for regional stability and peace. Nobuyuki Idei counsels that business should be more proactive about fulfilling its social responsibility with greater frequency. Hishamuddin Tun Hussein, Minister of Youth and Sports in Malaysia, gives a similar message of regional human understanding in his proposal for a regional collaboration. When more Asians follow the leads of Mr. Idei and Minister Hishamuddin, certainly the scope for regional tension will abate greatly. The fact that both are in positions of relative power in such different countries and sectors gives us hope that more Asians than one might otherwise suspect are receptive to such messages.

Asia's New Scenarios

H.E. Dr. Supachai Panitchpakdi
Director-General, World Trade Organization

Asia stands at a crossroads. The economic environments that provided for high and sustained growth levels in the 1980s and the beginning of the 1990s are a scenario from the past. Asia has grown up since then and has awakened to new circumstances.

Globalization used to be viewed in Asia as benign. Asians took easily to Western culture in food, dress, music and other living habits, along with the proliferation of economic and financial linkages. After the abrupt end to this prosperity, the 1997–98 financial crisis forced Asians to become more suspicious of this growing interdependence. Political parties that preached more inward-looking policies began to gain more profound popularity. Openness in economic policy can no longer be taken for granted and now is subjected to critical reconsideration.

The emergence of new market-economies such as China and the countries of Indochina has created more momentum for economic expansion and competition. Although Vietnam, Laos and Cambodia may not be, as yet, significant economies, they have already been members of ASEAN for a few years and are quickly moving along with the dynamism of ASEAN economies. Vietnam and Cambodia have both concluded bilateral trade agreements with the U.S., which should give them additional impetus to trade-related economic expansion. As a new member of the WTO, China's place in the world economy has gained in luster and real implications. The collective viability of the Asian economies should be enhanced, and we will return to this point shortly.

For a long time, Asia has been a continent without a serious effort at a region-wide economic integration. Dr. Mahathir's proposal of an East Asian Economic Caucus (EAEC), dating from the beginning of the 1990s, was found to be too exclusive and was seen as being similar to that proposed by the APEC. But in the last few years Asia seems to have rediscovered the niceties of regional or bilateral trade agreements and, in one way or another, all major economies in Asia, ranging from Japan and Korea to China and ASEAN, are now involved with them. The most significant of these is the latest consideration by the East Asian Vision Group — set up in 1999 by the leaders of ASEAN+3 (China, Japan, and Korea) — of the establishment of an East Asian Economic Community. China was the first nation to make a serious effort to entice ASEAN leaders to give their political will for an ASEAN-plus-China economic partnership. A free-trade arrangement is envisaged for this group within 10 years. Meanwhile, Japan has recently proposed an alternative in the form of a Japan-ASEAN comprehensive economic partnership.

Most Asian economies have become caught up in the new economic paradigm of an integrated, or international, production network (IPN). This production system is marked by the distribution of the sources of supply for various components in different countries, with the product to be finally assembled under one single brand name, the owner of which is generally a Western company. This IPN has linked Asian economies together in their production of IT products, electronic goods, and textiles and apparel. Intra-Asian trade is greatly influenced by IPN and is determined mainly by the cycles in product sectors of this network in fields such as electronics and textiles.

The relationship between trade and finance cannot be underestimated, particularly in Asia where, in the past, financial speculations could easily emerge as exchange rates were kept from moving flexibly for a prolonged period of time. Now that most countries have resorted to a flexible exchange-rate regime, this potential source of external disturbances seems to have been eliminated. However, since the process of financial reform (particularly in banking) and improvements in supervisory standards have only recently begun, the emphasis in the managed-floating-rate regime is on "managed", and because Asia's money markets are still quite shallow, the large impacts of exchange-rate movements should not be underestimated. As we have seen during the 1997–98 crisis, uncertainties in exchange-rate movements could easily induce sharp contractions in trade flows among countries.

COPING WITH CRISIS

When the World Bank was talking about "the Asian miracle" back in the 1980s, and Paul Krugman responded with his "myth of the Asian miracle", Asian economies were going through a purple patch as their openness produced strong impetus for growth that resulted in substantial reduction of poverty. Globalization was seen as the great catalytic force propelling economies in a fast-forward mode. Foreign investments poured in and foreign funds of all natures and maturities became available. Globalization had been a source of opportunities upon which further economic growth could have been built. Asia certainly did make use of this opportunity and might have made even more use of the globalization process had adequate attention been paid to the need to build up concomitant rules and capacities to cope with the process.

Internally, rules of law that could enhance fair competition were needed, as the economies were moving with strong currents of competition. The banking system needed to withstand the strain of fluctuating inflows and outflows of funds and be prudent in allocating credit. Social safety nets should have been constructed to lessen the pain of those who became losers from competition. Education and training that were geared to place skilled workers in a position to gain from growth and to turn unskilled workers into skilled ones were needed.

Having failed in some of these exercises, governments tended to look towards the politically expedient solutions of bailing out bankrupt firms and banks, and increasing farm subsidies, while keeping foreign competition under close scrutiny. Although multilateral trade agreements were being put into practice, some non-tariff impediments remained and were sometimes implemented with even greater frequency. Even in an advanced grouping like ASEAN, the increasing number of non-tariff protection measures in, say, the farm, petrochemical and some industrial sectors was alarming.

The need for flexible policy-making to match the pace of globalization remained. Rigidity in exchange-rate policy was the most glaring example. Technocrats groomed in the art of status quo could not bring themselves to look beyond tradition, and this situation was worsened by politicians and decision-makers who were not well-versed in international finance. The general feeling in 1997 was that, if the fixed exchange rate was kept long enough, the hoped-for economic miracle might emerge to bring support to exchange-rate levels. They did not realize the untenability of the exchange-rate levels. Moreover, the adjustment process after the financial crisis of 1997–98 and four years of financial reforms have not brought the kind of relief expected. Financial reform in Japan, with much larger sums, has already taken 10 years, with no end in sight. In the rest of Asia, with only partial reforms being put in place, one may anticipate a similarly long restructuring process.

Actually Asia was affected by another smaller crisis in 2001; the slump in the information-technology sector and stock markets in the U.S. took that economy out of the growth cycle and into a mild recession at the beginning of the year. The unprecedented growth in the IT industry, supported by the substantial outlays to prepare for Y2K, actually led to an early recovery in the export performance of East Asian economies, due to their strength as producers of IT equipment. This export-led recovery demonstrates once again the strong linkages between Asian economic conditions and the global economic scene.

The recent turnaround was not, however, sustainable. When Y2K-related investments died down, East Asia went into another round of dismal export performance in 2001. Although the depth of the second crisis is not as severe as the first, it is more widespread, affecting countries such as Taiwan and Singapore. Globalization appears to be deeply embedded into the economies of East Asia that are just beginning to learn how to fortify themselves against the tides of global interdependence.

MAINTAINING ECONOMIC GROWTH

As globalization tends to progress with technology, Asia will need to restructure even faster to stay competitive. Five years ago, before the 1997–98 crisis, this would not have posed such a meaningful challenge. But now that Asia has taken a long pause in its growth process, the commitment to restructuring seems to be clouded.

In order to prevent worsening unemployment, East Asian economies need to grow on average at a rate of 4–5% per annum. Under normal circumstances, this should not be hard to achieve, considering average annual growth rates of around 6–7% that were evident in the beginning of the 1990s. It should now be clear that, in the first half of this decade, even 5% would seem too ambitious. Thus, with an achievable rate of 3–4% , Asia's economies would have to exert tremendous effort to achieve a higher rate of 6% in the second half of the decade. This will be reached only through concerted efforts to implement needed reforms in the financial and real sectors, including liberalizing trade regimes so as to make the region attractive enough to pull in substantial amounts of foreign direct investment.

The likelihood of Asia achieving and maintaining acceptable growth rates and an open economic system aligned with globalization will be determined by several factors. These can be classified into the internal areas of economic policies, political cooperation and social changes; and external elements in the areas of trade liberalization and regional and multilateral cooperation efforts.

ECONOMIC POLICIES

Slow growth has inhibited domestic reform in Asia. Substantial sums of money have been drawn into the bottomless pit of cleaning up banks' balance sheets through asset-management companies, which use public funds to purchase non-performing loans. An example is the Indonesia Bank Restructuring Agency (IBRA), which has been struggling to resell purchased assets. Together with the ongoing fiscal expenditures to stimulate domestic economies, public debts and budget deficits are reaching alarming levels of 60% of GDP. Asia will soon have to plan fiscal spending with more circumspection.

Some Asian governments are faced with impossible options. One is to let the private sector and the market carry out the cleaning process of filing for bankruptcy that creates more unemployment. Or they can choose the costly alternative of using public funds to support recovery. The key element in either option would be the resuscitation of the banking system, which has generally been paralysed by the crisis. Ailing banks have mostly been taken over by the governments and have become more risk-averse as a result of their traumatic experiences. Capital increase is not a major problem as they adopt a defensive attitude in winding down their assets while struggling to restructure non-performing loans. The banks that have been resold, particularly to foreign banks, seem to stabilize their problems and begin anew. More banks should be sold to reputable foreigners to lessen the pressure on government budgets, but politics and nationalist feelings have been constraining this effort. Still, to avoid a long financial restructuring process, faster liberalization is a hard decision that must be taken sooner rather than later. Since this will not come easily, the recovery process is likely to cover the whole decade.

Can other solutions be sought in the meanwhile that would highlight the domestic stimulus effort and lend it more strength? Populist policies of debt relief to farmers (which results in a greater flouting of borrowing discipline by farmers and encouraging more delinquencies), the extension of interest-free loans to villages (encouraging more indebtedness), and government-sponsored health-care systems (creating more public debt with lower-quality health care covering only part of population) have been tried in several instances, creating more expectations from the electorates without really touching upon the root causes of systemic weaknesses. These contrived solutions will conjure a sense of false security while unemployment continues to grow and long-term funds are drained from the system.

In other cases, where farm prices have been depressed for a prolonged period, more subsidies have been extended to the farm sector. Politicians find it hard to resist demands from the poorest segment of their constituencies. This is why rising farm subsidies, particularly export subsidies by advanced countries, must be eliminated as soon as possible. If the causes of price depression can be removed, further price distortions which are unaffordable in Asia will disappear. The continuous process of agricultural negotiations to fight against domestic and export subsidies, in spite of the drive towards the knowledge economy, remains a key element in the reform policy in Asia.

With regard to the move into a knowledge-based economy, Asia provides a highly diverse background. The picture of a digital divide is emerging clearly in Asia as tele-density and Internet penetration strongly correlate with a country's GDP. It is still recommended that emerging and developing countries pursue reform as a route towards better performance. However, reforms through privatization and liberalization must always be supplemented by more direct investment, particularly from sources that can provide both technological know-how and funds to enhance financial feasibility. While Japan, Korea, Malaysia and India have striven to create an efficient telecom industry by encouraging an innovative competitive industry, other countries like China, Indonesia, Thailand and the Philippines are only set to promote tele-density and to mobilize additional investments. If Asia wants to stay competitive it must emphasize reform and investment in the telecom sector. Korea appears to be very much in the forefront and has succeeded in becoming so mainly because of strong political commitment to a knowledge-based society. This political will is a scarce commodity which will play a decisive role in Asia's commitment to globalization.

THE POLITICAL EQUATION

As the process of globalization accelerates and intensifies, questions are being increasingly raised over the issues of international agreements and national sovereignty. Trade negotiations and agreements used to have simple implications for areas such as tariffs and domestic trade rules. But as the agenda has become broader and more comprehensive, other related issues such as the protection of intellectual-property rights, sanitary and phyto-sanitary standards, environmental standards and labor rights have been introduced. The faster globalization moves forward, the more questions arise about equity and legitimacy, especially emphasizing civil society and the underprivileged groups left out of the process.

While there is a tendency to fall in line with the need for a system of global governance to make globalization work for all, people in general have begun to develop legitimate doubts as to whether existing international institutions are democratic enough to account for the unequal status of members. With regard to Asia in particular, questions arise as to the kind of democracy in Asia, with all the externalities and contingencies, that would be able to eventually face the challenges of globalization.

The Asian crisis has not only exposed flaws in Asia's economies but also laid bare deep structural deficiencies in the political and socio-economic systems of the region. Already far-reaching political reforms and restructuring have taken place in countries where political instability and social unrest have led to changes in government. However, the political dimension of the crisis is as important as the economic and the social. In various countries, the political system has failed to generate a sound and stable institutional framework for transparent rules and supervision and to provide for a balance between dynamic growth and system stability.

Politically, Asia has grown through the crisis. The roots of democracy are more firmly planted, and there is more public scrutiny of the political process. Long-standing regimes have been made to take into account more the voices of the people. In some cases, parliamentary watchdogs have also helped to guide the democratic process in the most responsible manner. Several court cases have been brought against well-known businesspeople who were involved in some malpractice. Laws will bring about a fairer and more responsible treatment of bankruptcy cases and public cases.

While, arguably, democracy gains from the crisis, more participatory democracy does not automatically mean more acceptance of globalization. Asians have become more skeptical of the negative side of globalization and in some cases, with political prodding, are becoming more nationalistic. If democracy is the most effective guarantee of good governance, then we should expect a close correlation between democratization and globalization in Asia. Elections will be fought more on the battlefield of economic and social policies. Asian politicians should become more strongly accountable to their electorate, who would be more demanding in their need to understand the consequences of globalization. As this new political equation endures, younger politicians should emerge with a more global sense of responsibility which is, nevertheless, deeply rooted in the regional characteristics of the Asian society. This should provide better balance vis-à-vis the international organizations and also enable better access to their benefits.

SOCIAL CHANGES

During the long period of economic growth in Asia, social policy has consistently been in the back seat in the national policy debates. In the aftermath of the crisis it has become glaringly evident that the absence or inadequacy of social safety nets needs to be urgently addressed. Various international institutions, such as the International Labour Organization and the World Bank, continue to draw attention to the pertinent issues of labor, women, absolute poverty, and the environment, and, at the international level, efforts are being made to manage the process of globalization to make it work for both rich and poor. The Doha Declaration of the Fourth WTO Ministerial Conference in November 2001, included, for the first time in the WTO, a significant program of negotiations on trade and environment.

As a result of the financial meltdown and rising unemployment, the social-security system has expanded to encompass large and small enterprises in the private sector. Additional health-care programs are being introduced while the debates intensify on the issue of protecting intellectual-property rights and the accessibility of essential drugs. Several countries in Asia are capable of producing these drugs, given the necessary licensing and R&D support from multinational pharmaceutical firms.

The financial crisis and the speed of globalization have pushed Asia to learn the hard lessons of the need for good governance and the accumulation of social capital as the keys to sustained growth. Transparent and responsive governments are bound to enhance the level of investment in rural infrastructure, agricultural research and extension, human-resource development and health care, and expand the reach of social safety-net programs.

Issues in the areas of core labor rights, such as eradication of child labor and gender equality, are being given the highest priority as part of the process of building social capital. At the same time, Asia is seeking an unprecedented growth in the production of science-oriented human resources, as witnessed in China and India.

In the areas of environmental protection, emphasis is being given to water treatment, urban air pollution and substantial reforestation efforts. And in order to make agricultural development ecologically sustainable, governments and the private sector have begun to invest heavily in promoting resource-conserving yet highly productive farming systems. Seen in this light, globalization has become a force for change and a promoter of social dynamism in Asia.

NEW REGIONALISM

Apart from the need to enforce domestic restructuring programs, globalization is also causing Asia to seek a new sense of direction externally. Collectively, in spite of rising doubts about trade liberalization, Asian economies should reap more benefits from further expansion of free trade. So we can expect Asia in general to remain faithful to the open-market regime. But, in spite of the fact that Asia has long been a proponent of multilateralism, regionalism is on the rise. Bilateral agreements are proliferating along the line of the so-called closer economic partnership to indicate cooperation not only in the areas of trade but also in investment and economic development in general. Financial cooperation in the forms of bilateral and multilateral swap agreements among Asian central banks are other forms of regional cooperation that have come about as a result of the financial crisis. It is to be expected that such agreements might eventually be developed into a full-fledged Asian Monetary Agreement that can supply liquidity as a last resort, as well as oversee much-needed financial reform in the region.

Firm political will in this regard can already be seen with regard to the so-called ASEAN+3 economic integration. An East Asia Vision Group, created in 1999 to formulate agendas for East Asian cooperation, has recently recommended the establishment of the East Asia Free Trade Area, including more cooperation in financial, political and security, environmental, social and cultural areas. In fact, practical work has already started, with the creation of an FTA between ASEAN and China that is expected to be completed within a decade. This, in turn, has been followed by the proposal by Japan's Prime Minister in January 2002 of an initiative for a comprehensive economic partnership between Japan and ASEAN, encompassing trade and investment, human-resource development, science and technology, and tourism.

China's accession to the WTO has become a great motivating force for markets in East Asia to join up so that the advantages accruing from economies of scale can be meshed with the wider diversity of production base, the availability of technical skills, the abundance of natural resources, with the ultimate aim of a more comprehensive Asia-wide integration that will probably include India, Australia and New Zealand. This new regionalism in Asia may sound tentative but it is truly based on Asian pragmatism to realize the need for regional governance of the globalization process.

CONCLUSION

As we move into the new millennium, the recognition that we are breaking into a new era of the knowledge-based economy is fully accepted in Asia. Because of its traditional embrace of an open economy and because of the traumas it experienced during the financial crisis, Asia has found a *raison d'etre* of twin policies combining domestic reforms in economic, political and social areas with regional, inter-regional and multinational cooperation. Asian production units have already been increasingly taken up as parts of the so-called international integrated-production network. The remaining trick is how to internalize the benefits from this network in creating more home-grown R&D, inventions and designs, and link them up with national endowments. It seems that, after all, globalization has become a powerful force of change that will accelerate the speed of institution-building in Asia as never before.

Towards Win-Win Growth Through Regional Trade

Xi Jinping
Governor of Fujian Province, People's Republic of China

 Since the adoption of reform and opening-up policies, China's economic growth has maintained a rapid upward momentum, exceeding the world's average annual GDP by about seven percentage points. China is now the seventh-largest economy in the world and, on the whole, its people's livelihood has reached a fairly comfortable level. The rapid and steady growth of the Chinese economy has made a significant contribution to the world economy, particularly in East Asia. We still remember the great difficulties that Asia's financial crisis brought to East Asian economies. By not devaluing the RMB and ensuring continued economic growth, China helped to lessen the unfavorable impact of the financial turmoil.

Again, in 2001, the world economy suffered a global slowdown, and uncertainty driven by terrorism added to the turbulence. However, China's economy continues to maintain a vigorous growth. China's GDP for 2001, however, has exceeded the expected rate of 7% set early in the year, and injected vigor into the world's economy. Given economic globalization, China's accession to the WTO has brought about new opportunities for cooperation between China and the rest of the world, in particular through bilateral cooperation with countries in East Asia. The Chinese government has committed itself to follow WTO rules and regulations, and laws inconsistent with WTO membership will be amended. On the whole, this will further enhance China's socialist market economy. This process will help China to join the world more quickly and make a greater contribution to the world economy. For Fujian, further efforts on reform and opening up will strengthen cooperation with East Asia and boost Fujian's overall economic development in a sustained manner.

Fujian is a relatively developed coastal province and was one of the first provinces to open up to the outside world. With Changjiang delta to the north and Zhujiang delta to the south, Fujian enjoys an ideal location and superior natural conditions. It is near to Hong Kong and Macau, facing Taiwan across the straits, and is part of the dynamic economic-development belt that includes Japan and the Republic of Korea. Fujian is also known as a major home for overseas Chinese: overseas Chinese from Fujian now reside worldwide; 90% of them are in Asia, further cementing close historical ties. Since the drive towards reform and opening up was initiated, Fujian has combined its natural resources, its connections to overseas Chinese, its close ties with Taiwan and its status as a special economic zone with policies and flexible measures granted by the central government and given them full play. This has helped its economy to enjoy a consistent and rapid development, and expand its aggregated economic strength in the past two decades through an annual provincial GDP growth rate of 12.9%, thereby exceeding the national average. Fujian has climbed in national economic rankings, from 23rd position in 1979 to 11th in 2000 in overall economic strength, and from 22nd in 1979 to sixth in 2000 in GDP per capita.

Among the key reasons for Fujian's economic development has been the adherence to a policy of expanding the opening-up, especially with East Asia. Since the adoption of reform and opening-up policies, Fujian's foreign trade volume has witnessed a sustained and rapid increase, reaching a total trade volume in 2000 of US$21.2 billion, a 20.5% increase over the previous year. Total trade volume accounted for over 44% of the province's GDP, and export volumes have grown from US$400 million in 1981 (6.8% of the province's GDP) to US$12.9 billion in 2000 (27.3%). Fujian's exports account for 5.2% of national exports, ranking it sixth among all the provinces.

East Asia is Fujian's most important trade partner, accounting for about 45% of the province's total. Trade with Taiwan is also strong, and exports from Fujian to Taiwan account for 10% of the national total. Exports to Japan, on the other hand, account for 18% of Fujian's total exports and exports to Hong Kong account for about 12%. In 2001, despite an adverse external trade environment the growth, in the province's foreign trade still managed to reach 6% overall, and 8% for trade with East Asia.

Fujian also enjoys strong foreign economic cooperation and investment. By the year 2000, the volume of foreign direct investment (FDI) had reached US$34 billion, of which some US$19 billion came from East Asia. Over 16,000 foreign-invested enterprises have been established in Fujian, and of those 10,000 are funded by East Asia, with Hong Kong, Macau and Taiwan accounting for the largest portion of FDI. Foreign-invested enterprises have made significant contributions to Fujian's development through growing exports, investment in fixed assets, tax revenues, employment opportunities and upgraded industrial patterns. In 2000, for instance, exports from foreign-funded enterprises accounted for 59% of the province's total exports. Foreign-funded enterprises accounted for 35% of the province's social fixed-asset investment from 1996 to 2000; 60% of provincial industrial output; and 25% of tax revenues. They also provide about one-quarter of employment for the province.

Overall, foreign-funded enterprises and, in particular, Taiwan-funded infrastructure facilities and enterprises, such as Top Victory Electronics (Fujian), China Picturetubes, and Southeast Automobile, have made a positive contribution in enhancing the quality of the province's basic industries. They have helped Fujian's basic industries to keep pace with the national economy.

Economic cooperation and exchanges between Fujian and East Asia have benefited Fujian and also pushed forward the economic development of East Asia in general. Of Fujian's imports, over 75% come from Asia, with over 61% coming from East Asia in particular. It should be noted also that Fujian continues to have a significant trade deficit with East Asia, meaning that East Asia gains more than Fujian in bilateral trade. The major sources of Fujian's imports are Taiwan, Korea and Japan, in that order, and the province maintains significant trade deficits with each partner. All of this shows that, by sustaining a rapid growth of imports from other countries in East Asia, Fujian has made significant contributions to the economic development and employment levels of these countries.

When East Asian countries invest in Fujian, the benefits are mutual. Fujian offers East Asian investors relatively inexpensive land, electricity and labor, as well as various preferential policies. These have contributed to their strong economic results. Since the reform and opening-up, most of the enterprises from the East Asian countries and regions who have made investments in Fujian have run their businesses well and have gained relatively good economic results. In addition, many of these foreign-funded enterprises from Japan, Korea, Hong Kong, Macau and Taiwan that were set up in the early or middle periods of reform and opening-up are small and medium-sized enterprises that had difficulties surviving in their own countries or were facing the possibility of elimination. The survival and growth of these enterprises have strongly promoted the transformation and economic upgrading of East Asia. In this way, Fujian has made positive contributions to promoting the overall economic development of these countries and regions.

Clearly, economic cooperation and exchanges between Fujian and East Asia have helped to boost the sustained and rapid economic development of Fujian and have pushed forward the rational division of industrial sectors and readjustment, optimization and upgrading of economic structures elsewhere in East Asia. This has effectively increased the overall competitiveness and stability of the East Asian economy. In short, economic cooperation and exchanges between Fujian and East Asia are mutually beneficial and complement each other's advantages. By now, both sides have realized that their common aim lies in these win-win results.

As we enter a new century, Fujian Province has set out on a new road of building a prosperous society, which has been sealed in the Tenth Five-Year Plan of Fujian Province, drafted in 2002. To reach the goal of 9% annual economic growth by the year 2005 and to implement the construction of a zone of prosperity on the west bank of the straits by 2010, Fujian must continue to open up and, especially, to strengthen economic cooperation and exchanges with its longtime friends in East Asia.

Opening-up is the biggest advantage and the future hope for Fujian. In the new century, Fujian Province will continue on this path, taking China's entry into the WTO as a milestone and a guide to the new requirements of economic globalization. We will continue to study new situations and changes in the world economy and further expand economic cooperation and exchanges with the rest of the world, especially with East Asia. We will continue to increase our exports; to introduce more foreign capital and advanced technology to constantly bolster the process; to promote the sustained, rapid and coordinated development of the national economy and social undertakings; and to accelerate the realization of the third step of the strategic goal of modernization.

The further opening-up of Fujian in the new century will provide new opportunities for the economic development of East Asia. Fujian actively encourages foreign investment in the modernization of traditional agriculture. It will also try to attract significant amounts of foreign capital to invest in high-tech and new technologies, such as electronic information, bio-engineering and new materials, and to develop machinery and petrochemical industries. We will also encourage foreign investment into the construction of highways, harbors, railways and other urban infrastructure facilities. In service and trade, Fujian will accelerate the development of emerging service industries.

It is fully expected that the implementation of the Tenth Five-Year Plan will provide opportunities for cooperation and development between Fujian and East Asia. The continuous adoption of economic-development measures such as expanding domestic demand, intensifying investment in fixed assets, and developing new technologies, will produce a rapid growth of imports. Current estimates show that Fujian's imports will reach about US$13 billion by 2005. Moreover, improvements in infrastructure will create favorable conditions for more economic cooperation between Fujian and other countries. The role of Fujian Province as the strategic window into the southeast coastal area of China will be further enhanced. In particular, before 2005, a coastal passage linking the Yangtze River Delta and the Pearl River Delta, and an east–west transportation passage linking the mid and western part of China will be built, which will further support the development of trade, and boost the rapid development of entrepôt and service trades. At that time, Fujian will play an even bigger role in the East Asian trade network, and cooperative economic relations between Fujian and other countries, in particular those in East Asia, will be closer.

The early- and mid-21st century will be a critical period for Fujian's modernization, as well as for the East Asian economy. Regional economic cooperation will enter a new era of development in line with the principles of promoting mutual benefit and complementary advantages. We sincerely look forward to strengthening economic cooperation and exchanges with other countries in East Asia, to making progress together, to realizing win-win results and to creating a better future.

Cambodia and the Quest for Regional and Sub-regional Integration

Keat Chhon
Senior Minister and Minister of Economy and Finance,
Cambodia

BACKGROUND

In April 1999 when Cambodia joined ASEAN, the vision of a united Southeast Asia came into being. This quest for regional integration constitutes one of the three pillars of the strategy of the Royal Government of Cambodia (RGC) to maintain peace and security in the country and in the region, embrace regional and world affairs and institute multi-faceted reforms. These will have far-reaching effects on the country's social and economic development.

Regional economic integration will generate positive externalities in stimulating economic development in Cambodia, and ASEAN membership brings many opportunities and challenges for the country. One challenge is to narrow the gaps between older and newer ASEAN members. The government is confident that promoting sub-regional cooperation and integration is also crucial for Cambodia's endeavors to promote economic take-off. In this regard, attention has been given to strengthening sub-regional efforts, such as the development of the Greater Mekong Sub-region (GMS), the establishment of economic growth triangles, such as the Northeastern Growth Triangle between Cambodia, Laos and Vietnam, and the Northwestern Growth Triangle between Cambodia, Laos and Thailand.

GREATER MEKONG SUB-REGION: THE RATIONALE FOR CLOSER ECONOMIC COOPERATION

Cambodia gives considerable importance to the development and cooperation within the GMS framework. The GMS is a huge region, with some 250 million inhabitants; it comprises five ASEAN members — Cambodia, Laos, Myanmar, Thailand and Vietnam — plus China's Yunnan Province; and has great potential for economic growth and development. Apart from sharing common borders, countries are linked by common histories, cultures and religions.

Most importantly the peoples of the GMS all make their living from the same source, the famous Mekong River. The history and livelihoods of the people in this region are more or less linked to the Mekong River. The river provides great potential for power and sources of invaluable natural resources. The GMS is rich in agriculture, forestry, fisheries and scenery.

In short, GMS countries possess complementary endowments in natural resources, human capital and historical sites. With adequate capital and wise investments, this sub-region could enjoy rapid, sustainable economic growth. For this reason, a vision of the GMS in the 21st century rests on three main features.

The first is the transformation of a region riven by internal conflicts and instability to an oasis of peace, security, stability and cooperation. Already much evidence exists to show substantive progress in this endeavor. Beyond the GMS, the vision of a united Southeast Asia has become a reality with the accomplishment of the ASEAN-10. A number of viable mechanisms have been put in place to foster consultations and strengthen security, political and economic cooperation. The backbone of these mechanisms is the ASEAN Regional Forum (ARF), which attracts the attention and participation of the major players and superpowers in pursuit of "preventive diplomacy" for regional peace and cooperation. The GMS is another important way to engage China as a direct partner in the cooperation with smaller economies and, to this end, the GMS can become a strategic gateway to China for Southeast Asia.

Strengthening regional cooperation is very important in that it represents several key opportunities. First, cooperation will help to resolve outstanding issues of common concerns in the region. Second, this kind of cooperation will provide countries in the sub-region with opportunities to develop through joint development projects in important areas such as communication, transport, power and telecommunication networks. Third, participating countries can act jointly to meet common, regional needs, such as investment promotion, technology development, human-resources training and knowledge transfer.

The enhancement of economic cooperation in the region through joint implementation of programs to foster free movement of goods, services and factors of production, as well as the coordination of economic and financial policies, legal systems, quality standards, and the establishment of an information-sharing network, will greatly facilitate the process of regional economic integration. This represents another opportunity for increasing economies of scale and enhancing the comparative advantage of regional countries through international competition and specialization.

The second feature is to transform this underdeveloped part of Asia into a center of growth and sustainable development. In view of the potential and emerging opportunities, many initiatives have been launched to support the region's development. As early as 1957, the Mekong Committee (MC) was established by Cambodia, Laos, Thailand and Vietnam to coordinate water-resources management of the lower Mekong Basin. In 1995, this committee became the Mekong River Commission (MRC).

During the past few years, more attention has been focused on the development of the Mekong Sub-region. In 1992, the Asian Development Bank (ADB) launched an initiative to promote cooperation in the GMS. Consultations between and among countries produced more than 100 projects in several important sectors, such as transport, power, telecommunications, tourism, environment, human-resource development, trade and investment. Sub-regional initiatives to promote tourism have been particularly successful, supported by the active involvement of the private sector. Environment cooperation is increasingly concerned with trans-border issues, such as the cumulative effects of development in the sub-region.

The GMS program is very different from ASEAN or other regional agreements since it is informal and guided only by a general set of principles and institutional arrangements. It is a pragmatic, results-oriented program whereby the six countries agree to plan and implement projects seen to be mutually beneficial. The projects selected for inclusion in the program generally have one or more of the following objectives or results:

- *facilitating sub-regional trade and investment:* for example, improvements in transportation and telecommunications systems linking the sub-regions
- *facilitating sub-regional development opportunities:* for example, energy projects or tourism promotion, access, and production development
- *facilitating resolution of trans-border issues:* for example, cooperation in protecting critical watersheds, mitigating the spread of communicable diseases, and harmonizing training standards

- *facilitating fulfillment of common resources or other needs:* for example, cooperation in meeting training needs or developing an environmental database for the sub-region.

These development projects cover many sectors and require large amounts of investment that may outstrip the capacity of the countries in the region. According to an ADB study, some US$9 billion will be needed to undertake projects in transport and telecommunications alone, not to mention other priority areas such as the environment, human-resource development, trade, investment, tourism and institutional capacity-building.

Given these huge needs, the main challenge for GMS countries is to identify potential sources of funding. This can be partially met by strengthening partnerships between regional countries and donors, especially the international and regional financial institutions. Governments participating in this cooperation should establish a national list of priority projects that are drawn from the framework of sub-regional development projects. Already some projects have been implemented within this framework, including the first GMS road-construction project, which improves the Phnom Penh – Ho Chi Minh City road.

As one of the engines for the region's growth, the private sector has a crucial role to play in these development projects. The private sector's financial resources, expertise, management skill and modern technology are needed to create and boost the dynamism for growth and development in each country. A top priority for all governments is to engage the private sector in this important endeavor.

Another challenge is to ensure that the many GMS initiatives and projects are complementary, rather than competitive or overlapping. There must be closer cooperation between initiatives such as the ADB's Greater Mekong Sub-region, the Forum on the Comprehensive Development of Indochina, the ASEAN-Mekong Basin Development Cooperation, the Mekong River Commission, the AEM-MITI Economic and Industrial Cooperation Committee (AMEICC) and other schemes under the umbrella of the UNDP and multilateral agencies. The crucial factor in this is to ensure effective coordination among cooperating countries with a view to maximizing the complementarities and ensuring the ownership of various projects and initiatives, rather than leave these projects and initiatives to the discretion of donors. To this end, attention should be given to national and institutional capacity-building at both national and sub-regional level. Countries in the sub-region should properly prioritize the GMS development projects, ensure a division of labor and mobilize our energy, resources and expertise to implement the agreed priority projects.

Should these development projects be implemented as planned, they will contribute to the alleviation of poverty, which continues to inhibit many millions of people in the GMS countries. In this respect, the third feature that characterizes the GMS in the 21st century is the transformation of a region stricken by poverty into an epicenter of prosperity. Peace and stability has brought the GMS friendship and cooperation.

REFORMS: THE RECIPE FOR ECONOMIC TAKE-OFF

Despite setbacks from the recent economic crisis, continued peace and market-based reforms have sustained economic growth and development in the GMS. For the ASEAN emerging economies, such as Cambodia, the challenge is to accelerate the internal reform processes. In this regard, Cambodia has made a concrete contribution to achieve the above vision.

Cambodia and Cambodians from all walks of life are at peace for the first time in many years. Cambodia now is one integrated, self-contained territory under one government, and political stability and security have helped to strengthen democracy, promote development and reduce poverty. The commitment to democracy, the respect for human rights, the prevalence of peace and national reconciliation in the country, the dismantling of the political and military organization of the Khmer Rouge — a major source of long-term instability in the country — all are of paramount importance to sustainable growth and development, not only for Cambodia but for all of Southeast Asia.

In the early 1990s, the Cambodian Government embarked on wide-ranging, macroeconomic and structural reforms and achieved some successes in stabilizing the economy. The economy expanded rapidly during the first half of the 1990s, despite the financial crises, while inflation was dramatically reduced.

To accelerate further this growth momentum, the new Cambodian coalition government, formed after the general election in 1998, has taken serious steps to ensure success for its "Triangle Strategy". The first side of this strategic triangle is building peace, restoring stability and maintaining security for the nation. The second side is Cambodia's rapid integration into the international community and normalization of our relationships with international financial institutions. The third side is to promote development based on the favorable conditions created by the implementation of key reform programs such as military demobilization, fiscal and judiciary reforms, land reform, eradication of corruption and cracking down on illegal logging, and environmental protection. As a result, growth in Cambodia rose again in 1999 and 2000, despite severe flooding, and inflation was kept at a very low level.

Although the tragic events of September 11 increased what were already significant downside risks in the region, the outlook for Cambodia is favorable. Certainly, some industries have been hit. For instance, tourist arrivals are likely to increase by 25% for 2001, instead of the projected 30%, and garment exports have also fallen short of targets. However, a bounce-back is projected for 2002.

In response to the current developments, the government has taken steps to attract visitors from Asia and promote Cambodia as a safe destination for tourism. Efforts are under way to diversify the economy by promoting investments in agriculture and agri-business.

Through these endeavors Cambodia has made concrete contributions to the common peace, stability, progress and prosperity within the GMS as well as in Southeast Asia. It is true that Cambodia will need assistance from development partners, especially the private sector, to shape a better future for our people. However, with successful reforms Cambodia will become a source of energy for the region and will contribute to strengthening the Greater Mekong's endeavors for stronger peace, stability, friendship, cooperation and prosperity.

ECONOMIC GROWTH AREAS

Regional cooperation represents a unique opportunity to complement strategies to combat poverty by: (i) stimulating growth in border areas that are often the poorest areas of the country; (ii) facilitating access to markets through infrastructure that could further enhance agricultural production and raise rural incomes; (iii) responding to the needs of ethnic minorities and other vulnerable groups; (iv) reducing the marginal cost of providing services, such as telecommunications and electrification to the rural areas through regional transmission links; and (v) strengthening the participation of all stakeholders. In this context, a key strategic thrust is to open borders to cross-border movement of goods and people.

Expansion of key transport corridors in the sub-region is also crucial for regional and sub-regional growth. More "growth corridors" that develop areas along the road network to turn them into agricultural, industrial, trade and investment development zones, are needed. An economic corridor is a well-defined area where infrastructure improvements are linked with production, trade and other development opportunities in order to promote economic development and cooperation among contiguous regions or countries. With the economic-corridor approach, the link between infrastructure development and the expansion of production investments increases employment and generates income, thereby helping to reduce poverty.

Another approach to narrow the gap in the levels of development and to reduce poverty and socio-economic disparities is to establish a socio-economic development triangle in the border areas. The Royal Government of Cambodia has envisaged the establishment of a growth triangle in the areas bordering with Laos and Vietnam, called the CLV Growth Triangle, as well as the areas bordering Laos and Thailand, called the CLT Growth Triangle.

As part of the CLV growth triangle, steps have been taken to institutionalize this cooperation by establishing working groups to discuss a wide range of issues relating to the potential for economic cooperation and the direction for development in the border zones of the three countries.

Such arrangements are designed to complement overall ASEAN economic cooperation. The Fourth ASEAN Summit and the ASEAN Vision 2020 have mandated the establishment and promotion of sub-regional economic arrangements among ASEAN members and between ASEAN members and non-ASEAN economies. They involve areas that may be at a considerable distance from their respective capitals but happen to be near one another. The economic development of these areas is stimulated through the promotion of trade and investment. The proximity of markets helps reduce costs. Foreign direct investments that are export-oriented should therefore find these growth areas attractive. Existing infrastructures should be improved to support the expansion of economic activities.

The rationale behind establishing growth triangles is that economic growth cannot be separated from education, human-resources development, science and technology and the environment. These areas can be connected together through special sub-regional initiatives for cooperation in information technology and for sharing our experiences and expertise in technical assistance. Transparency, openness and public dialogue are critical ingredients in forging the self-image of our people and countries.

With adequate infrastructure and policy coordination among the participating governments, this growth area should easily attract substantial foreign direct investments. In all the growth areas, the resources of the participating regions complement one another, enabling manufacturing firms to achieve vertical integration in their operations as well as economies of scale. The creation of a wider manufacturing base with resources that are similarly complementary should induce multinational corporations to consider the region as a whole in expanding their business activities.

This new concept for growth areas is to remove a number of *political, economic and social constraints:*

- The concept needs to be better understood, complex decision-making structures have to be simplified, border formalities have to be established and the inadequacy of infrastructures has to be remedied. Addressing these concerns requires time, expertise and financial resources.

- Private investors, international financial institutions and donors are invited to also be engaged in the massive development venture, initially involving roads and railway development to further stimulate growth in the region.

- There is a need for linking this growth triangle with the sub-regional initiatives such as the GMS and the ASEAN Mekong Basin Development Cooperation in order to complement the regional development plans of the Mekong Basin countries and mobilize the participation of the private sector in the projects and activities of the Cooperation.

- Linking the regional growth efforts with the ASEAN Investment Area (AIA), which is aimed at attracting greater and sustainable levels of investment flows to the region through developing further the attractiveness and competitiveness of ASEAN's investment regime, will provide a firm basis for ASEAN's efforts towards greater economic integration.

- A steering committee and working groups (road, electricity, water supply, finance) should be established to further institutionalize the Cambodia-Laos-Vietnam Growth Area.

In order to successfully implement the sub-regional cooperative efforts and strengthen economic integration in order to effectively engage in the process of regionalization and globalization, attention should be given to the following issues:

First, this growth region should offer to businessmen and investors immense opportunities for the exploitation of the region's rich resources and the complementary locational advantages which could easily suit any corporate strategy. Therefore, it is important to establish a very competitive environment in which governments have to take all necessary measures to boost efficiency, make our region an attractive base for investments and open up exciting opportunities for joint efforts between the public and private sectors.

Second, it is fair to argue that many of the regional and sub-regional economic initiatives were developed primarily to encourage private-sector development. Their establishment should generate a surge in tourism, infrastructure-related activities and trade in the sub-region. Therefore, it is important to discuss important issues related to attracting private investment, such as the need to establish a master plan for regional development, the adoption of a specific investment regime for the growth area, taxation and the like.

Third, the economic success of this cooperation and ability to attract sizeable FDI flows owe much to the peace, security and stability which we have assiduously built. The governments shall therefore remain firmly committed to this and shall take all steps to ensure that our region remains free of tensions and conflicts.

Fourth, the governments should link these growth areas to bigger ASEAN projects, such as the Trans-ASEAN Highway and the development of a railway link from Singapore to Kunming in Southern China.

Fifth, training or technical-assistance programs to develop human resources should be linked to the region-wide cooperation within the East Asia framework. This is a practical measure to help improve the management capacity as well as the ability to receive new technologies, which is crucial to the development of these border areas.

Environmental degradation, global terrorism, international crime and other transnational problems also demand our increased attention. It is crucial to have a more concerted drive against transboundary pollution, terrorism, the trade in illicit arms and drugs, money laundering, and the pernicious traffic exploiting human beings, particularly women and children. Perhaps it is time to formulate norms and common standards, if not binding agreements, to govern behavior and foster cooperation in these critical areas.

The broader and deeper sub-regional economic integration will pave the way for regional integration on a larger scale, thus facilitating a more effective participation of the region in the global cooperation process.

In this manner, our government has laid the foundations for a genuine sub-regional cooperation, built on the aspirations of our people to improve their lives and to live in harmony as good neighbors with one another. One must reach out for a new vision, a vision that will see our peoples as common stakeholders in the destiny of our sub-region. Our citizens on their own will stimulate the growth of closer people-to-people linkages, drawing strength from both our regional diversity and solidarity.

The Collaboration of Asian Civilizations

Hishamuddin Tun Hussein
Minister of Youth and Sports, Malaysia

 September 11, 2001 has altered global politics forever. The terrible atrocity and the frightening flurry of images — airplanes, explosions, buildings, destruction, people — has resulted in a dramatic change of mindset both in the United States of America and in Europe. Suddenly, the violence of the act became indistinguishable from words such as "religious extremism", "militancy", "security", "Afghanistan" and even "Islam". Suddenly these words and the ideas behind them bear an entirely new, deeply troubling set of connotations. For many in the West, Islam has become the "other": something that must be feared, loathed and fought against.

Furthermore, many people in the media have insisted on characterizing the attacks on American soil as *a priori* an assault on the world. In response to what was, without doubt, a terrible and bloody attack, the American people were forced to take action. Their desire for revenge and retribution is understandable. It is deeply human and unavoidable. In the immediate aftermath of the tragedy the world was more than willing to share the grief of the American people.

However, after a period of time, the world expected a more measured and thoughtful response. When in the wake of the terror, the U.S. launched a coalition for the global War Against Terrorism, many — especially in the Islamic world — were troubled by the perceived anti-Muslim tone of the Americans. For example, when the U.S. launched its war, President George W. Bush's clarion call to the world came in the form of an ultimatum: "You are either with us or against us".

Sadly, such rhetoric is far too simplistic for such a complex set of problems. As Ariel Sharon has discovered, violence begets violence. Force must always be measured and considered. It cannot be the sole factor in a nation's diplomatic toolbox.

Nonetheless, the divisive rhetoric has made it clear that a nation's political and economic competitive advantages are now determined by where they stand in the War Against Terrorism. Of course, as with any simplistic solution, there are obstacles.

The most important complication was the exclusion of most Muslim nations from this coalition against terror. In the terms laid down by President Bush, many Muslim nations who condemned terrorism but did not aid the U.S.'s military excursions against Osama Bin Laden and the Taliban in Afghanistan would be deemed as being "against the U.S.". Unfortunately, the reality was that the U.S.-led war against terrorism was being perverted into a clash between civilizations. In fact, Italian Prime Minister Silvio Berlusconi — perhaps in his hasty extremist support for the U.S. — went as far as to contrast Islamic civilization to the "superiority" of Western civilization. Thus, there were certain quarters that began to see the War Against Terrorism in terms of a war between the progressive, superior Western civilizations and the supposedly backward, extremist and weaker Islamic civilizations. Knowingly or otherwise, the resulting dichotomy caused the war to be interpreted as a clash of civilizations.

The simplistic solution of being "with" or "against" the U.S. is not the most effective answer to this challenge. The symptoms and causes of terrorism are complex and, therefore, its cure would also be equally complex. Hence, the first step towards solving a global problem must begin with a global response.

As has been repeated over and over again, the terrorist attacks on New York and Washington did not merely concern the U.S. They concerned the entire world. The entire citizenry of the world is a victim when it comes to terrorism. Therefore, the entire world has a part to play in the War Against Terrorism. To begin to find a global solution to terrorism, it is incumbent upon all citizens of the world to use every effort to foster a greater international unity and avoid a clash of civilizations at all costs. Because of its ramifications down the years, we must, instead, embrace a *collaboration* of civilizations.

MALAYSIA: A MODEL GLOBAL VILLAGE

There are few places in the world where there has been a true collaboration of civilizations along the lines of the "global village" concept. Whilst there are some who would seek to prevent a coming together, it cannot be stopped: the world is inexorably coming together. Our neighbors are no longer those who are just geographically next to us. Ethnic or cultural homogeneity, too, is slowly becoming passé. Our trading partners are no longer necessarily of the same race, cultural background or religion. We are living in a much smaller world but with a much greater diversity. The world community must cope with this fact. Multiculturalism will be the norm, and not just a buzzword. Hence, nations that are prepared for cross-cultural communication and a diverse community will be poised for the advantage to excel in this new millennium.

It is for all these reasons that Malaysia can and will play a very strategic role as a model global village. Ask any typical Malaysian on the street and you will realize that our diversity is our greatest strength. While the rest of the world is only now coming to terms with the global village concept, this has been an integral aspect of life in Malaysia since Independence over 44 years ago.

In cultural terms, the most striking aspect about Malaysia is the fact that it is the only society in the world where the great civilizations of Asia have come to a convergent point. Three great streams of civilization — Hinduism, Confucianism and Malay Islam — rich with history and culture meet at the riverhead of Malaysia. Perhaps it is no wonder that our Federal capital is called Kuala Lumpur (the word *kuala* is Malay for "meeting point", specifically at a river). It is here in Malaysia that Islam, Confucian China and Hindu India have come into direct contact with one another and all at once. Of course, there are also shadows and intimations of other cultures and civilizations — the Buddhist traditions that still remain firmly ensconced on mainland Southeast Asia; the rich and eclectic animistic beliefs; as well as Christianity in all its various forms, whether Catholic or Protestant.

It is the pride of the nation that we are a harmonious multi-racial and multi-religious country. Malaysia is perhaps the only country in the world where a government can be fully functional in the midst of a racially, religiously and even culturally diverse populace. Where else could you find a country in which the festivities of each culture and religion are celebrated with equal exuberance by the entire nation — ranging from Chinese New Year, through to Deepavali, Aidilfitri, Gawai or the Iban Harvest Festival and the Kadazan Kaamatan? What stronger evidence do we have of our sense of community than our practice of having *rumah terbuka*, the Malay term for "open houses", during festivals? I believe this experience is unique to Malaysia — that on a grand scale, our homes are opened up to guests, regardless of race, culture or religion, in the name of friendship.

Malaysians have been unique in our ability to take pride in celebrating one another's civilizations and their rich history, while still maintaining our united identity as Malaysians. This is perhaps the strongest example of what a global village should look like. Despite the obvious differences and problems that we have faced, we have still managed to maintain more than 44 years of relative political stability and economic prosperity.

The international business community has much to gain by learning from Malaysia's example. As multiculturalism becomes a reality in the world economy, businesses will need to adapt to accommodate this fact. Malaysia would be the ideal model in which to facilitate this.

MALAYSIA: A MODEL ISLAMIC NATION

Malaysia is also a model Islamic nation, regarded for its successful brand of progressive, moderate Islam. This has been evidenced by our political, economic and technological advancement.

Now, why is this an important point to note? The international community has rightfully denounced Islamic extremism and militancy that has resulted in terrorism. In its critique, however, it has failed to provide an alternative example for Muslim nations to follow. Many Muslims are left with a sense that they are heading in the wrong direction, when the problem is that they know of *no other* direction. A much better way would be for the international community to provide an alternative focal point for struggling Muslim nations to pursue.

The events of September 11 have brought the Islamic world under intense scrutiny. Even as the world sought to come to terms with these events, the foremost question on people's minds was "Why?". For the first time, many Americans were shocked and had to deal with the hatred expressed towards them. It was even sadder when news networks began running footage of people from Middle Eastern nations dancing in the streets at the news of the tragedy. What would cause people to revel at such disaster? Why is there such hatred?

Without going into too much debate, I will venture this: the problem with many Muslims is that they have only known the *jihad* by the sword. On the other hand, Malaysia has long propagated an alternative *jihad* by developing itself. It is Malaysia's firm belief that religion and modernity are not mutually exclusive. Instead, Malaysia is an excellent example of how religion and modernity complement each other, which is a result of our progressive, tolerant and moderate brand of Islam.

Now, when the international community begins to promote countries like Malaysia — by highlighting our technological and economic growth — they will provide a much-needed better direction and goal for these Muslim nations to follow. The international community will then be able to effectively address that sense of lost direction that I was talking about earlier. Then, Muslim nations will not be left with just a sense of going in the wrong direction when they know of no other direction to follow.

MALAYSIA: A COLLABORATION OF CIVILIZATIONS

There need not be conflict between civilizations. Each civilization has its strengths and, as a world community, we will be best suited to advance in the future if we are willing to learn from each other. We need to *work with* each other, not *impose* our views on each other. Consequently, Malaysia is ultimately best seen as an excellent example of how possible it is for civilizations to collaborate.

Malaysia has been able to operate as a model for how business and commerce would function in the new world. In the global village, business and commercial practices will need to adapt to this new environment. We must be vigilant and willing to adapt, or we will be caught unaware and washed away.

Malaysia has also been an effective model for how the world community can look in the coming global village. We are all getting closer to each other. We can choose to react to this by viewing each other with distrust, profiling each other according to whatever arbitrary category we decide; be it the way another person looks, speaks, dresses, or even their country of origin. Alternatively, we can take the higher road and choose to work with each other — to view each other as members of the same community, even as we maintain our unique diversity.

Finally, in the wake of September 11, it is important for Malaysia to play its part as a model Islamic nation. Criticism that is not constructive is useless. Muslim nations need an alternative to work towards, and Malaysia will actively seek to be that alternative example. This, I believe, is a much better solution to the problem of Islamic extremism, militancy and terrorism than merely forcing them into submission with military might.

GLOBALIZATION, GLOBAL VILLAGES AND COLLABORATION — WHERE WE GO FROM HERE

Having discussed how a microcosm of the global village concept has been successfully practiced in Malaysia, we now need to ask ourselves, "Where do we go from here? What can the rest of the world take from Malaysia's example?"

It is certain that a collaboration — and not a clash — of civilizations will be essential to the well-being of our future global community. It is time that we truly came together as a world, because we are beginning to realize that this is a small world after all. As globalization and all that it entails slowly encroaches upon us, there will be no place for superficial divisions between civilizations. We must find common grounds to collaborate; otherwise, we will be doomed.

One of the most important areas in which civilizations must collaborate begins at the very concept of globalization. To many nations throughout the world, globalization has been either embraced or feared. At any rate, it remains a force to be reckoned with. Globalization is the tool by which our global village will be created. However, we must not be too hasty to accept it just as it is. Globalization can be a double-edged sword. It can serve as a blessing, or it will bind us like a curse. As such, I do see a weakness with globalization as it is currently practiced. The problem that I see is this: will globalization help to ameliorate existing global inequality or will it legitimize it in the name of free markets?

Many nations from what was once called the Third World still fear globalization as nothing more than Western hegemony or colonization under another name. As a matter of fact, many who study popular culture are slowly raising the alarm at the dawning "McDonald-ization" of the world. When we talk about the global village, what exactly do we mean? Will there be a celebration of mutual prosperity, or will the poor nations be forced to accept a perpetually disadvantaged position? It is because of this perceived threat that many people are still wary of the concept of globalization and its implications.

This is why I would point the rest of the world community to look to Malaysia as a model of what globalization and the global village ought to look like. Any ordinary Malaysian will be able to attest to the unity in our diversity. I have already elaborated at length as to how Malaysia has successfully modeled a microcosm of the global village. We take pride in our ability to achieve unity without uniformity. Each of the three great civilizations of ancient history has come together in Malaysia and has maintained a healthy coexistence. We are able to maintain our unique cultural heritages and, yet, there is cause to celebrate in being Malaysian. Each of us has a unique flavor to add to the melting pot to blend together into something truly Malaysian. Can the world do this as globalization takes hold? Will we be able to retain our individual colors and add our unique palettes to the global village or will we just be whitewashed into one plain picture? Perhaps, if we begin collaborating as equals now, we will have a truly *global* village to look forward to.

Malaysia's approach to globalization has also caused us to pause and reflect on its implications for another major area; that is, the economy. At the time of independence, the existing economic inequality within Malaysia was a mirror image of current global inequality. Foreign and Chinese capital dominated the economy and the Malays were largely confined to the traditional subsistence sector of the economy. Without a determined government effort since 1970 to help the disadvantaged Malays, the inequality between the races would have persisted. The parallels to today's global economic situation are quite obvious. There are nations in our global village today who are poor and unable to fend for themselves in the face of a foreign-dominated world economy. How, then, are they supposed to take part in globalization's promise of mutual prosperity? Or, as I've cautioned earlier, will they be forced to accept a perpetually disadvantaged position?

Even as Malaysia continually equips itself for the reality of globalization, we are also aware of the challenges that it brings. It is for this reason that Malaysia has sought to pursue a more humane approach to modernization and globalization. As I've alluded to above, globalization, as it is currently understood or misunderstood, is being interpreted by weaker nations as the colonizing efforts of the more dominant civilization. In the light of such understanding, any effort to create a global village will be hampered. Why would this be so?

To truly be a community, one must feel as if one is a part of that community. Anyone who is left out, or unable to catch up with the rest of the community, will not be inclined to even care about the ideals of this community. It would be only natural for them to withdraw and to look out for their own needs. Likewise, this analogy holds when it comes to the more dangerous implications of globalization. How can we create a global village — a community of the world — when there are those among us who are poor and unable to fend for themselves? Why would people want to care about higher-level ideas such as democracy, mutual prosperity or even freedom when they are hungry? When people are in that state of existence, all they will care about is their next meal, and any perceived threat to their livelihood will be vehemently opposed. In view of this, it is obvious that what we need to do first is to address the hunger. Only then will they be more inclined towards higher ideas.

That is why Malaysia has sought to approach globalization and modernity with a human face. Malaysia has long realized that there was a need to create a sense of equality, especially when it comes to one's share of the economic "pie", before we could inspire our people towards a vision of unity. It was for this reason that Malaysia first implemented its New Economic Policy — the government's proactive efforts to create an economically stable Malay middle class as a social buffer for unity. We do not claim to be perfect, for we have had our mistakes. However, it was because of this initiative that we have been able to create stability in our nation and, therefore, lead our people towards a united vision of Malaysia.

Likewise, in our efforts to build our global village, we must also take proactive steps to ensure that there is at least some sense of equality in the world economy. When that sense of economic equality is evident in the world, then the citizens of the global village will be able to strive together towards a united vision. Shouldn't our global village look like this?

One final consideration before I conclude: recent events have made it necessary for me to address the issue of collaboration between religious civilizations and the secular civilizations of modernity. The need to address such an issue has been made even more significant in light of the events following September 11.

Islam has long been regarded by many in the West as a backward, intolerant and even repressive religion. In time, this has led to a misconception that Islam cannot coexist with the demands of modern civilization. Certainly, this is not true. I need not even begin to trace the glorious legacies of Islamic civilizations throughout history. Malaysia's own example has shown how its brand of modern, tolerant and progressive Islam has successfully coexisted with the demands of modernity. Further, Malaysia has also successfully modeled how Islam can coexist harmoniously with other religions.

In Malaysia, there is a collaboration between the sacred and the secular. Of course, there are those who would impose a dichotomy between the two, but Malaysia has shown this to be a false dichotomy. The sacred can collaborate with the secular because it is necessary that this be so. The sacred can influence the secular towards avenues of virtues — hence Malaysia's purposeful intention to adopt a more humane approach to globalization. At the same time, the secular can affect the sacred so that it continues to be relevant. With such a balance, we will be able to have a heart for heaven, yet with our feet planted firmly on the ground. Accordingly, religious civilizations and the secular civilizations of modernity are not mutually exclusive. They are able to collaborate, and I contend that they must if we are to avoid another September 11.

Therefore, I believe it is imperative that the global community take note of one of the largest religious civilizations in the world: Islam. They cannot ignore it, for Muslims are not going away. Thus, to create a global village, they must be prepared to collaborate with the Islamic civilizations, just as Islamic civilizations need to be prepared to collaborate with the rest of the world.

CONCLUSION

Since the September 11 tragedy, the world has been made even more aware of how vulnerable we really are. However, military prowess alone will not deliver the global security we all seek. We must address the root causes of terrorism collectively. We must denounce ALL forms of extremism and acts of terrorism. There must be no double standards. Islam must not be demonized.

At the same time, all of us must also be prepared to face the realities of globalization and the advent of the global village. To do this, we must begin to see ourselves as equals and start actively pursuing avenues of collaboration. The collaboration of civilizations must be heralded if we are to build a truly global village.

This is where the Malaysian model of Islam and modernity becomes a vital resource and an essential learning experience for the international community. While the world now struggles to come to terms with the meeting of many different civilizations, Malaysia has long been in the vanguard. Since our independence 44 years ago, we have actively pursued a collaboration of civilizations as a way of life.

I have raised several issues and points of discussion in this article regarding globalization, the global village and the collaboration of civilizations. At the same time, however, I am convinced that Malaysia, as an example, successfully illustrates and addresses these issues. In light of this, perhaps it would be opportune for the international community to take a closer look at Malaysia?

Globalization and Regional Monetary Cooperation

Oh Jong-Nam
Commissioner of the National Statistical Office,
Republic of Korea
(Position is at the time of printing)

BENEFITS AND RISKS OF GLOBALIZATION

Globalization has been a key word in the international community since the 1990s. Theoretically, globalization aims to maximize economic benefits by promoting competition, furthering the division of labor and enhancing productivity and efficiency through technological transfer and investment. In financial markets, especially, the speed of globalization has accelerated, with the rapid progress of information and communications technology as its primary driving force. This has created pressures for the harmonization of systems such as accounting and corporate governance. Now, the dynamism of globalization appears inevitable and irreversible.

However, globalization may also have adverse impacts and global convergence may benefit all countries only initially. For emerging economies, in particular, globalization may have detrimental economic effects, particularly in countries with weak economic foundations. In this regard, some countries are becoming integrated into the global economy more quickly than others, and they are seeing faster growth.

Second, though active cross-border capital flows theoretically achieve a more efficient allocation of resources, at the same time they pose a great risk if the rapid increase in international capital flows is reversed. A case in point is the contagion from the Asian currency crisis in 1997 spreading over to Russia and Latin America.

Third, the financial-market integration that comes with the rapid progress of globalization brings with it increased uncertainty, especially for small, open, emerging economies (SOEs) such as those in Asia. In the past, external shocks of the world economy, such as a U.S. business-cycle downturn or a hike in the international oil price, had a delayed impact on these SOEs.

Now, international financial-market integration has created a situation in which the altered monetary policy of major countries and capital movements by large hedge funds affects, immediately and in real time, the domestic financial markets of SOEs. This implies that the risk of contagion from a financial crisis in one economy transmitting to other economies has increased. For example, Korea's position may have become more vulnerable because it has a higher share of foreign portfolio investment than of foreign direct investment. Foreign holdings in the Korean stock market had risen to 35.5% of market capitalization in October 2001 from just 11.9% at the end of 1995. The establishment of a free-floating exchange-rate system in December 1997 also increased uncertainty for policy-makers, exporters and importers.

REGIONAL MONETARY COOPERATION TO ALLEVIATE RISKS OF GLOBALIZATION

In this regard, the need to cooperate regionally on monetary policy has been discussed as a way to minimize the downside risks associated with globalization. Among the proposals given attention by the media, policy-makers and academia are the Asian Monetary Fund (AMF) and the ASEAN+3 Chiang Mai Initiative. In fact, since the Asian currency crisis, several measures have been adopted to forestall contagion from financial crises. These include the tightening of disclosure requirements to achieve greater transparency and accountability, the establishment of robust domestic financial systems that can resist external shocks, and closer international and intra-regional cooperation and coordination during temporary liquidity crises.

One view of regional monetary cooperation sees it as synonymous with a regional mechanism that would help prevent financial crisis within the region and limit contagion. Proponents of these ideas view existing international financial institutions, including the IMF and the World Bank, as lacking sufficient resources. Not only are they slow to provide financial support, but they do not adequately take into account Asian perspectives in finance and development.

Others consider regional monetary cooperation in the context of closer regional economic integration. This functionalist view sees regional monetary cooperation as part of long-term structural efforts toward further regional integration. Debates on adopting international best practices, harmonizing macroeconomic policies, intensifying trade and financial cooperation within the region have often taken this as their sub-text. The ultimate goal of cooperation in these matters is seen as being the establishment of a regional free-trade area and a currency union.

The strengthening of regional cooperation may appear at first to be in conflict with economic and financial globalization and it is not easy to synthesize these two agendas. Regional monetary cooperation can, however, be reasonably grasped by understanding the relationship between globalization and regional cooperation. Through globalization, Asia's economies have become more closely linked and their monetary policies tend to take into account not only domestic concerns but also international trends, as has been the case with the recent series of interest-rate cuts undertaken by the Federal Reserve, the ECB and the Bank of England.

KOREA'S EFFORTS TOWARD GLOBALIZATION

Ironically, the currency crisis of 1997 provided momentum for the acceleration of Korea's drive for financial- and corporate-sector restructuring. In particular, Korea's three-year IMF tutelage under the stand-by arrangement, which expired in December 2000, brought several achievements.

First, macroeconomic fundamentals have improved, and vulnerability to crisis lessened in the immediate aftermath of the crisis. Unemployment has been reduced and inflation contained, exports are stronger (despite recent softening with the global slowdown), foreign direct investment and portfolio inflows have increased, and foreign reserves have been built up to record levels.

Second, wide-ranging structural reforms have made Korea's economy more open, competitive and market driven. Significant progress has been made towards stabilizing the financial system, addressing corporate distress, strengthening the institutional framework for corporate governance and financial-sector supervision, liberalizing capital markets and foreign investment, enhancing transparency and creating an environment in which market discipline plays an increasingly important role.

The IMF pronounced itself satisfied that the program for Korea has been very successful and that its objectives — namely, to restore confidence, stabilize financial markets, lay the foundation for a sustained recovery in the real economy, and lower the chances of future crises — had been realized. Moreover, the reforms initiated following the crisis will continue to yield benefits for years to come and, in many cases, these will increase as practices and ways of doing business change. In particular, financial- and corporate-sector restructuring helped Korea to regain international confidence. Through these efforts, Korea is now widely recognized as a country that works to meet global standards.

Financial-Sector Restructuring

The restructuring of the financial sector was central to the structural reform program. The Korean government's strategy comprises four key elements:

- Emergency measures to quickly restore stability to the financial system through liquidity support, a blanket (but time-bound) deposit guarantee, and intervention in systemically important non-viable institutions.
- Restructuring measures to restore the solvency of the financial system by intervention in non-viable institutions, the purchase of non-performing loans (NPLs), and recapitalization.
- Regulatory measures to strengthen the existing framework by bringing prudential regulation and supervision in line with international best practice.
- Corporate restructuring measures to reduce corporate distress and the vulnerability of financial institutions with exposure to the highly indebted corporate sector.

Emergency Measures: At the height of the crisis, the most urgent need was to restore stability to the financial system. The first task was to maintain public confidence in the banking system. Before the onset of the crisis, in January 1997, the authorities had introduced a deposit-insurance scheme which provided for full coverage of all deposits not exceeding 20 million Won per individual depositor. In addition, in August 1997, the Korean government announced that it would ensure that Korean financial institutions were in a position to meet their foreign liabilities, effectively guaranteeing these liabilities. The withdrawal of foreign credit lines in the second half of 1997 suggested that the authorities' external guarantees were not viewed as entirely credible. Thus, further action became necessary and, in mid-November of that year, the government announced that it would guarantee all deposits with financial institutions until the end of 2000, and would provide liquidity support to banks in order to facilitate the extension of maturing foreign-currency liability to foreign banks. The efforts to reassure domestic creditors via the blanket deposit-insurance largely succeeded and no major bank runs took place.

Restructuring measures: The next stage was to restore the solvency of the financial system. The first step in this process was to distinguish non-viable institutions from weak but viable institutions. This involved a systemic evaluation of credit and banking institutions. For institutions seen as non-viable, rehabilitation plans specifying measures to achieve minimum capital adequacy and restructuring were required. Failure to comply with the performance targets triggered prompt corrective-action procedures, including suspension and eventual closure.

Prudential regulation and supervision: Supervisory surveillance has been significantly strengthened and prudential regulation brought closer in line with international best practices. Steps have also been taken to improve the quality of supervision. Supervision has been consolidated under a single independent agency, the FSC (Financial Supervisory Commission) and its executive branch, the FSS (Financial Supervisory Service). The FSC/FSS now has supervisory as well as regulatory authority for all bank and non-bank financial institutions, including specialized and development banks. In addition, new legislation delegated the FSC (rather than the Ministry of Finance and Economy) with the responsibility to issue and revoke licenses of all financial institutions. With the consolidation of supervisory functions in a single agency, the potential for regulatory arbitrage, a problem in the past, has been reduced.

Prudential measures introduced so far have addressed a wide range of concerns, including loan classification and provisioning standards, capital adequacy, accounting and disclosure standards, connected lending, cross guarantees, and foreign-exchange liquidity and exposure.

*A **convergence towards international best practices***: More-stringent rules on the classification and provisioning of non-performing loans have been put in place. At the end of 1999, the introduction of loan classification and provisioning based on "forward-looking criteria", which take into account the capacity of borrowers to service all their obligations rather than focusing on delinquency criteria, was especially noteworthy.

Large exposure ceilings for commercial, merchant, and specialized and development banks were reduced, and more-comprehensive definitions of single and interlinked group exposure were laid down. This will help to limit the ability of major corporations to become over-leveraged. Prudential requirements for commercial banks have also been imposed on specialized and development banks.

Restrictions on connected lending to shareholders and their affiliates have been significantly tightened and disclosure requirements strengthened. In addition, since 1999, all connected lending and the terms on which it is provided must be audited and disclosed in annual financial statements.

Market-to-market accounting was introduced, for example, to new funds invested in ITCs (Investment Trust Companies), and to all traded securities and derivative positions other than for hedging assets valued at historical cost.

Controls were introduced for prudent management of banks' foreign-currency liquidity. Both commercial and merchant banks are now required to report the maturity of their liabilities and assets. In addition, internal liquidity controls based on a maturity-ladder approach have been introduced for these institutions. To further improve Korea's external-debt profile, the monitoring of external debt and reserves has been strengthened through more-frequent reporting and improved coverage.

Accounting and disclosure standards for banks, securities companies and insurance companies now fully comply with the requirements of the International Accounting Standards (IAS) or the U.S. GAAP as an alternative benchmark.

Corporate-Sector Restructuring

In response to the crisis, the government made corporate restructuring, and restoring the health and competitiveness of the corporate sector, one of its key priorities. This aimed to address the structural weakness which opened Korea to financial crisis. Unlike interventions in the past, the government sought to limit its role to strengthening the institutions in order to allow investors and creditors to monitor firms and create an environment where market discipline could play a stronger role in driving the restructuring process. Given the scale of the corporate sector's problems and the use of public funds to restructure the financial system, however, a substantial government role was unavoidable. The strategy for corporate restructuring had three main elements:

1. Promoting greater competition. Reforms focused on opening markets to greater competition, both domestic and foreign, by liberalizing the foreign-investment regime and strengthening the role of the Fair Trade Commission (FTC).
2. Improving corporate governance. Among the measures used were strengthening investors' rights, enhancing the transparency of financial accounting and disclosure, raising the accountability of managers and major shareholders, and improving the efficiency of insolvency procedures.

3. Improving capital structure and profitability. Through a combination of direct enforcement and market incentives, the government pushed corporations to lower excessive debt levels, improve capital structure and eliminate cross-subsidization of weaker affiliates. The government adopted a flexible approach to restructuring, depending upon the size and nature of the problem, and the available financing options.

PROGRESS OF REGIONAL COOPERATION

In turning to globalization, there has been a marked move toward regionalism or regional cooperation in various parts of the world, which has embraced both trade and financial relations. For example, in Europe, there has been a deepening and widening of integration with the introduction of the Euro and the commitment to eastward expansion of the E.U. In the Americas, there have been proposals to expand NAFTA and the adoption of the dollar is currently being considered by some Latin American countries. In Asia, we have begun to see some steps being taken toward closer cooperation, including an AMF scheme and the ASEAN+3 Chiang Mai Initiative.

Those forces which are driving globalization are also bringing about closer integration of economic and financial activities. Regional cooperation has become even more important as globalization progresses rapidly and, in fact, if managed properly, promotes globalization. If common platforms for discussion or frameworks for solving problems are established in regions where countries have similar economic conditions and policy orientations, the global negotiations could become easier in the event of international policy conflict. In this way, regional cooperation may supplement the framework of a global cooperation.

Regional Cooperation in Asia

Asia is extremely diverse in culture, politics and religion and this may create difficulties in regional cooperation. In fact, the pace of regional cooperation in Asia has been slower than in several other regions. The bitter experience of the currency crisis in 1997, however, made Asians alert to the risks of spillover and contagion. The consequent momentum for more intra-regional cooperation will serve as a basis for globalization.

In promoting regional cooperation, three important points should be observed. First, mutual surveillance should be strengthened; second, countries in the region should share a common view of the future direction of the regional economy; and, third, joint participation in global efforts should be exerted to ensure the stability of the international financial system. It is increasingly important for Asian countries to speak with one voice, especially where policy is debated, such as at the Financial Stability Forum and meetings of the Group of Twenty (G20) Finance Ministers and Central Bankers.

One of the important trends of globalization is that once international standards are developed by the international institutions such as BIS, the OECD, the IMF and the World Bank, other countries are forced to comply with these standards regardless of an individual country's specific conditions.

For a small country in Asia, leading an international debate on a particular agenda is truly impossible. Instead, Asian countries tend to take the international standards imposed from outside as given constraints. However, by forming a regional alliance on issues that pose a common threat for Asia, it becomes possible to create new standards that account for Asian situations.

Asian regionalism can be distinguished from other regionalisms such as that of the E.U. in at least three ways.

First, Asian regionalism is pluralistic. There is no single dominant organization that guides continental regional integration in the manner of the E.U. in Europe. Membership of the main existing organizations — the Association of South East Nations (ASEAN), the ASEAN Regional Forum (ARF), and the Asia Pacific Economic Co-operation (APEC) forum overlaps, and there are rival notions of the appropriate scope of the Asian regional space.

Second, regional organizations in Asia are much less institutionalized than the E.U. They are more explicitly state-led and their chosen mode of interaction is intergovernmental. For example, APEC has no more than a modest secretariat and operates through regular meetings of national officials and annual summits of national leaders. It has no collective aspiration to build a binding body of international law. This sets APEC apart from both the E.U. and NAFTA.

Third, Asian regionalism has more modest goals than the E.U. APEC proposes to eliminate trade and investment barriers between its richer members by 2010 and by 2020 for its poorer members. It is, in other words, no more than an aspirant free-trade area. Even Asia in its original conception was not really an economic agent.

Regional Lender of Last Resort

One path to remedying the possible international financial disorder would be to set up regional lenders of last resort. Asia can look to other regions for examples. The Arab Monetary Fund was set up in 1976 by the League of Arab States to assist member countries to eliminate payment and trade restrictions, to achieve exchange-rate stability, and to develop capital flows among member countries. The Latin American Reserve Fund, established in 1991 as the successor to the Andean Reserve Fund, aims to assist members in correcting payment imbalances through loans or guarantees, to coordinate monetary and exchange-rate policies, and to promote the liberalization of trade and payments in the Andean sub-region.

In the same vein, it would be reasonable for Asian countries to form a regional lender of last resort or to pool foreign-exchange reserves.

The volume of international capital flows through each small developing country is far more than the multiple of its foreign trade and services. These small developing countries are thus better off sharing their foreign-exchange reserves to cope with surges in capital flows. This would enable the authorities to prevent overshooting exchange rates that tends to result from massive capital flows. A reduced volatility in exchange rates would help facilitate the domestic utilization of resources.

Each member country would have greater access to rescue funds than those available from the IMF, with it biased quota system. In addition, as there would be fewer member countries in the regional group than in the IMF, each of them could take out a larger share in borrowings from the common fund.

When countries are geographically close and have similar and linked economies, they are highly vulnerable to contagion from a financial crisis that occurs in a neighboring country. So a country in crisis would not be the only party to benefit from a regional lender of last resort. Its neighboring countries, which contribute to the resources of the fund, would find it in their interests to prevent the crisis from spreading. Regional economies are increasingly linked with each other through trade, investment and financial transactions. In these circumstances, each country has a strong stake in the financial status of its neighbors.

There is also a strong case for regional surveillance and monitoring because it is better tailored to local circumstances and situations.

Given that small developing countries in most regions typically do not possess extensive foreign-exchange reserves, pooling these reserves might still not suffice as a common buffer. The regional lender of last resort might have to tap funds from commercial sources to supplement members' contributions. Such a lender of last resort would not operate on a concessional basis and more private participation would mean greater market discipline and accountability.

CONCLUSION

The proposals for a regional monetary arrangement are a further repercussion of Asia's frustration at the performance of the IMF and the World Bank on this region's behalf. The AMF can be understood as one possible form of a do-it-yourself approach. If the global mechanism is not appropriate when a country is in a desperate liquidity crisis, some kind of regional mechanism is needed to cope with potential threats.

It does not have to be a monetary fund. It could be an arrangement between central banks, some kind of swap arrangement — multilateral or bilateral — or an agreement between regional countries with regard to crisis lending or cooperation.

The leadership of the IMF and the World Bank need to listen more carefully to the voice of Asia. Asia right now is under-represented in the quota shares that determine voting rights. For instance, Korea would have a much larger quota if the quota formula faithfully reflected Korea's economic strength. Such reform measures for rationalizing the governance structure of the international financial institutions have been stalled because of vested interests within the institutions.

Under current circumstances, an urgent concern is the task of developing an Asian regional financial market where regional funds could be recycled instead of relying too heavily upon the global financing system centered in the U.S. If Asian financial companies could raise money in an Asian financial market, they could create one of the strongest barriers against a financial crisis. It is crucial, therefore, for Asia to develop a well-functioning Asian money market and capital market. This would be mutually beneficial for Asia and the global economy by enhancing efficiency of capital flow and forestalling potential crisis at an early stage.

The Evolving Role of Central Banks in Asia: A View from the Philippines

Rafael B. Buenaventura
Governor of Bangko Sentral ng Pilipinas
(Central Bank of the Philippines)

INTRODUCTION

Some time ago, some economists wrote of the "demise" of the central bank. They argued that, with the global convergence toward low inflation, the tremendous expansion of capital markets alongside rapid technological innovation, and the advent of electronic-based payment systems and currencies, central banks are slowly losing their influence and are in danger of becoming irrelevant.

As a central banker, of course, my reply is that nothing could be farther from the truth. The reports of the death of central banking as we know it have been greatly exaggerated, and I would like to offer a few ideas on what the future holds for central bankers in the Asian region.

The central bank's basic institutional role in the modern market-based economy is likely to endure. Central banks were established to provide stability to the economy by preserving the value of the currency and maintaining the soundness of the financial system. In these ways, they help lay the foundations for long-term sustainable economic growth.

The role of central banks in Asia will continue to be built around these core functions. And because much of the region's economic future lies in addressing decisively the problems highlighted by the financial crisis and the recent global economic downturn, Asia's central banks will be tasked to provide not only economic stability but also to help advance the cause of economic reform.

In the Philippines, the Bangko Sentral ng Pilipinas (BSP) remains staunchly committed to its strategic role of promoting economic growth by maintaining stable prices and a sound banking system. The BSP has been instrumental in bringing about improving macroeconomic fundamentals, which include low and stable inflation, and a stable banking and financial sector.

MONETARY POLICY

Preserving the value of the currency remains the fundamental task of central banking, and a large part of the evolving role of central banks in Asia will continue to focus on the design and conduct of monetary policy.

Framework for Monetary Policy

Over the past few decades, the role of the central bank with respect to monetary policy has evolved from that of achieving a number of goals such as maintaining full employment and the competitiveness of the exchange rate, to that of focusing on a single objective; namely, price stability. It is now well established among economists and central bankers that price stability is a key ingredient to promoting stable, long-term economic growth. Achieving long-run price stability is a difficult and continuous challenge, requiring constant efforts to detect and address the build-up of internal and external imbalances. For this reason, fighting inflation is likely to remain the enduring challenge for central banks in Asia and elsewhere. In addition, because of time lags in policy effectiveness, the central bank's role to promote price stability will require a forward-looking approach to monetary policy.

Inflation-targeting represents one such approach. This framework is becoming increasingly accepted as a focused and forward-looking way of strengthening central bank commitment to stable prices. A recent assessment of the decade-long experience of pioneer inflation-targeters such as the United Kingdom, Canada, New Zealand and Australia concludes that inflation-targeting has indeed been successful as a policy framework. The pioneer countries moved from a high-inflation to a low-inflation environment and experienced higher output growth as well as reduced volatility in prices and output growth. Inflation-targeting is also gaining acceptance among developing economies, notably Brazil and Chile.

In the case of the Philippines, efforts to promote long-run price stability are centered on the formal adoption of inflation-targeting as a framework for monetary policy, beginning January 2002. We believe that this approach provides a more focused, consistent and effective way for the BSP to ensure stable prices. Under the new framework, the BSP will be committed to achieve the government's average annual inflation target of 5–6% for 2002 and 4.5–5.5% for 2003. These rates represent a trend decline from the 2001 average inflation rate of 6%, which is the low end of the government's 6–7% target for the year. Moderation in consumer prices during the year could be attributed to stable food prices, lower oil prices and the continued prudence in the BSP's monetary policy.

Central Bank Independence

Promoting price stability under any framework will also require central bank independence. Empirical evidence suggests that, on average, countries with more independent central banks also tend to have lower inflation, but not at the expense of output growth or the variability of growth. Country experiences suggest that an independent central bank that has responsibility for price stability can overcome the inflationary bias associated with policies of national governments that do not have tight fiscal discipline. Therefore, part of the efforts on price stability will also likely include measures to strengthen central bank independence.

In recent years, a good number of central banks (for example, Argentina, Chile, France, Mexico, New Zealand, Spain and the United Kingdom) have undergone charter changes that provided them with greater autonomy from political authorities. A common thread among these changes was the need to insulate the process of monetary policy formulation and implementation from political influence. The greater level of independence was seen to enhance the degree of central bank commitment to fighting inflation, thereby reducing the inflationary expectations of the public.

In the case of the Philippines, major steps were taken in the early 1990s to ensure greater independence of the Bangko Sentral. The New Central Bank Act of 1993 (Republic Act No. 7653) not only explicitly identifies price stability as the primary objective of the BSP, it also strengthens the foundations for central bank independence. The law specifically provides for the operational (or instrument) independence of the BSP and sets clear limits to the BSP's financial assistance to the national government. Fiscal independence thus allows the BSP to pursue its main objective of price stability without being constrained by fiscal considerations.

e-Central Banking

The advent of electronic money also poses some serious questions about the role of central banks. Specifically, economists are divided over whether the central bank can still conduct monetary policy if privately issued e-money erodes the central bank's monopoly over the control of base money. In theory, the argument goes, the use of electronic currency could weaken the connection between base money and economic activity, and undermine the effectiveness of traditional monetary tools.

If we really think about it, however, it is hard to imagine our physical currency being completely replaced by the electronic kind, in much the same way that the widespread use of electronic media has not obliterated the demand for paper. Moreover, history tells us that various forms of money can, in fact, coexist. For the same reasons that households and businesses still require hard copies of electronic-based documents, so will demand for physical currency — and the central bank's ability to conduct monetary policy — endure. e-money is only a partial substitute for traditional currency for several reasons: (1) it carries a higher risk than central bank notes because the issuer may not be a risk-free agent; (2) it does not grant anonymity to the parties involved, since transactions are recorded; and (3) it carries a high risk of loss or theft, given the problems associated with network security. Thus, it is my view that the demand for traditional currency will continue to exist.

In the extreme case that demand for currency does disappear altogether, demand for central bank base money will be reduced but will remain, since currency is only part of base money — the other part is bank reserves. Moreover, as long as electronic-based settlements among banks are settled against reserve balances with the central bank, then demand for base money will remain, and the central bank will retain control over short-term interest rates.

A related issue is the major changes in payment systems worldwide that are expected to happen in the medium term. The payment system represents a major component of the infrastructure system of any modern economy, and the systemic failure of the payment system can undermine the effectiveness of monetary policy and adversely affect the real sector. Monetary authorities, therefore, have a natural interest in promoting an efficient and sound payment system and in finding ways to minimize systemic risk because of its implications for monetary policy, the soundness of the financial institutions and the economy at large.

In this era of electronic-based transactions, the BSP continues to play a major role. In response to current trends towards increased use of the Internet in banking, the BSP has laid down the requirements for banks seeking to provide electronic banking services. This is to ensure that banks planning to provide these services have in place a risk-management process that is adequate to assess, control and monitor associated risks.

Room for Monetary Flexibility

In the years ahead, the basic task of economic stabilization will remain crucial for central banks. Macroeconomic instability has become more common, as evidenced by the two major global slowdowns witnessed in less than a decade. Policy-makers will need to preserve discipline in macroeconomic policy and maintain a forward-looking approach to dealing with rapidly changing economic and financial conditions. As the IMF has noted recently, there are stronger downside risks to world economic and financial conditions, and monetary authorities must find the appropriate policy responses to the situation. In this regard, the major industrial countries have taken the lead in easing monetary policy to help sustain demand. Central banks in emerging markets will need to assess the scope for monetary policy stimulus in their respective economies, given the outlook for inflationary pressures.

In the Philippines, subdued inflation, spare capacity and broad currency stability enabled calibrated monetary easing during the past year. The BSP has reduced its policy rates by a total of 725 basis points since December 2000. The overnight borrowing and lending rates now stand at 7.75% and 10%, respectively. The reduction in policy rates was undertaken to support domestic growth in the face of a weak external environment due to the expected downturn in the U.S. economy and other global uncertainties. Moreover, the reduction in interest rates by many central banks in the advanced economies has provided the BSP with leeway to cut policy interest rates, without fueling concern over a shift away from peso-denominated assets inasmuch as interest rate differentials do not narrow. These factors are seen as positive for the peso, which in turn can help keep inflationary pressures in check.

MAINTAINING A SOUND BANKING AND FINANCIAL SYSTEM

The task of maintaining broad oversight of the financial system constitutes another evolving role for central banks. The role of supervision aims to preserve the health and soundness of the banking and financial system, with a view to preventing or containing financial shocks and disruptions. This role is likely to become increasingly complex over time, especially given the increased potential for contagion from financial crises due to the increasingly seamless nature of capital flows. While greater capital integration has made domestic financial systems more efficient in allocating resources, it has also made the systems quite vulnerable to shocks from other economies.

For this reason, Asian central banks are likely to retain their lender-of-last-resort function. Preventing systemic risk is a function that remains unique to central banks, and is likely to be so in the future. As former U.S. Fed official Lawrence Lindsey has noted, it is a role that cannot be ceded to supranational bodies such as the IMF, simply because national central banks have both the capacity to generate liquidity and the political accountability to handle the consequences that an institution like the IMF lacks. The possibility of increased incidence of financial crises suggests that the central banks' function as lender of last resort could probably be more important in the future than it is at present.

Equally important to dealing with financial crises is preventing them, and financial supervision will likely remain a key role for central banks. Considerable progress has been made in rehabilitating Asia's financial systems, but more work needs to be done. Asian countries appear to have followed varying strategies in pursuing financial reforms. Some have favored a gradualist approach, arguing that the banking and corporate sector should be first given time to recover and strengthen before restructuring can take place. Others have argued for more aggressive and comprehensive reform efforts, in the belief that the weaknesses need to be addressed speedily for lasting recovery to take place.

However, universal policy prescriptions are difficult to draw, given the wide range of experience and initial conditions. Authorities in individual countries must decide on the most appropriate set of solutions for their own financial systems. At the same time, reformers must be aware that there are no "quick fixes" to financial-sector problems, and only a strong dedication to financial reform will produce a sustainable recovery and greater resilience to crises. Just as strong financial systems act as stabilizers when the domestic economy is battered, weak financial systems amplify the scope and extent of the problems, making bad situations even worse. In the end, financial stability can only be ensured through the collective interaction of three main factors: sound leadership at the bank or financial institution level, effective market discipline, and strong prudential regulation and supervision.

In the case of the Philippines, the domestic financial system has had a long history of continued policy reforms, enabling it to serve as an efficient channel for the transmission of monetary policy, and to perform its roles of intermediating funds and managing risks appropriately. The BSP's initiatives in reforming the banking sector have continuously focused on developing a stable, sound and globally competitive banking system. Major banking reforms were implemented to: (1) improve banks' risk management by shifting to a risk-based capital adequacy framework; (2)

strengthen the prudential supervisory and regulatory framework in accordance with international standards; (3) promote good governance in banks by improving transparency and disclosure as well as strengthening accountability; and (4) create a stronger, more competitive banking system through mergers and consolidations and freer entry for foreign banks.

Other BSP initiatives include implementing the General Banking Law (GBL) of 2000, which represents the overarching framework for financial regulation. In this regard, the BSP has issued rules and regulations pertaining to foreign stockholdings, outsourcing of banking functions, adoption of risk-based capital adequacy standards aligned with international norms, and guidelines on micro-finance.

Together with other concerned agencies, the BSP also successfully pushed for the passage in Congress of the anti-money-laundering law on September 29, 2001. The anti-money-laundering law will preserve the integrity of the financial system and help ensure financial stability. It will help ensure that the reputation of Philippine banks and financial institutions will not be compromised and that the trust and confidence of domestic and foreign investors in them will not be undermined.

Moreover, the BSP is pursuing continually the proposed amendments to its charter to reinforce its authority and capacity to regulate and supervise the banking system and implement monetary policy more effectively. Among the amendments that are proposed are: (1) granting authority to the BSP to conduct more frequent banking examinations; (2) implementing prompt corrective action in the case of problem/distressed banks; (3) imposing stronger criminal and administrative penalties for violation of banking laws and regulations; and (4) enhancing the BSP's administrative efficiency and restoring its tax-exemption privilege as far as open-market operations are concerned.

Drawing strength from the sustained efforts of the BSP to push forward key reform initiatives and to implement preemptive policy measures to address critical problems, the Philippine banking system continued to hold its ground amidst a challenging environment. The banking system continued to be resilient. Its resources grew by 7.6% year-on-year to ₱3.4 trillion as of the end of September 2001. This growth in resources was underpinned by increased deposit mobilization and build-up in capital. Asset quality remained manageable, with the non-performing loan (NPL) ratio of the banking system recorded at 17.5% as of September 2001. For commercial banks, the NPL ratio was recorded at 17.92% in September and 18.8% in October 2001. It is worth noting that no public funds have been used in the Philippines to purchase non-performing assets or recapitalize financial institutions. Moreover, the capital buffer of the banking system has remained adequate, as its capital adequacy ratio (CAR) reached 16.47% as of September 2001 while the commercial banks' CAR was posted at 16.10%. This was well above the statutory floor of 10% and the BIS standard of 8%.

CONCLUSION

From where I stand, central banks fulfill a crucial institutional role in the modern market-based economy: to provide stability through their influence on the monetary sector and the financial system. This role is the product of centuries of social and economic history, and is likely to endure in the future — albeit perhaps in a different form. We are likely to see some changes in the role of central banks in the Asian region, but it is unlikely that they will lose their influence. Asia's central banks will still be tasked with, among other things, promoting stable prices, overseeing the financial system and acting as lender of last resort. These functions will remain central to the overall efforts of Asian countries to build a path to long-term sustainable economic growth.

The Future of Asian Capital Markets: Towards a Regional Equity Market?

Georges Ugeux
Group Executive Vice President International,
New York Stock Exchange, U.S.

 **OVERVIEW**

Anybody who has been a participant or an observer of the world's equity markets will have been struck by the enormous potential and the very limited realizations that have characterized Asian equity markets so far. While the American markets are becoming increasingly seamless and the European markets are striving with several forms of integration, Asia's equity markets remain fragmented, and only the Australian, Singapore and Hong Kong exchanges seem to have actively pursued avenues of cooperation.

The reality of the Asian equity markets is marked by elements of similarity, but fundamental differences make such cooperative efforts difficult to implement. In order to try to clarify the main challenges and opportunities that lie ahead for Asia, this paper will distinguish between several interlinked issues, thereby artificially insulating them. The main challenge for Asia will be to integrate the solution to these issues into a common vision. However, it is only the people and nations of Asia that will be able to do so.

The input of an outsider can only be the sharing of experience and this is what this paper is about: we have no lessons to teach Asia, but maybe our successes and errors can help Asia to choose its own way to develop its equity market. No other country in the world has ever handled the size of the population and the diversity that exists in Asia. The experience of strategic discussions with Asian stock exchanges might also provide both the objectivity and the proximity to make these observations helpful.

THE MACRO LEVEL: THE THREE ASIAN POLES

Trying to understand the potential for integration in Asia requires more than a mapping of the current stock exchanges and equity markets. There are currently more than 20 stock exchanges in Asia, but the dominant market is **Japan**. How many remember that 12 years ago the world's largest stock market was the Tokyo Stock Exchange, that the Nikkei crossed the 1000 mark in 1962, at the same time as the Dow, but reached 42,000 during the 1980s? There is an interesting parallel to be made between the recent bubble on the Nasdaq and the evolution of the Japanese markets. While the Nikkei 225 went as high as 42,000, good analysts were recommending NTT at the time of its privatization at 250 times earnings, justifying these incredible price/earning ratios because of the "Yen Factor", meaning the Yen would increase in value for ever. There were plenty of press reports on the Japanese "circles of excellence". Today, the Nikkei is 25% above the Dow Jones Industrial and the Tokyo Stock Exchange's domestic market capitalization is only one-quarter that of the New York Stock Exchange (NYSE), slightly higher than the London Stock Exchange and the Nasdaq.

Japan had the opportunity to develop a world-class equity market and become a regional leader. While it is hard to point to one single factor to enhance its ability to do so, the most important one is probably the simplest: Japan needs to develop a vision of regional leadership, within the wider context of a global role. As we continue to look at the Asian challenges, we will look at Japan as a single market. Most non-Japanese companies are de-listing from the Tokyo Stock Exchange (TSE). The key reasons for this are the cost of filings (and the use of exorbitantly expensive official translation into Japanese) and the bureaucracy. Those companies would be prepared to bear that cost if the Japanese market had been providing liquidity to their stock in Japan. Here again, the expectation came from a vision of an ever-growing Japanese investor base. The reality, however, was different. The liquidity needed by the major institutional investors was not available in Tokyo. As to retail investors, for regulatory and traditional reasons, they don't buy stocks, but put their money in bank deposits.

Will this change? The regulatory changes put in place in the last few years could change the Japanese investor's reluctance to buy stocks. But this change will come slowly and will only translate into Japan's emergence as a regional market through a regional vision. The TSE's trading volume is now predominantly coming from non-Japanese brokers, but it is almost entirely limited to Japanese stocks. The de-mutualization of the Tokyo Stock Exchange is now effective but will this lead to a more globalized future? Japan is a very special case: as of today it has to be seen more as the center of liquidity for Japanese stocks worldwide, not as a regional leader, let alone a global market. The New York Stock Exchange has invited the TSE to join the Global Equity Market (GEM), a partnership of 10 exchanges around the world to enhance liquidity and global trading.

Where is **China**? That question is probably the most intriguing of the Asian landscape. Compared with Japan, China is smaller and fragmented. In order to cover the Chinese markets, one needs to include Shanghai and Shenzhen, Hong Kong, Taiwan and Singapore. Among these, only Hong Kong and Singapore have a fully convertible currency.

However, China has a vision, and the rest of the world needs to pay attention to the recent evolution of the mainland Chinese markets. The dynamics of the Chinese markets are very interesting. The key player is the Beijing government and the economic growth of the People's Republic of China (PRC) will be the sustaining factor for the entire Chinese market. The emergence of China as a global leader is possible in the medium term (five to 10 years) but will only be completed when the currencies are fully fungible, and when the liquidity of the stocks from mainland China is unified.

Today, the mainland market is limited to the "A-shares", shares in Chinese companies that are exclusively distributed to mainland citizens. The access to "B-shares" is restricted to Chinese investors who own foreign currency. But the buoyancy of Shanghai and Shenzhen should not be underestimated. The trading volume is growing fast, and the system infrastructure is modern and sophisticated.

Hong Kong has emerged as the global portal for the Chinese equity markets. The first reason for this is that the Chinese government has given Hong Kong a global mission: trade and list those mainland companies that are allowed to raise capital in Asia and beyond. These companies trade under the denomination of "H-shares", and trade at different (generally lower) prices than in Shanghai or Shenzhen. The Hong Kong SAR thinks globally, as does its regulator and its Exchange.

The role of **Singapore** in the evolution of Asian capital markets is also regionally focused. The Monetary Authority of Singapore and the Singapore Exchange (SGX) are joining forces in a way that leaves no doubt about the political will to make the SGX a regional leader. Singapore is looking at opportunities to create niches that facilitate the development of the derivative markets. Singapore is looking for, and building, links. The recent announcement of the partnership with the Australian Stock Exchange (ASX) gives a measure of its eagerness to develop beyond the borders of Singapore. Interestingly, the Singapore government remains hesitant about allowing Singapore companies to list overseas.

Taiwan is predominantly a technology market, and a very active one. It probably has the highest turnover of its shares (up to seven times a year in 2000) of any market in the world. This fact reflects the fascination of Taiwanese investors for stock trading. Taiwanese companies have accessed foreign markets and trade very actively abroad. The NYSE trades several leading Taiwanese technology companies. However, the fact that there are restrictions to the convertibility of the Taiwan dollar does not make Taiwan a likely immediate candidate for global leadership.

The third large player, **India,** presents a picture of contrast. The 23 Indian stock exchanges are not yet fully connected electronically and the liquidity of Indian stocks is limited by the absence of retail and institutional investors. The regulatory restrictions and recent scandals have raised questions. However, while these handicaps are compounded by the limited convertibility of the Indian Rupee, India's potential is exceptional. Two exchanges, Mumbai and National, have become the main source of liquidity for Indian stocks, with the active support of the London Stock Exchange and the NYSE. Their sheer size and the development of world-class companies make India a global player. Most importantly, India wants to be global and is gradually applying global rules. These efforts are remarkable, even though their enforcement is often difficult. But India is not the only country to have such enforcement difficulties.

India has developed in the last few years a prudent vision of a global player. Sometimes, traditional Indian groups are still more interested in partnering with foreign companies in India rather than opening up for competition. But economic reform is accelerating. However, restrictions to the capital-account convertibility of the Indian Rupee remain one of the main factors limiting the reform and the growth of liquidity in Indian stocks.

The absence of privately managed mutual funds and pensions funds has also been a handicap to the development of Indian markets. The scandal associated with the dealing of U.T.I., the largest, government-sponsored, mutual fund of India, is creating a serious credibility gap.

The likelihood of India emerging as a regional leader is not immediate. But any regional platform will have take account of India's depth and importance.

Three Asian equity markets — Japan, China and India — will have, because of their size and weight, a deep influence on the development of an integrated Asian market. What does this mean, however, for the other markets? These three markets are the largest and should, therefore, be the integrators of regional liquidity. But their evolution has been slow. Smaller markets such as Hong Kong, Singapore and Taiwan have developed much faster and challenge the leadership of the largest markets.

Several factors will play a significant role in possible alliances. Within Northeast Asia, the key questions are the future of the Taiwanese and the Korean markets. Both have global companies. Both have international reach. Both have currency restrictions. Both also have "natural" partners with whom they have had political difficulties in the past. The integration of the other stock markets could be made easier if the only considerations were the proximity of investors and the positioning of listed companies. Unfortunately, political considerations will make it tougher to realize. There is clearly a potential for a Southeast Asian market where Jakarta, Bangkok, Kuala Lumpur, Singapore, Manila and Hong Kong would have common interests.

BUILDING INVESTOR CONFIDENCE

The most frequently asked question on Asian markets comes straight from investors: "Can we trust the Asian markets? " The question covers several issues that need to be treated separately. Investor confidence is based on an expectation that the management and the dominant shareholder — if any — will make sure that all shareholders are being treated fairly. In addition, the same level of disclosure must apply evenly among shareholders, and rules of corporate governance cannot authorize privileges for some categories of shareholders, for the management or for the employees. They also need to be convinced that the markets themselves are adequately regulated to prevent insider trading, to ensure adequate capitalization of financial intermediaries, and to establish priority trading rules in order to create a level playing field for investors.

Disclosure has long been one of the most difficult subjects. Japanese companies have never made a secret of their reluctance to publish profits and/or revenues by business segment. Indian companies are renowned for their reluctance to consolidate financial statements, and shift assets and liabilities among subsidiaries. The definition and the disclosure of non-performing loans by Asian banks have been the subject of contention. We could continue the list of issues at length. The IOSCO (the International Organization of Securities Commissions) has developed a set of non-financial disclosure rules that were adopted by all regulators. These are in the process of being applied to individual countries. They should make disclosure substantially similar around the world.

The application of International Accounting Standards (IAS) will undoubtedly improve the comparability of reporting of Asian companies. Japan is moving towards IAS. Other Asian countries are also in the process of transforming their national legislation to these principles.

The use of privileged information — by definition, not publicly disclosed — has been so widespread in Asia that it probably is one of the keys to the creation of a climate of confidence. Many Asian companies are still controlled by governments or family groups: these shareholders are learning to respect outside shareholders. They often learn it through trial and error, but there is no doubt that progress is happening. The basic principle of equal information for all investors is increasingly admitted.

Corporate governance is a much more delicate issue. It starts at the top. Although every country of Asia is working on the development of corporate-governance standards, the situation presents a paradox: most governments want to improve their corporate governance, while continuing to behave as if those standards did not apply to themselves as shareholders. Governments or public institutions can only expect corporate-governance standards to apply if they become the champion and model of such standards.

Similarly, the question of the corporate governance of the markets themselves needs to be addressed. Stock exchanges have undertaken changes that will affect their corporate governance. The most spectacular of these is the de-mutualization of the Tokyo, Australian, Singapore and Hong Kong exchanges. This process is not limited to those exchanges who decide to be publicly listed. De-mutualization in itself has a major objective from a corporate-governance standpoint; that is, to ensure new governance structures that reflect the interest of a wider shareholder base than market participants. Markets are too important to be left to the sole interests of the financial intermediaries.

The application of corporate-governance principles by the authorities and the markets themselves are an important condition to implement governance principles on companies. The Japanese authorities, the Hong Kong regulator, the Chinese Securities Regulation Commission (CSRC) and the Indian SEBI have made major advances in this field. Local progress is important, since corporate governance cannot be imposed from outside of the territorial jurisdiction of the regulatory body. What is expected from those companies is the strict application of local rules and regulations. Progress in this field is therefore largely dependent on the evolution of corporate-governance standards in the home country. The principle of equality of treatment of shareholders is the cornerstone of these standards.

While the existence of regulation is absolutely essential, another issue is implementation: most Asian countries have not granted statutory powers allowing their regulators to enforce regulation. This is linked also to the self-regulatory powers that are granted to the stock exchanges. In India, the regulator, SEBI, is represented on the boards of the exchanges, making the regulator a participant to the decision process of the exchanges. In China, the CSRC is effectively running the exchanges. In Japan, the influence of the Ministry of Finance on regulatory issues is overwhelming.

Enhancing investor confidence is a challenge. There is limited coordination on those issues inside the region despite the efforts of the Asian Corporate Governance Association, which aims to define and ensure the implementation of global corporate-governance principles in Asia.

FINANCIAL INTERMEDIARIES

The globalization of capital markets, even at a regional level, has generally been the result of the development of global financial intermediaries. Whether they are originally from the United States or from Europe, these institutions are global wholesale players. One common characteristic of the Asian markets is the underdevelopment of collective instruments of savings and the lack of "popular capitalism".

Japan is definitely the most advanced country in this field, having created major securities companies that enhanced the Japanese market. International competition has been growing fast in the brokerage field. Japan is probably the only market in Asia where trading is almost evenly split between local and foreign brokers. However, direct share ownership is extremely limited, and an important part of Japanese equity is owned in the form of cross-shareholding. Furthermore, the level of capitalization remains insufficient. Direct ownership by Japanese households has been discouraged. The fact that the Bank for International Settlement (BIS) standards have allowed Japanese banks to count as equity the difference between the cost of their share portfolio and the current market price was a major concession to the Japanese banking system, and probably one of the reasons why this sector is under severe pressure today and unable to play a role as a major collector of savings towards equities. It will take several years before Japan manages to enjoy the benefits of a healthy full-fledged financial intermediation.

In several countries in Asia, the domestic brokerage structure remains limited to retail trading. Most commercial banks have not played a key role as distribution channels of securities, let alone of equities, among their customers. The development of "popular capitalism" is in its infancy. New leaders are emerging in India and China, and they will build a securities infrastructure without which the Asia markets will continue to be heavily dependent on foreign capital and, therefore, excessively volatile.

CURRENCY CONVERTIBILITY AND OWNERSHIP LIMITATIONS

The development of a regional Asian equity market has encountered another specific difficulty: the limited convertibility of several Asian currencies.

The currencies of China, Taiwan, India, Korea, Malaysia and Indonesia do not enjoy full convertibility. The immediate consequence of this situation is a fragmentation of their equity markets between equities held by domestic investors and those held by foreign investors. This results in a segmented liquidity, very often with a different price discovery.

Ownership limitations have, in many countries, produced the same result. Several Asian markets have both ownership limitations and limited currency convertibility. The first victims of this type of situation are the companies of those countries. Pricing that is not the result of a joint price discovery between the domestic and the international markets is detrimental to their competitive position and their cost of capital.

Investors are also put to a disadvantage since they cannot benefit from this sustainable price level. In most cases, foreign investors pay a premium on the domestic market. In the case of China, the reverse is true. Chinese investors pay a premium relative to foreign owners.

The solution to this problem will be gradual: a sudden full convertibility or change of ownership would create severe disruption. The solution lies in a managed process of progressive equalization of supply and demand that ensures that prices converge globally and gradually. In other words, develop a better liquidity of the market that is suffering from under-supply, and move to full convertibility as soon as the two markets are more balanced.

One of the arguments used by monetary authorities and central banks against full convertibility is the risks linked to a massive sale of domestic equities by foreign investors in times of crisis. From a foreign-exchange standpoint, this is understandable. But equities have a unique characteristic: they do not need to be repaid and will not put the same pressure on foreign-exchange reserves as bonds and loans do when they need to be redeemed. Therefore, the money will not come from the issuer, but from the market.

One of the prerequisites for the creation of an integrated regional market in Asia is a concerted move by the monetary authorities to a gradual full convertibility of their currencies, at least for equities. Unless ownership or convertibility barriers are removed, there will be little possibility to expand the liquidity of individual stocks by mobilizing the resources of the region.

EXPANDING THE INVESTOR BASE

To various degrees, as we noticed before, the development of a regional investor base has come from U.S. and European investors, rather than regional ones.

Japan is the most advanced country in this field: the combination of record savings and major institutional investors explains the remarkable development of the Japanese economy. This combination also made Japan a global market and made it possible for foreign borrowers to launch Yen-denominated bonds in Japan. But Japan does not have a significant domestic retail-investor base since most Japanese savings are in bank accounts.

Outside Japan, the lack of pension funds, mutual funds and other ways to channel savings into equity, coupled with the lack of interest or ability by commercial banks to develop such distribution channels, are probably the biggest hurdle to the development of Asian capital markets. The liquidity built in Hong Kong and Singapore is the result of the development of a very modern and sophisticated network of financial intermediaries. They managed to gather global money in search of Asian opportunities. Most of it, however, was not money from the region itself.

The development of a true retail-investor base in a region of 2.5 billion people is the biggest single opportunity in equity financing. But it will happen if banks running branch networks make it a priority to develop collective saving instruments and add to their services the ability for their customers to buy and sell securities. In several Asian countries, some banks have started developing such networks and they are in the vanguard of a new generation of financial intermediaries.

Pensions are the most socially sensitive issue of the modern economies. In most Asian countries, once again with the notable exception of Japan, pensions are entirely the responsibility of the governments, not simply for their armies of bureaucrats and civil servants, but also for the entire ageing population. The creation of pension funds is a key political priority. Investing part of pension-fund money into equities will undoubtedly boost the depth and the liquidity of Asian markets, and they will go beyond the borders of an individual country. This is precisely what is currently happening in Europe, where the Euro has made cross-border investments a major growth area.

SUMMARY

The development of a regional Asian equity market is full of challenges and opportunities. Not dissimilar from the European situation, the Asian markets will in all likelihood be multi-polar, with Japan, China and India being the largest players. These three have the key ingredients: size, people, companies and growth. Whether they will have the leadership, the vision and the political consensus to make it happen is for them to decide.

The path to that project is complex: it includes the improvement of investor confidence, a change in regulatory framework, a truly credible corporate governance for the markets themselves, the development of equity investments among the population and the development of pension funds.

This is by no means an easy development. But the movement has already started. In my interaction with Asian governments, investors, companies, stock exchanges and financial intermediaries, I have seen an increasing awareness of the challenges and the opportunities lying ahead. The degree of development is not the same across Asia, and leaders like Japan, Hong Kong and Singapore, sometimes with the strong backing of Australia, are clearly aiming in this direction. The corporate-governance efforts of the CSRC and SEBI, among others, are impressive. The emergence of global Asian banks is adding to the global role played by Japanese financial institutions.

The New York Stock Exchange has seen, in the last three years, its listing and trading of Asian securities develop more quickly than any other region in the world. The NYSE started to develop the GEM partnership, including Tokyo, Hong Kong and Australia in the first Asia-Pacific partnership. In this ambitious endeavor, the NYSE is a partner for Asia, its markets and its companies. A vibrant regional Asian equity market is good for the domestic markets, good for the region and good for the world.

Glory and Dreams: Shenzhen's High-tech Industry

Yu Youjun
Mayor of Shenzhen, People's Republic of China

 At present, the world information industry is facing the need to restructure. Multinational companies are in the process of restructuring their operations by relocating parts of their manufacturing and R&D capacities to developing countries. In conditions of global economic slowdown, China and other Asian countries can meet the challenge by upgrading their investment environments and technological levels, and making full use of their rich human resources.

Shenzhen is a fast-growing city that symbolizes China's reform and opening-up. Since its establishment 21 years ago, Shenzhen's main economic indicators, such as GDP, total industrial output, foreign trade volume and fiscal revenue, have been growing at an average annual rate of between 30% and 40%, placing it at the forefront of China's major cities. In recent years, the growth of the high-tech industry has been especially remarkable and, in 2000, high-tech products accounted for 42.3% of the city's total industrial output, and the information industry accounted for 15% of the total output value of that industry nationwide.

The high-tech development of Shenzhen features leading industries and competitive products. The manufacturing capacity and technological level of products such as telecommunication equipment, computers and audio-video products are among the country's best. In 2000, Shenzhen produced over 23% of program-control switches and 50% of all wireless-network equipment in the country. Shenzhen has become the largest manufacturing base for computer and telecommunication equipment on the mainland.

STRONG INDUSTRIAL ASSEMBLING CAPACITY

Altogether, there are 1,600 related companies, with an annual assembling capacity of 30 million computers. An IT supply chain which centers around Shenzhen and covers the Pearl River Delta is able to provide over 90% of computer parts.

Foreign-funded and local enterprises have also enjoyed parallel progress, and more than 40 multinationals, including IBM, Compaq, Intel, HP, JDS, Seagate, Philips, Nortel, Matsushita and Epson, have invested in the high-tech sector in Shenzhen. They have brought with them advanced technology and management expertise and helped to accelerate the overall development of the city's high-tech industry. This has created a number of Chinese companies and native brands with their own intellectual-property rights, which accounted for 50% of the total industrial output in this sector. This suggests that Shenzhen's high-tech industry, centering around IT, is gradually shifting from processing and assembling alone towards both processing and R&D. Gradually, an IT grouping comprising the Chinese firms Huawei, ZTE, Great Wall and others has been formed in Shenzhen, and Shenzhen companies now account for 15 of the top 100 IT enterprises in the country.

The focus on R&D has served Shenzhen well, and gradually a market-oriented and enterprise-based technology-development system has been established. In 2000, over 90% of R&D centers, staff and funding in Shenzhen were located within enterprises. The city's R&D centers have also linked up with key higher education institutions in China, and many companies such as Legend, TCL and Oracle have established, or will soon establish, their own R&D centers in Shenzhen. In 2000, fully 2.9% of the city's GDP was invested into R&D.

The benefits of this investment created an environment in which, despite a global downturn in 2001, the high-tech industry in Shenzhen achieved a growth rate of 24%, accounting for 44.4% of the total industrial output value and increasing export volumes by over 27%. Global high-tech giants such as IBM, Intel and Sony have also increased their procurement and orders in Shenzhen, and Sumitomo recently made an initial investment of nearly US$100 million in a local fiber-optical project. Total investment on this project is expected to reach US$700 million over the next three to four years.

Over the next several years, the high-tech industry will remain a strategic area of growth. Shenzhen's plans to become a major high-tech manufacturing and R&D center are focused on upgrading the industrial scale and technological advancement in several key areas through to 2005:

Computer Hardware: The output value of computer hardware is expected to reach RMB100 billion.

Communications equipment: An emphasis on mobile, fiber-optical transmission, digital and satellite communications equipment, with an expected output value of RMB100 billion.

Digital audio-video products: An emphasis on the digital TV, digital set-top box, DVD, and digital cameras, with an expected output value of RMB100 billion.

Micro-electronics and elements: An emphasis on IC design and large-scale production, with an expected output value of RMB45 billion.

Software: Plans are being made to build up to five software parks, which will focus development on embedded software, specialized and cross-industry application software, information security products, service software and system integration software. The expected output value is RMB30 billion, with an export volume of US$0.5 billion.

Bio-related industries: The biological, pharmaceutical and medical-instrument sectors are expected to yield RMB25 billion by 2005. The emphasis in development will be on the application and industrialization of key technologies such as genetic treatment, biological chips, and genetically modified organisms so as to make Shenzhen a key biotechnological production center and modern medical industry base. Shenzhen will also be an important center for battery-centre for materials and nano-materials, with an expected output value of RMB15 billion for new materials and new energies. The environmental-protection industries will focus on the treatment of urban wastewater and garbage, control over vehicle exhaust, the de-sulphurization of seawater, the development of clean energy, and cleaning products. Several well-known brands of environmental protection-related products will be cultivated. The expected output value of this sector will be RMB3 billion.

SHENZHEN'S FUTURE AS A HIGH-TECH R&D CENTER

In order to make Shenzhen a high-tech R&D center, we will improve capacity for technological innovation, protect independent intellectual-property rights and improve the regional R&D support to create a market-oriented system based on enterprises, supported by universities and research institutes and assisted by the municipal goverernment. Independent intellectual-property rights and commercial confidentiality will be properly protected. A system of management shareholding and technological equity will be further encouraged, backed up by more policies to attract and retain high-tech talent from home and abroad. The development of higher education and the building of Shenzhen University City will be accelerated in order to enrich the city's human resources.

The venture-capital market is expected to mature, complemented by high-tech incubators. The China High-tech Fair, a state-level international fair held annually in Shenzhen, will continue to be a highlight.

Building Information Services

The emphasis will be on telecommunication services, computer and network services and information consultation. We will increase our efforts to introduce information technology into the local economy and social life through a broadband network that will upgrade the city's IT application level to that of developed countries in three to five years. A better overall information service will also improve government administration and the management of modern enterprises. By 2005, we anticipate that information services will be worth RMB45 billion.

Constructing a High-tech Belt

Shenzhen's first high-tech industrial park, with 11.5 square kilometers, was established in 1996 and is now one of the top six national high-tech parks. To further expand the space for high-tech development, in 2001 Shenzhen decided to construct a high-tech belt that will have an area of 100 square kilometers. It is scheduled for completion in five years. The aggregate industrial-output value is expected to reach RMB200 billion by 2005, and double that by 2010. The high-tech belt will be a great asset to Shenzhen's development in coming decades.

China's admission into the WTO presents Shenzhen with many challenges and the city is taking action to meet these through:

- Improving the investment environment to support high-tech progress
- Improving government efficiency through new administrative systems
- Strengthening the legal system to make it more transparent
- Protecting intellectual-property rights and optimizing market order
- Providing high-quality human resources to attract further investment
- Improving the living environment.

Economic globalization and technological progress are creating a broader vista for cooperation between countries, regions and cities and over the next five years, foreign investment in Shenzhen is expected to reach US$20billion. Despite the global economic slowdown, China has maintained considerable momentum in its economic development. This, in addition to China's entry into the WTO and its development potential, makes it one of the safest places for investment. Shenzhen is one of the fastest-moving cities in China and we welcome any opportunity to work with other Asian and foreign friends and to share the fruits of progress in our world.

A Common Responsibility to Promote Stability and Growth

Nobuyuki Idei
Chairman and Chief Executive Officer, Sony Corporation, Japan

The recent global economic downturn and the widespread ripple effects of September 11 reveal just how tightly knit we have become as a global society. This global society is still fragile. There are no guarantees of peace or stability, and economic growth is not evenly distributed. Despite these difficulties, it is clear that a key word for the global era is "interdependence". How can corporations contribute to building a more peaceful and secure world? They can begin by recognizing the growing interdependence of society and business.

Good business can promote social stability and prosperity, but corporations can only grow in an environment conducive to good business. That is why it is in the best interests of corporations to actively engage in socially responsible activities that will promote the development of such an environment. In addition to respecting the basic principles of human rights, labor and the environment, corporations can help foster the fundamental tools for societal development; namely, building the educational infrastructure necessary for success in this knowledge era. Our prosperity, indeed our long-term survival, is dependent on whether we can narrow the digital divide and provide opportunities for developing communities to integrate with the global community.

SOCIAL RESPONSIBILITY IN THE AGE OF INTERDEPENDENCE

The nature of social responsibility has changed because interdependence today is a more complex web connecting both macro and micro elements of the global society. It is no longer just business-to-government or business-to-business relations that corporations have to consider. Corporations are now interconnected with local communities and individuals more closely than ever. Technology such as the Internet has made this possible. It has opened up new avenues of communication, empowering individuals in this knowledge-based society. Even those who are not connected to the Internet often have their stories told by proxies to a wider audience.

The degree of global interconnectedness is constantly rising as a result of such technological innovation and the falling cost of intercontinental transportation and communication. Although the global economic recession and the event of September 11 put a temporary halt to the cross-border movement of goods and capital, global trade continues to rise. One indication of this is that, as *The Economist* notes, the volume of global trade rose by an average of 7% a year in the 1990s. From a long-term perspective, according to Stephen Roach of Morgan Stanley, global trade today accounts for 24% of the world's GDP, compared with 17% 25 years ago. This trend is likely to continue as technology permeates even more areas of the world, bringing remote communities into our own backyard. As a result, corporations must understand local cultures and how a corporation and its products fit into local communities. The tools to gain knowledge are in our hands, and we must utilize them effectively.

Corporations must consider the concerns of individuals, whether on human rights, labor or other related issues. This is not only because these issues are widely publicized through the Internet or by the media, but because, if left unresolved, these issues will start a wave of local discontent. In this global age, there are no walls to contain such waves, and discontent at the local level can quickly turn global. In this sense, nothing is truly local anymore.

The events of September 11 showed this to be true. One cause of this tragedy may have been the growing digital divide between the haves and have-nots, fueling a bubble of resentment that finally burst. No country, no matter how politically, economically or militarily powerful, is safe from the dangers of poverty and social discontent brewing halfway around the world. This tragedy was just a reminder of how once "local" matters can explode onto the global scene overnight.

TROUBLE SPOTS IN ASIA

This is true for Asia as well. The Asian currency crisis of 1997 showed that no country is immune from the virus of financial instability and fear.

This instability prompted social unrest in many parts of Asia, not least in Indonesia, where ethnic conflict threatened an implosion in the unstable country. This would have had a tremendous impact on the entire region, as it would have led to a massive exodus of refugees and a threat to the straits vital for the transport of natural resources to East Asia. Disillusionment with the global capitalist system is also widespread in other poverty-stricken areas of Asia. The Philippines, for example, has recently been identified as one of many havens for terrorist organizations working to undermine the process of globalization. The government has made exceptional efforts to stem these terrorist activities, but the fundamental root of the problem — poverty and alienation from the global community — must be addressed in the long run.

Perhaps the biggest concern in Asia now is China, because its immense population and uncertain political future warrant both optimism and fear from surrounding countries. Following its accession to the WTO, China is likely to change in many ways, opening its market to foreign firms and creating wealth from previously untapped resources. However, the income disparity within the country is likely to grow, causing large segments of the population to express dissatisfaction with the system, perhaps even leading to mass unrest and disorder. An unstable China would lead to regional instability, with immigrants flowing into neighboring countries. Japan is already experiencing problems with illegal immigrants seeking opportunities they are denied at home. These are just a few examples of how "local" issues are no longer local, and governments of these developing countries often lack the means to address these problems adequately.

A GRASSROOTS EFFORT TO PROMOTE KNOWLEDGE-BASED SOCIETIES

Resolving these social issues and quelling discontent will take time. It will be a gradual, often painful, process. With this in mind, corporations can begin at the grassroots level by, for example, promoting human rights, providing equal employment opportunities for women, and connecting local villages to the worldwide network. It goes without saying that many areas of the world are still left without network connections. According to the August 2001 Nielson Netratings report, the populations of only 30 countries account for 93% of the estimated number of individuals in the world with home-based Internet access. Of those with access, 40% reside in the U.S. and Canada. This is a clear indication that the fruits of technological innovation have only been enjoyed in exclusive areas of the world. Indeed, the term "selective globalization" appropriately describes the uneven path the process of global integration has taken.

Thomas Friedman mentions in his book *Lexus and the Olive Tree* how the Internet connectivity level of a country is a sign of the direction in which that country is headed. I believe there is truth to this. Internet connectivity represents the shift towards a knowledge-based society, which is the next step in the evolutionary process of social development. Knowledge-based societies create wealth from the most important asset of society: the human mind. The human mind has creative potential without limit and, unlike other tangible resources, it can never be depleted. The more effectively it is used, the more powerful it becomes.

A knowledge-based society needs few natural resources to thrive. All that is required is the right social environment. Unfortunately, many countries, villages and communities around the world do not have the means to even begin planting the seeds for a knowledge-based society. They require help from the outside. As "good citizens" of the global community, corporations can help by providing some basic needs to the underprivileged. This goes beyond simply writing a check. It means actively engaging in the community to foster sustainable growth and development by cultivating especially those intangible assets — providing knowledge and expertise for eventual self-sustenance. Education is the key to success in this knowledge society and, for that matter, education will also sow the seeds for social stability.

EDUCATION IN THE KNOWLEDGE ERA

My previous point coincides with what I believe is an important trait for the success of both business and society as a whole: the idea of continuous learning. Education is a continuous process, and this is especially the case today with the pace of changes surrounding us and the "Knowledge Revolution" that has empowered individuals with the ability to choose from an ever-expanding pool of information.

Because we are living in the knowledge era, education should be geared towards nurturing innovation and creativity, two skills necessary for success in this knowledge-based society. This means teaching children how to "think outside the box", to develop their critical-thinking skills and their ability to transform disparate information into useful knowledge. Children must also learn to think for themselves and to formulate their own unique ideas from an early age. Only by fostering this habit of active thinking can we create societies in which the creative powers of individuals realize their full potential.

This applies not only to children but to everyone, regardless of age. We often hear of the necessity to continue studying even after graduating from school and entering the workforce. There are stories of grandparents in their 70s and 80s going back to school to get their college degrees. These are truly remarkable stories, but unfortunately, still all too rare. The spirit of learning should be timeless. And we should make a consistent effort to learn new things previously foreign to us.

We should make use of technology like the Internet to create a network of colleagues with diverse spectra of knowledge from different regions of the world and strive to actively learn from each other. Through such networking, we may acquire alternative perspectives on preconceived ideas. We are, indeed, living in an age when we must form a habit of continuously challenging our most basic assumptions. This is another reason why it is in the interests of corporations to provide expertise and infrastructure to those communities that are unable to utilize the technological advances of the IT revolution. By connecting more people to the Internet, the pool of knowledge will increase substantially, creating an even broader web of information that benefits all.

A RESPONSIBILITY SHARED BY ALL

Some of the turbulence we have experienced recently is due to the fact that not all of us have been able to make the transition to a knowledge society. We are all at different stages of development, and because we are all mutually dependent now, those who are ahead in the game must lend a hand to those who have had a late start. The process can begin by helping poor communities build the framework and infrastructure necessary for basic education. From there, the next step would be to develop the infrastructure for network connections. Corporations can do this on their own or work together with governments and NGOs. Whatever the means and methods, corporations must take an active role because, as already mentioned, the responsibility lies with everyone who has a stake in this global community.

In this age of interdependence, the responsibilities of corporations are greater than ever, not only from a humanitarian point of view, but also because how we act as global citizens will determine whether we continue to move forward as one global community or as a fragmented world. We cannot take peace and stability for granted, as we saw on September 11. Likewise, we cannot wait for others to take up the mantle of responsibility. It belongs to each and every one of us, and it is up to each of us to contemplate what needs to be done today.

Index